6 servings

meat 300g.
2 onion
3 potatoe   Water 800cc

① cut meat & vegetable into
   bite size pieces
② Heat oil /3 tablespoon in a pan
③ fry meat & vegetable. in pan
④ add water 1800cc Boil 20 minutes
⑤ after well done — add curry

⑧* Mr. Mrs. Hirotsugu Enomoto
   3-114 Ishikawa-cho Naka-Ward
   Yokohama Kanagawa Japan
   045-662-8727

* Mrs Michie Minato (Tokyo)
   1-12-14 Higashi Nagata
   Minami - Ku , Yokohama
   Kanagawa 232 Japan
   0457-16-3386

Ayaka Enomoto (daughter)
Slippers (abg + feet)
Ring (silver)
post cards - Bay Bridge
flower cards
Book Marker
paper folders
— good meals —

Paper fold doll

ナツメ社

Traditional Japanese Culture & Modern Japan

【日本文化を英語で紹介する事典】

杉浦洋一＋John K. Gillespie❖共著

まえがき

　どんな人でも文化でも、自己を知ることは他者を知ることよりずっと困難です。私たちは日頃日本人であることを意識することはありませんが、海外へ行ったときとか、あるいは日本国内で非日本人と接触したときに、初めて自分が日本人であることを意識させられます。そのようなとき、改めて自己の文化について何事かを語ろうとして、自分がいかに無知であるかを思い知らされるのです。日本人だから日本文化に詳しい、などとはゆめゆめ考えてはなりません。一方、海外からは日本に対する誤解や偏見が、相変わらず後を絶ちません。

　それなら、一体日本とは何なのか？　日本文化とは何なのか？……これは、「自分とは何か」と自分に問うのに似て、日本人にとって永遠に問い続けなければならない種類の疑問であり、それゆえ答は一定ではありえません。

　そこで、永遠に問い続ける問いの、最初の答のきっかけとして役立つよう本書は企画されました。本書に収録された説明をもって、相手に何事かを伝えたなどとは考えずに、これをきっかけとして自らの答を探る旅に出ることをおすすめします。

平成5年10月（1993.10）

日本文著者：杉浦洋一
英文著者：ジョン・K・ギレスピー（John K. Gillespie）

目　次

もくじ
Mokuji
CONTENTS

2．現代日本人の生活様式

日本人の精神

社会生活

娯楽

本書の使い方

1）本書は歴史と自然を考慮して、次のように大きく３部に分かれています。
　　　①日本の伝統文化
　　　②現代日本人の生活様式
　　　③自然を通して見る日本
2）日本文化を英語で説明する必要が生じたときに、本書の「目次」で該当項目を探してください。
3）「目次」に該当項目がないときは、巻末の「索引」を検索してください。索引には、見出し項目以外にも重要と思われるキーワードが収録されています。
4）キーワードについて
　　　①本文中に太字で示してある単語（日本語はゴシック体、英語はボールド体）は、「キーワード」として巻末の索引に一括して収録されています。和英単語表として活用してください。
　　　②見出し語として採用されている語は、必ず「キーワード」になっています。

＊英語はなるべく日本語と対応するように、センテンスを超えた意訳は避けました。日本人読者が対照して理解できるように配慮したつもりです。

●凡例

<英語の表記について>
・英文中における日本語の表記はローマ字表記とし、イタリック体で示しています。
　（例：*bunraku, bukkyō...*）
・ローマ字表記の長音は、原則として　 ̄（長音記号）を使用しています。
　（例：*bōeki, dohyōiri...*）
・日本語であっても、すでに英語として認められていると考えられる単語は、英語の
　表記に従っています。（例：神道→Shinto、歌舞伎→Kabuki、能→Noh...）
・日本人の氏名の表記は、日本式に姓を先、名を後に表記しています。但し従来の慣
　例との混乱を避けるため、姓はスモール・キャピタルをもちいています。
　（例：MATSUO Bashō、ENDŌ Shūsaku）
・日本語原稿と同様、キーワードは太字（ボールド）で示してあります。
・英語の中の書名等のタイトル名はイタリック体ではなく" "でくくってあります。

・・・・・・・・・・・・・・・・・・・・・・・・・・・

●写真提供・協力一覧

筑前琵琶連合会
東京都台東区立下町風俗資料館
東京浅草「木馬亭」
札幌市役所
秋田市役所
福岡市役所
(社)青森観光協会
(社)京都市観光協会
(社)長唄協会
(社)落語芸術協会
国立劇場
国立能楽堂
国立文楽劇場

＊ご協力ありがとうございました。

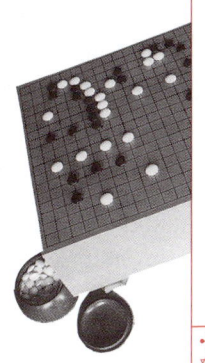

日本文化を英語で紹介する事典

1. 日本の伝統文化

芸能

【歌舞伎】 Kabuki かぶき

　日本の代表的な伝統演劇の１つで、1603年ごろ出雲大社の巫女・阿国が京都で念仏踊りを興行したのが初めとされています。人気が出ましたが、女性の歌舞伎は風紀を乱すと禁止され、以後は男性のみで演じられるようになりました。その後次第に技芸本位となり、演劇、舞踊、音楽の集大成ともいうべき総合芸術として完成されました。女性役も男性が演じる、**隈取り**という派手な舞台化粧をする、舞台装置に独自の工夫がなされているなどの特徴があります。第２次大戦後はヨーロッパやアジア、アメリカなど海外公演も盛んになり、ヨーロッパ歌舞伎会議やヨーロッパ日本演劇研究センターなど西洋人学者の研究組織も設立されました。

Kabuki : This is one of the representative traditional theater forms of Japan, said to have begun around 1603 when Okuni, a female attendant of the Izumo Shrine performed "*Nenbutsu* folk dances" in Kyoto. These were very popular, but all-female Kabuki came to be outlawed as corrupting public morals; subsequently Kabuki performances came to be enacted by males only. Later, those performances gradually became to put emphasis on artistry, and was perfected as composite art that brought together theater, classical Japanese dance, and music. It is principally characterized by that even the female roles are played by male actors, use of **Kabuki stage makeup**, and distinctive inventions on stage installations. After the Second World War there were abundant performances in Europe, Asia, the United States, and other places, and research organizations of Western scholars such as the European Kabuki Conference and Japanese Theater Research Center were established.

回り舞台／revolving stage

セリ／trapdoor

花道／elevated runway

　歌舞伎の舞台には、いくつかの独特な装置があります。

　花道は舞台の延長として客席を縦断して設けられた通路で、役者の登場・退場に使われるほか、重要な場面がここで演じられることもあります。舞台には**回り舞台**や**セリ**という仕掛けがあり、幕を使わずに場面を変化させたり、役者を下から出現させたりできます。そのほかに大道具が後ろに倒れて別の場面が現れる装置などもあり、それらが緻密に計算され、効果的に使われることにより、**歌舞伎**の美しさ、面白さが増すのです。

Kabuki stage has a number of unique installations. The **elevated runway** is a passage built as an extension of the stage that cuts through the audience; in addition to being used for actors' entrances and exits, important scenes take place on it. On the stage, with the mechanisms of a **revolving stage** and a **trapdoor**, scenes can change without using the curtain and actors can appear from below. In addition, there are installations in which large props fall backward and separate scenes appear; by calculating such actions in minute detail, the beauty and appeal of **Kabuki** increases.

【能】
のう Nō

　能とは筋立てをもつ芸能という意味で、日本最古の音楽劇です。14世紀以降に盛んになりました。筋は「謡」と呼ばれる歌で語られ、役は主役である**シテ**と、わき役である**ワキ**に大別されます。役者はそれぞれ木製で漆塗りの面をかぶり、豪華な錦織りの衣装を着て演じます。面をかぶらない役柄もありますが、その場合でも顔を面に見立てて演じ、顔の表情を作るようなことはしないのです。

　動きも地味で、役者は感情を声に出さないため、能では人間の陰の部分が表現されるのですが、一方でその神秘的な動作と単調な音楽が「幽玄」といわれる奥深い美しさを醸し出しているのです。

N **oh :** Noh is a performing art with plot and is Japan's oldest form of musical theater. It has flourished since the fourteenth century. The story is spoken in a recitation known as *utai*, and the roles are divided into the leading role of *shite*(the **protagonist**, meaning "doer" or "actor") and the supporting role of *waki*(a **deuteragonist**, meaning "bystander" or "onlooker"). The actors wear **lacquer**-coated masks made of wood and colorful brocade costumes. There are also roles without mask, but even then the face is used to resemble a mask, with no attempt at expression.

　Because movements are restrained and the actors put no sentiment in their voices, Noh expresses the darker aspects of humanity; on the other hand, the mysterious gestures and monotonic music yield a deep beauty known as *yūgen*(the **subtle and profound**).

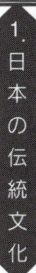
【能舞台】
Nō-butai.
のうぶたい

能や**狂言**の専用舞台は、屋根を支える太い4本の柱が舞台を囲み、前3方は開け放たれています。役者は橋掛りを通って舞台に現われます。

能では一切が**謡**の文句と音楽、役者の動きによって表されるため、能舞台には舞台装置が施されていません。ですから、逆に観客は自由な幻想を抱くことができ、どんな装置も及ばないような、雄大な舞台面を描き出すことも可能となり得るのです。

Noh stage : The stage exclusively used by **Noh** and **Kyogen** is framed by four thick pillars that hold up its roof and is open on three sides. Actors appear on the stage by walking along the corridor connecting the backstage to the stage.

In **Noh**, everything is expressed through the phrases and music of the **Noh chant** and the movements of the actors, so the Noh-*butai* has no stage props. As a result, by contrast, the spectators can embrace the illusion, and it is possible to portray sublime scenes that surpasses any prop or stage setting.

【狂言】
Kyōgen
きょうげん

狂言は日本の古典喜劇で、**室町時代**（1392〜1573）に**能**と同様、**観阿弥**、**世阿弥**父子によって確立されました。当初は**能**の合間に演じられていましたが、現在は単独で上演したり、狂言役者が**能**の中の役を演じたりすることもあります。

能に比べると狂言は庶民的です。面をかぶるのは一部の役柄に限られ、化粧もほどこしません。神や**鬼**など特殊な役柄を除いては15世紀の日常着が衣装となります。狂言の筋には人間肯定の精神があり、盗人なども真の悪人としては描かれません。また、**能**が歌舞中心であるのに対し、狂言にはせりふや劇的行動が伴うという特徴もあります。

Kyogen is classical Japanese comic theater and, like **Noh**, was established in the **Muromachi Period**(1392-1573) by the father and son pair, **Kan'ami** and **Zeami**. At first, Kyogen plays were performed in the intervals between **Noh** plays, but now they are staged independently and sometimes Kyogen actors take roles in **Noh** plays.

Compared to **Noh**, Kyogen has mass appeal. Masks are only used in a few roles, and no makeup is put on. Except for the special roles of deities and **ogres**, the costumes are the daily clothing worn in the fifteenth century. Kyogen plots have an affirmative human spirit and do not draw thieves and the like as truly wicked people. In addition, in contrast to **Noh** which centers on chanting and dance, Kyogen's outstanding characteristic is the spoken lines accompanied by dramatic movement.

【日本舞踊】 Nihonbuyō にほんぶよう

　日本舞踊は15世紀ごろ、「踊」という跳躍運動を主としたものに、旋回運動を主とした「舞」と、演劇的表現の強い「振り」の要素が取り入れられて生まれたものですが、狭義の「日本舞踊」では主に歌舞伎舞踊をさします。これは1603年に出雲の阿国が興行した「かぶき踊り」から**歌舞伎**が誕生した後、**歌舞伎**をもとにして発展したもので、歌舞伎舞踊を基盤とする舞踊の流派の多くは、18世紀後半に振付師や**歌舞伎**俳優によって始められています。

　現在は花柳流、藤間流、西川流をはじめとして100以上の流派があり、女性の稽古こととしても広く行われています。

Classical Japanese dance : *Nihonbuyō* was born in the fifteenth century bringing together dance called *odori* that is the elements of mainly jumping movements with another dance called *mai* that principally involves circling movements and poses called *furi* that give a strong dramatic impression. In the narrow sense, *nihonbuyō* indicates chiefly Kabuki dance. It developed through **Kabuki** after **Kabuki** was developed from the *Kabuki odori* performed by Okuni of Izumo in 1603. Most schools of *buyō*, which are based on Kabuki dance, began in the latter part of the eighteenth century with choreographers and **Kabuki** actors.

Currently, there are more than 100 schools, starting with the Hanayagi, Fujima and Nishikawa schools, and it is also popularly practiced as one of accomplishments for women.

【雅楽】 Gagaku ががく

雅楽とは古代に中国・朝鮮などから輸入した音楽と舞、およびそれを模倣した日本製の楽曲です。笙、ひちりき、楽箏、楽琵琶、楽太鼓など独特の楽器が使われます。宮廷音楽として**平安時代**（794〜1185）に栄え、寺社でも演奏されました。

雅楽には舞のあるものと舞を伴わないものとがあり、前者を**舞楽**、後者を**管弦**といいます。**舞楽**と**管弦**とでは同一の曲でも速度や楽器編成・強弱法などが異なります。現在は一般ではほとんど演奏されず、わずかに宮内庁楽部などが継承して、祝いの際に演奏するくらいです。

Ancient court music : *Gagaku* is Japanese musical composition modeled on the music and dance brought from China and Korea in ancient times. Unique instruments are used such as a reed instrument, Shinto flute, thirteen-stringed *koto*, Japanese lute and drum. *Gagaku* flourished in the **Heian Period**(794-1185) and was performed at temples and shrines.

There are *gagaku* pieces with dance and without dance, the former called an **ancient court dance and music**(*bugaku*) and the latter the **orchestral music with wind and string instruments**(*kangen*). With *bugaku* and *kangen*, even when the music is the same, the tempo and the composition of the musical instruments and dynamics are different. Rarely performed today, *gagaku* has been taken over by groups like the music department of the Imperial Household Agency and is performed only on celebratory occasions.

【琴】 Koto こと

　日本の伝統的な弦楽器です。木製で長さは約180センチ、幅は約30センチあり、右手の親指、人差指、中指に爪を付けて弾きます。13本の弦が柱と呼ばれる駒の上に張ってあり、柱の位置で音の高さが決まります。**江戸時代**（1603〜1867）には琴の演奏は女性のたしなみとされ、良家の娘の多くは小さいころから琴の稽古をしました。現在でも女性には多くの愛好者がいます。

*K*oto is a traditional Japanese stringed instrument, made of wood. It's about 180 centimeters in length, about 30 centimeters in width, and it is played with plectrums attached to the thumb, index and middle fingers of the right hand. Thirteen strings are stretched over bridges and the pitch is determined by the position of the bridges. In the **Edo Period**(1603-1867), performance was regarded as one of accomplishments of woman, and many of daughters of decent families practiced *koto* from a young age. Even now there are many devotees among women.

【三味線】 Shamisen しゃみせん

　バンジョーに似た形の弦楽器で、フレットのないのが特徴です。３本の弦を**ばち**で弾いて演奏し、**歌舞伎や文楽、民謡**の伴奏に使われます。中国から沖縄を経て日本全国に普及し、独自の発展を遂げました。**江戸時代**（1603〜1867）以降、日本の代表的な楽器となりました。

*S*hamisen : This is a stringed instrument shaped like a banjo, but its outstanding feature is that it has no frets. It is played by striking its three strings with a **plectrum** and is used as accompaniment for **Kabuki** and *bunraku* plays and for **folk songs**. It came from China through Okinawa and spread throughout Japan, in which it developed independently from the original style. It became the representative instrument of Japan since the **Edo Period**(1603-1867).

【尺八】
Shakuhachi
しゃくはち

尺八は**竹製**の管楽器です。長さが日本の昔の度量衡で、1尺と8寸であることからその名が付けられました。構造は竹筒に穴をあけた簡単なものですが、息の吹き込み方や唇と吹き口との間隔、指の押さえ具合などで音階や音色に微妙な変化が出るのが特徴です。西洋の**笛**にはない独特な音が出るため、ジャズや現代音楽にも取り入れられて、表現の幅を広げています。

Five-holed bamboo clarinet : *Shakuhachi* is a wind instrument made of **bamboo**. Its length, by the old Japanese standard of weights and measures, is one *shaku*(about one foot) and eight(*hachi*) *sun*(a tenths of a *shaku*), so that is how it got its name. It is made by simply putting holes in a bamboo tube, but its chief characteristic is the curious changes in scale and tone coloration that come out with the style of blowing into it, with the space between the lips and the mouthpiece and with the manner of controlling the fingering. Because a unique sound, not found in Western **flutes**, emerges, the *shakuhachi* has been incorporated into jazz and contemporary music, extending its range of expression.

【琵琶】
Biwa
びわ

琵琶は東洋の弦楽器の1つです。起源はペルシア・アラビアとされ、インドや中国を経て**奈良時代**（710〜784）に日本に伝わりました。木製で楕円形をした胴に4本ないし5本の弦が張ってあり、**ばち**を使って弾きます。『平家物語』などを語るときに伴奏に使われることで有名で、女流演奏者による演奏会も行われています。

Japanese lute : *Biwa* is an Oriental stringed instrument. It originated in Persia and Arabia and came to Japan through India and China in the **Nara Period**(710-784). The body, which is made of wood and oval shaped, is strung with four or five strings, and it is played with a **plectrum**. It is well-known for being used in chanting of "Heike-monogatari," and there are concerts by female artists.

【文楽】Bunraku ぶんらく

文楽は人形劇の1つで、17世紀から盛んになりました。能、歌舞伎と合わせて三大古典演劇といわれています。三味線の伴奏と語りからなる浄瑠璃に合わせて人形が操られ、物語が展開していきます。人形を使うことを除けば歌舞伎とよく似ており、人形の動きの巧みさには観客も思わず引き込まれてしまうのです。実際、劇作家・近松門左衛門が文楽と歌舞伎の両方の脚本を書いたことが、両者の発展に大きく寄与しました。文楽の人形は顔、胴、手、足、衣装からなり、大きさは1～1.5メートルです。通常、3人の人形つかいが舞台の上で1つの人形を操りますが、その動きの巧みさゆえ、人形つかいの存在は観客に意識されません。

Bunraku is puppet theater that has flourished in the seventeenth century. It constitute the three major classical theater with **Noh** and **Kabuki**. Puppet manipulation is combined with *jōruri*, the **ballad drama** that is formed by narrative chanted to *shamisen* accompaniment, and plot lines are developed. Except for the puppets, it is very similar to **Kabuki**, and spectators are unconsciously drawn in by the skillfullness of the puppets' movements. The playwright CHIKAMATSU **Monzaemon** wrote scripts for both *Bunraku* and **Kabuki** and greatly influenced both forms. *Bunraku* puppets have faces, bodies, hands, feet and costumes, and are from one to one and a half meters tall. Usually, three puppet operators are on stage to manipulate one puppet, but, because of the skill of their movements, spectators are not conscious of the operators.

【浄瑠璃】

Jōruri.
じょうるり

浄瑠璃とは、**三味線**伴奏による**語り物**です。もともと**室町時代**（1392〜1573）に誕生した語り物の中に、牛若丸と浄瑠璃姫のロマンスを題材にした物語があり、人気を博したことから、その後、新しい語り物を浄瑠璃と総称するようになりました。

江戸時代（1603-1867）に入ると、浄瑠璃は多くの流派に分かれました。現在はそれぞれ独立したものとして扱われており、「浄瑠璃」といえば、そのうちの有名な一派である**義太夫節**を指すこともあります。また、浄瑠璃と人形劇を組み合わせた人形浄瑠璃の１つに**文楽**があります。

Ballad drama : *Jōruri* is chanted narration with *shamisen* accompaniment. It originated in the narratives of the **Muromachi Period**(1392-1573), taking as its material the romance of young *samurai* Ushiwakamaru and Princess Jōruri, and, after its popularity became widespread, new narratives came to be called *jōruri*.

In the **Edo Period**(1603~l867), *jōruri* split into several schools. At present, these function respectively as independent entities, and the term *jōruri* sometimes indicates *gidayū-bushi*, one of the well-known schools. In addition, there is *bunraku*, a form of puppet *jōruri* which combines *jōruri* and puppet theater.

【薪能】
Takiginō
たきぎのう

　薪能とは「薪の宴の能」という意味で、本来は奈良の興福寺に薪を献進する際に行われた**能**のことでした。その後いったんは絶えたものの、近年簡略化して復興しました。最近は、夕方暗くなってから、薪の火を照明代わりにして野外で行う納涼能のことも薪能と呼んでいます。夜の海や林を背景にして薪の明かりで演ずる**能**は、**幽玄**がさらに増して迫力があり、新たな人気を呼び起こしています。

Firelight Noh : *Takiginō* means "a **Noh** for the firewood party" and was originally **Noh** performed on the occasion of offering firewood to the Kōfukuji, a temple in Nara. Later it was discontinued for a time and in recent years was revived in a simplified form. Recently, outdoor **Noh** performances in the evening cool after dark, useing light from the burning firewood in place of lighting, are also called *takiginō*. **Noh** performed in the firelight with the sea and woods at night as background yields *yūgen*, the **subtle and profound**, all the more intense and has aroused renewed popularity.

【義太夫】
Gidayū
ぎだゆう

　義太夫は**文楽**とともに発展した**浄瑠璃**の一派で、「**義太夫節**」の略称です。17世紀末、**三味線**の名手である**竹本義太夫**が**浄瑠璃**を大成したことにちなみ、このように呼ばれています。

　浄瑠璃のほかの派に比べると最も語り物的性格が強く、登場人物の感情表現がはっきりしているのが特徴で、伴奏に使う**三味線**は低音域で力強い音色のものが使われます。

G*idayū*, a shortened form of *gidayū-bushi*, is a school of **ballad drama**(*jōruri*) that developed together with *bunraku*. The name comes from TAKEMOTO **Gidayū** an accomplished *shamisen* player at the end of seventeenth century, who brought *jōruri* to its highest form.

Compared to other schools of *jōruri*, *gidayū* has a strong narrative aspect, marked particularly by its characters' clear expression of feelings, and the accompanying *shamisen* uses strong tone coloration in the low notes.

【落語】
Rakugo
らくご

　落語は**江戸時代**（1603〜1867）に発達した**寄席演芸**で、寄席と呼ばれる演芸場で演じられます。落語家は**着物**姿で高座という舞台に座り、主に対話形式で、語呂合わせや洒落を用いながらこっけいな話を独演します。話の終わりには「**落ち**」がつくのが特徴です。小道具には**扇子**や手拭いが使われます。落語家はこれらをいろいろなものに見立てながら、観客を想像の世界へ導くのです。

　落語は男性が語るために改良が重ねられてきた話芸で、**歌舞伎**と同様に、男性が女性をも演じられるように工夫されています。しかし、最近女性の落語家が現われて話題になっています。

Comic storytelling : *Rakugo*, a **vaudeville performance** developed in the **Edo Period**(1603-1867), is performed in entertainment halls called *yose*. The *rakugo* artist sits on stage on a dais, wearing a **kimono**, and performs his humorous piece solo, with puns and wordplay, usually in the form of a dialogue. The main feature is applying the "**punch line**" at the end of the piece. **Folding fans** and hand towels are used for props. In making these sorts of props come alive, *rakugo* artists lead the spectators into an imaginative world.

Rakugo is a conversational art form in which the refinements that have piled up come from men doing the reciting; it uses the same device as **Kabuki** with men taking female parts. However, recently female *rakugo* artists have emerged and are much talked about.

【漫才】 Manzai まんざい

主に2人の芸人が1組になり、面白おかしく言葉をやりとりして観客を笑わせる**寄席演芸**の1つ。新年を祝う歌舞が**寄席演芸**に変化したもので、**昭和時代**（1926～1989）初期に対話中心になりました。**落語**に比べ漫才は現代的です。2人がこっけいな役割を分担し、やり取りの面白さやアドリブの巧みさが客を楽しませます。**落語家**と同様、漫才師もテレビのバラエティー番組で大活躍しています。

Comic dialogue : This is a kind of **vaudeville performance** in which two comedians as a team make spectators laugh by their humorous verbal exchanges. The singing and dancing that once served to celebrate New Year changed into a **vaudeville performance**, and in the early part of the **Showa Period**(1926-1989) became dialogue-oriented. Compared to **comic storytelling**(*rakugo*), *manzai* is contemporary. The two comedians divide their comic roles and entertain the spectators with the skillfulness of their humorous, ad-libbed exchanges. Like ***rakugo*** storytellers, *manzai* artists appear regularly on television variety shows.

【講談】 Kōdan こうだん

講談は**落語**同様、**寄席演芸**の1つで、17世紀に始まったとされています。釈台と称する小机を置き、講釈師はそれを張り扇で打ちながら、軍記や武勇伝などを独特の調子で語るのです。1920年代以降は映画や軽演劇に圧倒されたり、講釈の名手が亡くなったりして不振となった時期もありましたが、近年は女性講釈師の活躍も目立ち、新作も発表されるなど、再び盛り返しの兆しを見せています。

Historical narrative : *Kōdan*, a typical **vaudeville performance**, like **comic storytelling**, began in the seventeenth century. While tapping a small table called a *shakudai* with a paper-covered folded fan, the professional storyteller relates tales of war and martial valor in a unique tone. After the 1920's, there was a period of stagnation, being surpassed by movies and light theatrical performances, and with master storytellers disappearing. But in recent years they have shown signs of making a comeback in which female storytellers are conspicuous and new compositions are being released.

left : *koto*, center : *shamisen*, right : *shakuhachi*

【邦楽】
Hōgaku
ほうがく

邦楽とは広義には日本の音楽のことですが、一般には近世に発達した**三味線**、箏、**尺八**などの音楽のことをさし、**雅楽**や**民謡**は含まれません。

邦楽を大別すると、**浄瑠璃**をはじめとする語り物と、**長唄**や**小唄**をはじめとする歌い物とに分けられ、いずれもその主たる伴奏楽器が**三味線**であるという共通点があります。

邦楽は伝統音楽であるため、現在では万人向けというよりは、主に専門家や愛好家によって演奏され、楽しまれています。しかし最近は、和楽器と洋楽器を組み合わせることによって邦楽と西洋音楽とを融合させ、新たな音楽を生み出そうとする若手のバンドも出現しています。

Traditional Japanese music : *Hōgaku* in the broad sense refers to the music of Japan, but it usually indicates such music as that of **_shamisen_**, *koto* with 13 strings, and a **five-holed bamboo clarinet**, which developed in the modern era(after around 1600), and does not include **ancient court music** and **folk songs**.

The general classifications of *hōgaku* can be divided into narrated stories, including **ballad drama**(*jōruri*), and sung or chanted pieces, including **long epic songs** and **little ballads**. Both have in common the **_shamisen_** as the principal accompanying instrument.

Because *hōgaku* is traditional music, it is at present mainly performed and appreciated by specialists and enthusiasts, rather than by everybody. However, recently there are some young music bands, trying to create a new kind of music through using Japanese and western instruments in combination, thus uniting the two kinds of music.

【詩吟】 しぎん Shigin

　漢詩に節をつけて吟詠するのが詩吟です。**琵琶**を伴奏とする**琵琶歌**の中から吟詠の部分だけを取り出し、そのほかの部分を削り落とした形で世間一般に詠（うた）われるようになりました。**琵琶歌**に比べ習得しやすく、声を出すことで健康増進にもなることから愛好者も多く、流派、宗家などの数も毎年増え続けているようです。

Recitation of Chinese poems : Putting music to Chinese poetry and reciting it is called *shigin*. It came to be recited by general public in a form of only taking the part for recitation from **Japanese lute songs**, which accompaniment is **Japanese lute**, and leaving out the rest part. Since it's easy to master compared to **Japanese lute song** and lifting the voice is good for the health, there are many *shigin* lovers. Every year the number of schools and head families continues to increase.

【謡】 うたい Utai

　能の声楽部分が謡です。旋律的な部分だけでなくせりふの部分をも含みます。しかし、**能**の一要素にとどまらず、**室町時代**（1392〜1573）ごろから独立した芸能としても愛好され、単独での演奏、鑑賞も行われてきました。現在も庶民に根強い愛好者がいて、このことが**能**の存続を支える基盤ともなっています。

Noh chant : The vocal part of **Noh** drama is called *utai*. It includes not only the melodic parts but the spoken lines as well. However, it is not an element confined to **Noh** drama but has been loved as an independent performing art since the **Muromachi Period**(1392-1573), and performance and appreciation of *utai* by itself has been held. Even today, there are strong devotees among the people, and this fact has become the basis supporting the continued existence of **Noh** drama.

【長唄】
Nagauta
ながうた

　長唄は**三味線**に合わせて歌う長編の歌い物で、**江戸時代**（1603〜1867）中期に大きく発達しました。それまでの江戸（今の東京）の文化はすべて京都や大阪の文化の模倣だったのですが、江戸生まれ・江戸育ちの奏者が独自の曲調を生み出し、彼らが演奏することによって、初めて江戸独自ともいえる文化が誕生したのです。

　もとは**歌舞伎**の舞踊曲として生まれた長唄ですが、その発展過程で**謡**、**狂言**、**民謡**などの歌詞や節回しが取り入れられたため、きわめて多様性に富んでいるという特徴があります。また、時には舞踊から独立し、**三味線**だけの伴奏で物語風の長唄が演奏されることもあります。

L ong epic songs : *Nagauta*, long pieces sung with *shamisen* accompaniment, developed on a grand scale in the middle years of the **Edo Period**(1603-1867). Up until that time, the culture of Edo(present-day Tokyo) was an imitation of the culture of Kyoto and Osaka, but performers born and raised in Edo produced their own unique melodies and, based on their concerts, a culture came into being that for the first time could be called uniquely Edo.

Originally, *nagauta* were created as dance music for **Kabuki**, but an outstanding feature is that they are rich in diversity, given that in their process of development they adapted words and melody of **Noh chant**, **Kyogen**, and **folk songs**. In addition, *nagauta* on occation have become independent of dance and are performed as storytelling with only *shamisen* accompaniment.

【小唄】
Kouta
こうた

　小唄も今日に引き継がれている邦楽の１つで、**三味線**に合わせて洒落や風刺のきいた歌が歌われます。**江戸時代**（1603〜1867）の小品の三味線唄である**端唄**から派生したもので、**明治時代**（1868〜1912）後期に今日のような形になりました。現在では家元がたくさんあり、小唄の愛好者も多く、手軽にできる宴会芸としても人気があります。また、小唄の**三味線**では**ばち**を使わず、爪弾いて演奏するのが特徴です。

L ittle ballads : *Kouta* is a kind of Japanese music handed down to today and features songs of humor and irony sung to *shamisen* accompaniment. *Kouta* ballads are derived from the little **Edo Period**(1603-1867) *shamisen* songs known as a **short love songs**(*ha-uta*), and they assumed their present form at the end of the **Meiji Period**(1868-1912). Today there are lots of needs of the schools and many lovers of *kouta*; it is also popular as informal entertainment at dinner parties. In addition, an outstanding feature of *kouta* is that the *shamisen* is played with the fingers, not with a **plectrum**.

【大道芸】
Daidōgei
だいどうげい

　一定の演じる場所を持たず、人々の多く集まる道ばたで演ずる芸をいいます。演じて喜捨を乞う場合と物を売るために演ずる場合とがあります。**浪花節**など日本の伝統芸のいくつかも、最初は大道芸から出発しました。物を売る場合は初めに口上を述べて人々の関心を引きつけ、最後に物を買わせるという手順を踏むため、その口上自体が芸となったものもあります。がまの油売りはその典型例です。

S treet performances : These are performances with no fixed locale on roadsides where a lot of people gather. They are performed either to receive donations or to sell things. Some of the traditional Japanese arts, like the *naniwa-bushi* **reciting**, first started from *daidōgei*. It usually took a procedure of drawing people's attention by delivering a lively monologue in order to sell things at the end, and some, among those monologues, themselves had become the performance. Selling "toad's grease," saying that it heals chaps and cracks in the skin is a typical example.

【民謡】
Min'yō
みんよう

　民謡は、庶民の集団生活の中で生まれた民衆の歌謡です。生活感情や地域性などをよく反映しており、多くの人々に長く歌い継がれてきました。**田植え**のときに歌われた**田植歌**、**茶摘み**のときに歌われた**茶摘歌**、水夫が船を漕ぎながら歌った**舟歌**などをはじめとして、いろいろな種類があります。高音域の美しさや細かい節回しが特徴です。伴奏には**笛**や**太鼓**、**尺八**、**三味線**などが使われ、夏に行われる**盆踊り**では民謡に合わせ、大勢が輪になってにぎやかに踊ります。新作も多く、テレビ番組でのコンテストも人気があります。

Folk songs : *Min'yō* are popular songs born of the collective life of the common people. The songs often reflect life's emotions, regionality and so on, and have been sung and handed down by a lot of people for a long time. There are various kinds of these songs, including **rice-planting songs**(*taue uta*) sung when **planting rice**, **tea-picking songs**(*chatsumi uta*) sung when **picking tea**, **boat songs**(*funa uta*) sung by sailors while rowing their boats. They feature a beauty of high notes and delicate melodies. **Flutes**, **drums**, **five-holed bamboo clarinets**, and *shamisen* are used for accompaniment, and during the **Bon Festival dance**(*bon-odori*) the general practice is to form a circle and dance in a lively way together with *min'yō*. There are a lot of new compositions, and its contests on television programs are popular.

【わらべうた】
Warabeuta

　童謡は子供のために作られた歌ですが、その中で、特に生活の中で子供が歌い、遊び仲間を通じて伝承されてきた歌はわらべうたと呼ばれています。作詞作曲者は不詳で、自然に広まっていったというところは**民謡**と似ています。

　日本のわらべうたの原形は、**平安時代（794～1185）**にできたといわれています。多くは手まりや**お手玉**、**なわとび**、**かくれんぼ**といった遊びのなかで歌われてきました。そのほか、自然、動物や年中行事に関するものも多くあります。

　年月が経つにつれ、歌の内容は変化してきましたが、日本の伝統的な音階に基づくという特徴は変わっていません。

Children's songs : *Dōyō* are songs created for children. Specifically, *warabeuta* are songs that children sing in their daily lives and that are handed down through their playmates. They resemble **folk songs** in that the lyricists and composers are unknown, and they became widespread spontaneously.

　The original form of *warabeuta* was probably established in the **Heian Period**(794-1185). Most of them have been sung in games like traditional Japanese handball, **beanbags**, **rope skipping** and **hide-and-seek**. In addition, there are many sung in connection with nature, animals and annual events.

　With the passage of years, song contents have changed, but the main characteristic, based on the traditional Japanese musical scale, has not changed.

【浪花節】
なにわぶし
Naniwa-bushi

浪曲ともいいます。美談や悲劇を**三味線**の伴奏で歌い語る、日本独特の演芸です。悲しさや怒りをことさら強調することによって**人情**や**義理**などの典型的な日本人の心情を演じ、庶民の抑圧された心を代弁しました。そのため1960年ごろまでは非常な人気を獲得し、**落語**や**講談**とともに庶民の人気娯楽でした。やがてテレビ時代の到来とともに浪花節は急速に衰え、歌謡曲の歌手に転向した浪曲師もいました。現在でも「浪花節的」といえば、それは合理性に対して**義理人情**を優先させる人を形容するときに使う言葉です。しかし、最近は**義理人情**だけでない新しい試みが少しずつ若い層のファンを獲得しつつあります。

***N**aniwa-bushi* **recitings :** It is also called *Rōkyoku*. It is a uniquely Japanese performing art in which admirable stories and tragedies are musically recited with *shamisen* accompaniment. By especially emphasizing sadness and indignation, *naniwa-bushi* enacted prototypical sentiments of the Japanese people, like **humane feelings** and **moral obligations**, and spoke for the oppressed hearts of the common people. Hence, until around 1960 they had enormous popularity and, along with **comic storytelling** and **historical narrative**, were a popular amusement for the common people. In the long run, with the arrival of the television age, *naniwa-bushi* suddenly faded away, and some of the reciters even turned to become singers of popular songs. Even now, the word "*naniwa-bushi*-like" is used to describe people who prefer **moral obligations and humane feelings** over rationality. However, recently experimental *naniwa-bushi* works, that are not only based on **moral obligations and humane feelings**, are gaining younger fans.

文化・芸術

【日本画】
にほんが
Nihonga

　日本の絵画は、中国から伝わった技法の影響下に成長しました。**奈良時代**（710〜784）から**平安時代**（794〜1185）には徐々に日本的な絵画の特質が現れ始め、大和絵として確立しました。**鎌倉時代**（1185〜1333）にはやはり中国から**水墨画**が伝わり、**室町時代**（1392〜1573）に日本独自のものが完成します。**江戸時代**（1603〜1867）には**浮世絵**が誕生しました。狭義で日本画と呼ばれるものは、伝統的な材質、技法、形式で作られた絵画で、絹布や和紙などの上に、**墨や岩絵の具などの顔料**を使って筆やはけで描きます。画面には**ふすま**や**屏風**、色紙などが用いられるほか、絵巻の形でも描かれ、その大きさも形式もさまざまです。

Japanese paintings : The paintings of Japan developed under the influence of techniques brought from China. From the **Nara Period**(710-784) to the **Heian Period**(794-1185), the particular quality of Japanese-style painting gradually began to appear and was established as classical Japanese painting. In the **Kamakura Period**(1185-1333), **ink painting** was introduced, again from China, and its uniquely Japanese style was perfected in the **Muromachi Period**(1392-1573). In the **Edo Period**(1603-1867), *ukiyoe* flourished. In the narrow sense, works called *nihonga* are paintings done with traditional materials, techniques and form; they are painted with brushes and paints, such as **India ink** and mineral pigments like the rock paints, on silk and Japanese paper. *Nihonga* come in various sizes and shapes. In addition to **paper sliding doors**, **folding screens** and square poetry paper being used as surfaces for painting, they are also painted in the form of picture scrolls.

【水墨画】
Suibokuga
すいぼくが

　水墨画は墨を使って描く絵画です。墨の濃淡や描線の強弱、ぼかしといった手法を特徴とするもので、描く紙の品質によっても雰囲気が変わってきます。

　鎌倉時代（1185～1333）に中国からもたらされた後、室町時代（1392～1573）に最も栄えました。当初は禅宗にちなんだ宗教画が多かったのですが、15世紀ごろになると風景や花鳥などの画題が扱われるようになりました。

　日本における水墨画は雪舟（せっしゅう）という画僧によって大成されました。彼は本場中国で水墨画の画法を学んだ後、独自の画風を作り上げたのです。

Ink painting : *Suibokuga* are pictures painted in **India ink**. Their special characteristic is the method of shading the **India ink** and making strong and weak strokes, and the atmosphere changes with the quality of the paper on which they are painted.

After being brought over from China in the **Kamakura Period**(1185-1333), ink painting was at the height of its popularity in the **Muromachi Period**(1392-1573). At first, there were mostly religious paintings connected with teaching of the **Zen sect**, but, by the fifteenth century, it started to deal with subjects such as landscapes, flowers and birds.

Suibokuga in Japan came to perfection with the painter priest **Sesshū**. After learning the art of *suibokuga* at its source in China, he created his own particular style of painting.

【浮世絵】 Ukiyoe うきよえ

浮世絵は**江戸時代**（1603〜1867）に発達した絵画で、その多くは版画として普及しました。17世紀後半、**菱川師宣**が木版画を1枚の絵として独立させたのが初めとされています。当初は墨1色でしたが、18世紀中ごろには多色刷りの技法が**鈴木春信**によって開発されました。

浮世絵の画題には美女や役者、**力士**など人物のほか、風景や庶民の生活状況なども使われました。中でも**喜多川歌麿**による美人画や**東洲斎写楽**による**歌舞伎**役者の絵、**葛飾北斎**の風景画などが有名です。また、浮世絵の画法はゴッホなどのフランス印象派に影響を与えたことでも知られています。

Pictures of the floating world : *Ukiyoe* are paintings developed in the **Edo Period**(1603-1867), most of which became widespread as woodblock prints. They began in the second half of the seventeenth century when HISHIKAWA **Moronobu** made a woodblock print to stand as one independent picture. At first, only India ink was used, but in the eighteenth century SUZUKI **Harunobu** developed the technique of printing with several colors.

In addition to the human subjects of *ukiyoe*—beautiful women, actors and *sumō* **wrestlers**—landscapes and the living conditions of the common people were also illustrated. Famous among these are the prints of beautiful women by KITAGAWA **Utamaro**, **Kabuki** actors by TŌSHŪSAI **Sharaku**, and landscapes by KATSUSHIKA **Hokusai**. In addition, *ukiyoe* art is known for its influence on Van Gogh and the Impressionists.

【陶磁器】
Tōjiki
とうじき

　土で器を作り、うわ薬を塗って焼いたものを**陶器**といい、光の透過性はありません。一方、**磁器**は硬度が高く、光の透過性があります。これらを総称して陶磁器といいます。

　日本の陶磁器は実用に使われるだけでなく、鑑賞用として芸術性の高い作品が多くあります。**華道**や**茶道**において花器や茶碗など器そのものの鑑賞も重要視されてきたためそれが陶磁器のいっそうの発展に結び付いてきたのです。

　陶磁器のことを、「**瀬戸物**」とも呼びますが、これは有名な産地である愛知県瀬戸市の名前からきています。代表的な**陶器**には滋賀の信楽焼、岡山の備前焼があり、**磁器**では佐賀県の伊万里焼、石川の九谷焼が有名です。

Ceramics and porcelain : Vessels made of earth, coated with a glaze and baked are **ceramics** and are not permeable by light. Meanwhile, **porcelain** are very hard and are permeable by light. These are all generally called *tōjiki*.

Japanese *tōjiki* are not only for practical use but are often works appreciated for their high art. In the art of **flower arrangement** and the **tea ceremony**, the very appreciation of the flower vases and tea cups as vessels for their own sake is regarded as important; those arts, therefore, were connected all the more to the development of *tōjiki*.

Tōjiki are also referred to as ***setomono***, a term taken from Seto City in Aichi Prefecture, a well-known production site. Representative **ceramics** are Shigaraki ware from Shiga and Bizen ware from Okayama; among **porcelains**, Imari ware from Saga Prefecture and Kutani ware from Ishikawa are famous.

【漆器】

しっき Shikki

　漆器は漆を塗った工芸品で、東南アジア一帯で２千数百年前から使われてきました。ウルシの木の樹液を濃縮した塗料に顔料を混ぜたものを、**竹**や木や布の素材に塗って作ります。日本では**仏教**が伝来した６世紀に唐文化の影響を強く受け、漆器作りの技術が飛躍的に向上しました。その後も家具や食器として生活の中で幅広く使われ、やがて美術工芸品としての漆器も作られるようになります。15〜16世紀にはポルトガルやオランダとの貿易でヨーロッパに広く紹介されたため、漆器は英語で「ジャパン」と呼ばれるのです。漆器の特長は湿気や熱に強く、耐久性に優れていることです。現在も輪島塗や会津塗などが作られています。

Lacquerware : *Shikki* is craftwork coated with lacquer, and it has been in general use in all over Southeast Asia for more than 2,000 years. **Bamboo**, wood and cloth materials are painted with a mixture of paints and concentrated lacquer tree sap. In Japan there was a strong influence from China in the sixth century when **Buddhism** was introduced, and the techniques of making *shikki* improved rapidly. Subsequently, *shikki* was used widely in daily life for furniture and tableware and before long it even came to be made for industrial art objects. In the trade with Portugal and Holland in the fifteenth and sixteenth centuries, it was widely introduced into Europe and in English was called "japan." The chief characteristics of *shikki* are its strength against humidity and heat and its outstanding durability. Even now, Wajima lacquer and Aizu lacquer are being made.

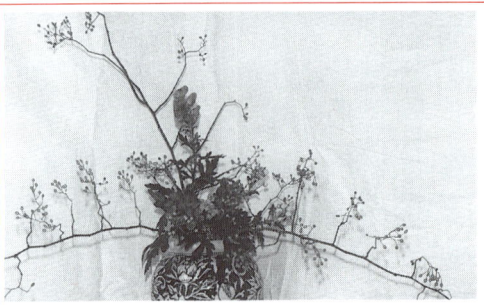

【華道・生け花】
Kadō,Ikebana
かどう・いけばな

華道は、16世紀ごろから盛んになった日本の伝統的な芸術の1つです。生け花とも呼ばれ、6世紀に**仏教**の**僧**が仏前に花を捧げたのがその起源だといわれています。自然の花を使って天（宇宙）、地（地球）、人の3要素をバランスよく表現する、という考え方が基本です。広口で平たい花器に水を張り、金属板にたくさんの太い針が上向きに並んだ剣山で花を固定し、盛り上げるように花を生ける、という様式が一般的です。はさみで長短をつけたり、葉の形を修正したり、手で反りを加えたりして、自然の美や心情を表現するのです。現代では芸術の1ジャンルとして、植物を使わない前衛的な生け花も行われています。

Flower arrangement : *Kadō* is a traditional Japanese art that has flourished since the sixteenth century. Also called *ikebana*, its origin is said to date from the sixth century when **Buddhist priests** offered up flowers before Buddha. Its fundamental concept is to express the three elements of heaven, earth, and mankind in a balanced composition,using natural flowers. The general style is to fill a wide-mouthed, simple vase with water, and stick and heap up the flowers on *kenzan*, that is a metallic plate with a lot of thick needles pointing upwards. Natural beauty and one's feelings are expressed by using scissors to adjust the length of the stems and to modify the shape of the leaves and by using the hands to add curvature. Today, avant-garde *ikebana* that does not even use plants is one genre of the art.

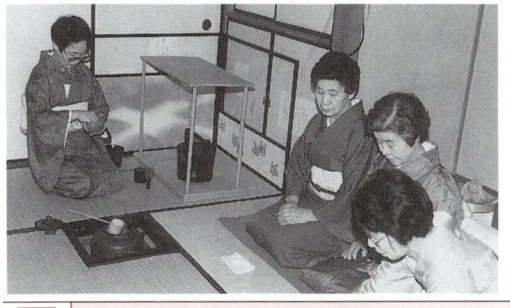

【茶道】

Sadō
さどう

　茶道は、来客の際の茶の入れ方や飲み方の伝統的な作法で、**茶の湯**ともいわれます。茶道では抹茶といって、日常飲む煎茶とは違うものを主に使用します。茶碗に粉末の抹茶を入れ、湯を注いで茶せんでかき混ぜ、泡立てて飲みます。

　16世紀に**千利休**が**わび**、**さび**といわれる簡素な趣や「**一期一会**」の心を取り入れ、茶道を大成しました。「**一期一会**」とは一生にただ1度の出会いという意味で、主人は出会いを大切にするために、**床の間**に飾る掛け軸や花、茶碗などの道具を心を込めて用意します。一方、客はそれらのものから主人のもてなしの心を思い、感謝の気持ちを持つのです。

Tea ceremony : *Sadō*, also called *chadō* or **cha no yu**, is the traditional etiquette of preparing and drinking **tea** when one has guests. In *sadō*, special powdered tea, different from ordinary Japanese tea is chiefly used. The powdered tea is put into a teacup, hot water is poured on it, it is whipped with a bamboo whisk till it foams and it is drunk.

In the sixteenth century, **Sen-no-Rikyū** brought *sadō* to perfection by incorporating the simple aesthetic values known as *wabi*(**subtle taste**) and *sabi*(**elegant simplicity**) and the concept that **every single encounter never repeats in a life time**(*ichigo ichie*). To make the encounter important, the host prepares with deep sincerity implements such as a hunging scroll or flowers to put in the **alcove** or the teacups. From such activities, meanwhile, the guests know the host's warm hospitality and are filled with gratitude.

	楷書 kaisho	文	心	魚	音
	行書 gyōsho	文	心	魚	音
	草書 sōsho	文	心	乭	音

【書道】
Shodō
しょどう

　書道は**毛筆**と**墨**で文字を書く芸術で、精神的な深みや美しさが表されます。もともと中国から伝わったものですが、日本では表意文字の**漢字**に加え、日本で発明された表音文字の**仮名**を組み合わせて独特の文字芸術を作り上げてきました。**毛筆**は墨を含ませれば、ペンと違って文字の太さや濃淡を自由に調整できます。そのため書く人の精神や観念が表現できるのです。書体は標準的な**楷書**のほか、やや崩した**行書**、さらに崩した**草書**などに書き分けることができます。**年賀状**などを除いては、ふだんはあまり**毛筆**で文字を書くことはありませんが、小学校の授業には書道が取り入れられています。

Calligraphy : *Shodō* is the art of drawing characters with a **brush** and **India ink** to express spiritual depth and beauty. *Shodō* originally came from China, but in Japan **Chinese characters**(*kanji*) were combined with the **Japanese syllabary**(*kana*), devised in Japan, to create this unique character art. With a **brush** soaked in **India ink** one can freely control, unlike with a pen, the thickness and the tone of the characters. That is how the calligraphers are able to express their spirits and ideas. Beyond the standard **square style of writing**(*kaisho*), calligraphic style can be divided into the somewhat simplified **semicursive style**(*gyōsho*) and the still more simplified **cursive style**(*sōsho*). Except for **New Year's cards** and the like, a **brush** is ordinarily not used for writing, but *shodō* is included in the elementary school curriculum.

【俳句】
はいく

Haiku

俳句は5・7・5の17音で構成される定型詩です。5・7・5と7・7を交互に繰り返す連歌の、最初の5・7・5の部分から派生したもので、**江戸時代**（1603～1867）に**松尾芭蕉**が現在の形に確立させました。俳句という呼称が一般に広まったのは、**明治時代**（1868～1912）に**正岡子規**が活躍するようになってからのことです。短い形式の中で自然の美や人の心の中を表現することができるため、現在では世界的な広がりを見せ、アメリカでは教育にも取り入れられています。本来の俳句には、季節を表わす**季語**が詠み込まれます。季語によって、その語の背景にあるものが連想され、わずか17音の中で句に広がりと深みが出てくるのです。

Poems in seventeen syllables : *Haiku* is poetry structured in the set form of 17 syllables, arranged in groups of 5, 7, and 5. It derives from the first line of the linked verse which alternately repeats a line in groups of 5, 7, and 5 syllables, and a line in groups of 7 and 7 syllables; in the **Edo Period**(1603-1867), MATSUO Bashō established its present form. The designation *haiku* became widespread with the work of MASAOKA Shiki in the **Meiji Period**(1868-1912). Because *haiku* can express the beauty of nature and the depths of the human heart in a brief form, it now has spread throughout the world and in the United States it is even part of one's education.

A **season word**, indicating the season, is included in *haiku* in the original style. The **season word** brings out ideas associated with the background of the word, and, within the space of just 17 syllables, it adds breadth and depth to the verse.

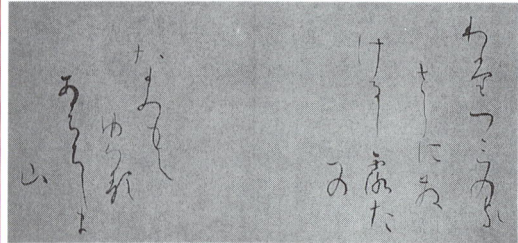

【短歌】
たんか
Tanka

　短歌は、5・7・5・7・7の5句31音で構成された短い叙情詩で、前半の5・7・5と後半の7・7の2部構成です。8世紀に編まれた日本最古の歌集『万葉集』にも、すでにこの形式で詠まれているものが多く見られます。

　『古今和歌集』の序文には「大和歌は人の心を種として、よろづの言の葉とぞなれりける」とあります。単純な形式で喜怒哀楽を表現するには、言外に感じられる余情を含まなければならないのが特徴であり、また欠かせない要素です。文字には表されていない余情や、深い趣を連想させることができるのが、優れた短歌の条件の1つであるともいえるでしょう。現代にも多くの愛好者がいます。

Poems in thirty-one syllables : *Tanka* is short, lyrical poetry structured in 31 syllables arranged in groups of 5, 7, 5, 7 and 7, syllables, in a two-part form with the first part in 5, 7, 5, and the second part in 7 and 7. Even in the "**Man'yōshū,**"(*the Collection of Ten Thousand Leaves*) which is the Japan's oldest anthology of poetry, compiled in the eighth century, many of the poems were already composed in this form.

 It is written in the preface of "**Kokinwakashū,**"(*the Collection of Japanese Poems from Ancient and Modern Times*) that "the Japanese poetry grows out of people's feelings to become leaves of words for everything in the world." Its main feature is that, in expressing the gamut of feelings in a simple form, it must contain–and this is an indispensable feature–a suggestiveness felt beyond the words. Perhaps a requirement for an outstanding *tanka* is that it causes associations with a suggestiveness not expressed in words and a deep elegance. Today there are many lovers of this art form.

【日本の人形】
Nihon no ningyō
にほんのにんぎょう

　日本には、埴輪や土偶など人の形をしたものは古代からありましたが、いわゆる「人形」と呼べるものは、9世紀に出現しています。しかし当初は信仰に関連したものが多く、玩具としての人形は、紙で作られた簡単なものしかありませんでした。

　美術的、工芸的な要素を持った人形は、人形浄瑠璃が出現した後、18世紀から作られ始めたとされています。その後は、茶を運ぶぜんまい仕掛けのからくり人形など複雑なものも現れ、**ひな祭り**が盛んになると豪華な**ひな人形**も作られました。現在では郷土色豊かな人形が日本各地で生産されています。

Japanese dolls : In Japan, figures in human form, like *haniwa* and *dogū*, have existed since ancient times, but the term "doll" emerged in the ninth century. However, early on they were mainly associated with religious belief; dolls as playthings were simple objects made only out of paper.

Dolls with artistic and manufactured elements began to be made in the eighteenth century, after the emergence of ballad using puppets. Later, puppets that carried tea emerged, with complex mechanical construction using springs, and, when the **Doll's Festival** became widespread, colorful **dolls for the Doll's Festival** appeared. Today, dolls rich in local color are made as specialities of certain famous regions in Japan.

【こけし】Kokeshi

こけしは女児の姿を表した木製の郷土人形です。円筒形の胴に丸い頭が特徴で、ふつう手足はついていません。東北地方の特産で、17世紀から18世紀ごろ、**温泉**の湯治客の土産用に作られていたものです。現在でもその愛らしく素朴な姿に根強い人気があってコレクターも多く、観光土産の1つとして東北地方以外でも製造・販売されています。

こけしの原木には主にミズキやサクラが使われます。その原木をろくろに取り付け、回しながら削ります。そして形を整えた後、髪や目鼻を頭部に、**着物**を胴体に、それぞれ筆で描いていくのです。この技術は職人芸といえるもので、師から弟子へと受け継がれていきます。

Kokeshi **dolls :** *Kokeshi* are wooden folk dolls representing little girls. Their main characteristic is a cylindrically-shaped body with a round head, generally without hands and feet. They are products indigenous to the Tōhoku region, and in the seventeenth and eighteenth centuries they were used as souvenirs for visitors to the **hot springs**. Even now, with the deeply-rooted popularity of this charming, simple shape, there are a lot of collectors, and the dolls are made and sold beyond the Tōhoku region as tourist souvenirs.

Wood from dogwood and cherry trees is used as pulp for *kokeshi*. The pulp is put into a lathe and whittled down while spinning. After the shape is completed, the hair, eyes and nose are painted on the head and **kimono** on the body. This technique is worth being called a craftsman art and is passed down from master to apprentice.

【根付】 Netsuke ねつけ

江戸時代 (1603〜1867) までの日本人は**和服**のみを着ていたため、必ず**帯**を締めていました。その**帯**に、主に男性がたばこ入れや印籠、巾 着などをひもで挟んで下げました。そのひもの先端に付けてある小さな彫刻のことを根付といいます。珊瑚、めのう、象牙などを使って人物、動物などを精巧に彫刻したもので、現在では芸術品として高い評価を得ています。

Miniature carvings for suspending a pouch : Until the **Edo Period**(1603-1867), the Japanese only wore **Japanese-style garments**, which they invariably tied with a **sash**. From the **sash**, men generally would attach and hang by string, a tobacco container, a medicine or seal case and a purse. The small carvings attached to the end of the string are called *netsuke*. They were delicately carved humans and animals, using coral, agate, ivory and so on, and today they bring high value as art objects.

【香道】 Kōdō こうどう

日本人は伝統的に菜食が中心であるため、ヨーロッパや中国のように体臭を消すために強い香りを必要とすることはありませんでした。日本では、**室町時代** (1392〜1573) 末期は**茶道**が大成されようとする時期にあたり、花とともに香りも**茶道**のなかで鑑賞の対象となったのでした。

香道とは、香木を炊いてその香りを鑑賞し、「**わび・さび**」の美を追求することです。

Incense ceremony : Because the Japanese traditionally ate a vegetarian diet, a strong fragrance to cancel body odor, as in Europe and China, was not necessary. In Japan, at the end of the **Muromachi Period**(1392-1573) when the **tea ceremony** was coming to perfection, fragrances also, together with flowers, became elements for appreciation in **tea ceremony.**

Kōdō refers to appreciating the fragrance from burning aromatic wood and to seeking after the aesthetic value of "**subtle taste and elegant simplicity**."

【七宝焼】

Shippō-yaki
しっぽうやき

　「七宝」とは**仏教**で金、銀、珊瑚などの7種の宝物をさしますが、七宝焼とはその七宝をちりばめたように美しい焼物という意味です。銀や銅などの金属や**陶器**の素地にガラス質のうわ薬を焼き付け、花や鳥などの模様を表し出します。それを高温で熱し、うわ薬が2、3分でガラスのような状態に変化すると、それを磨いて仕上げます。アクセサリーや皿などがよく作られます。

　8世紀ごろ、ペルシア、ヨーロッパ地域から中国経由で伝えられましたが、いったんすたれました。その後、再び17世紀に朝鮮からその製法が伝わり、現在に至っています。手軽にできる手工芸の1つとしても人気があります。

Cloisonné ware : *Shippō* indicates the seven treasures in **Buddhism**, including gold, silver and coral, but *Shippō-yaki* means beautiful ceramic ware as if it's inlaid with these seven treasures. A glass-like glaze is baked onto metals like silver and copper and onto the **ceramic** foundation, with designs of things such as flowers and birds. After the objects are heated to a high temperature, the glaze changes in a few minutes to a glass-like state and they are completed by polishing. They are often used as accessories or plates.

　Shippō-yaki came to Japan in the eighth century from regions in Persia and Europe by way of China, and for a time it died out. Later, the manufacturing process was brought in a second time, in the seventeenth century from Korea, and has continued to the present time. It is popular as a handicraft that is easy to make.

【屏風】
Byōbu
びょうぶ

屏風は風を防ぐため、あるいは仕切りや装飾のために室内で用いられる家具です。高さは5尺（約1.5メートル）、幅は2尺（約66センチ）を標準とするものを2枚から6枚ほどつなぎ合わせて波状に折り曲げ、倒れないように立てるのです。側面には紙が張られ、片面には金箔や銀箔を使って大和絵などが描かれています。

朝鮮から贈られたという記録が最初で、**平安時代**（794～1185）には、宮廷貴族の間で用いられていました。その後、寺院でも使われるようになり、**安土桃山時代**（1573～1603）以降武士や庶民にも広まりました。現代では**結婚式**などの儀式のとき以外、日常生活ではあまり使用されません。

Folding screens : *Byōbu* are household items used in rooms to ward off breezes or as partitions or decoration. They consist of from two to six connected panels that have a standard height of about one and a half meters and width of about 66 centimeters; the panels are set up in half folds so that the screen will not fall over. The sides are covered with paper, while one side has classical Japanese paintings with gold and silver leaf.

They were first recorded to have been sent from Korea, and in the **Heian Period**(794-1185) they were used by court nobles. Subsequently, they also came to be used in temples, and in the **Azuchi-Momoyama Period**(1573-1603) they spread to the warrior class and to the common people. At present, beyond ceremonies such as **weddings**, they are not really used in daily life.

【十二単】

Jūni-hitoe

じゅうにひとえ

　十二単は、**平安時代**（794〜1185）以後の宮廷婦人や武家の娘の正装です。**奈良時代**（710〜784）の女官が着用していた衣装が変化したもので、現在でも**皇室**の結婚の際は十二単が着用されます。最近では1993年の皇太子の結婚式に雅子妃が着用して、テレビで全世界に報道されました。一般人が着用する**着物**とは違い、下着の上に色鮮やかな**着物**を、ふつうは12枚重ねて着ます。すそは長く伸ばし、引きずって歩くのです。

　なお、十二単を着るときは「すべらかし」という、後ろに長く垂れ下げた髪型にし、手には桧扇を持つことになっています。

Twelve-layered ceremonial robe : *Jūni-hitoe* is a ceremonial robe that was the proper attire for court ladies and daughters of the warrior-class families in the **Heian Period**(794-1185) and after. It was a modification of the clothing worn by court ladies in the **Nara Period**(710-784) and even now *jūni-hitoe* is worn on the occasion of weddings of the members of the **Imperial Family**. Recently, in the wedding in 1993 of the Crown Prince, Princess Masako wore it and the news was broadcast by television throughout the world. It is different from the **kimonos** worn by ordinary people, usually having brightly-colored **kimonos** worn on top of each other in twelve-layers over undergarments. The skirt has an extended train that trails behind when walking.

　In addition, when wearing the *jūni-hitoe*, the hairstyle is gathered at the neck to hang down the back(*suberakashi*) and a fan made of Japanese cypress is held in the hands.

【日本刀・刀】

Nihontō, Katana

にほんとう・かたな

日本刀は、日本固有の方法で鍛えた刀で、その優れた切れ味と美しさによって海外にも早くから知られていました。片刃で反りがあるのが特徴です。柄の根元には、敵の刀を受け止めたり、柄を握る手を守ったりするため、つばという金具を入れます。

刀は武士の魂といわれ、**江戸時代**（1603〜1867）には武家社会の象徴ともされていました。**明治時代**（1868〜1912）に入ると武士は廃業を強いられ、刀も禁止されました。その後は軍隊の将校が地位の象徴として持っていました。戦後はその澄み切った清らかさと美しさから芸術品として鑑賞する以外には、所持することを禁じられています。

Japanese swords : *Nihontō* are swords tempered with a peculiarly Japanese method, and early on they became known overseas for their superior sharpness and beauty. Their main feature is that it is single-edged and slightly curved. At the bass of the hilt, there is a metal piece called a sword guard which serves to ward off an opponent's *katana* and to protect the hands gripping the hilt.

The *katana*, said to be the soul of the samurai, was regarded in the **Edo Period**(1603-1867) as a symbol of feudal society. In the **Meiji Period**(1868-1912), samurai were forced to give up their position, and *katana* were also prohibited. Subsequently, military officers wore them as symbols of rank. After the war, it was forbidden to possess them, except to appreciate them as art objects for their limpid purity and beauty .

【熊手】
Kumade
くまで

　熊手は穀物や落ち葉をかき集めるための道具で、ふつうは竹でできています。熊の手のように爪が広がっているため「熊手」といわれ、現在でも一般に広く使われています。

　この熊手が昔、祭礼の日に**神社**の境内で売られることがありました。とりわけ、商売繁盛の神がまつられた**神社**で熊手がよく売れたことから「熊手で金儲けができる」といわれ始めました。さらにそれが「熊手は金銀をかき集めて取り込む」と発展し、さまざまな飾りが付けられ、**縁起物**の１つとして売られるようになったのです。

　毎年11月に**神社**で行われる**酉の市**では、今でも**縁起物**として人気を集めています。

Bamboo rakes : *Kumade* are implements for raking up grains and fallen leaves and are usually made of bamboo. They are called *Kumade* which means bear claws for their prongs extending like the claws of a bear, and they are still commonly used.

Kumade used to be sold within **shrine** compounds on festival days. Because *kumade* sold especially well at **shrines** housing gods for business prosperity, the saying started that "you can make money with *kumade*." This developed further as "*Kumade* rake in the money," and they came to be decorated in a variety of ways and sold as **good luck charms**.

Even now, at the **festival of the rooster** that occur at **shrines** every year in November, they are popular as **good luck charms**.

【日本庭園】
Nihon-teien
にほんていえん

　日本庭園は、幾何学的に作られた西洋のものと比べ、自然景観を重視した作りになっています。土を山の形に盛ったり、池を海に見立てたり、水を引いて川を作ったりして自然世界を模倣したものが主で、飛び石を配置し、腰掛けを置いた茶庭(ちゃてい)を取り入れることもあります。

　そのほか、代表的な日本庭園の形式に**枯山水**があります。これは水を使わず、石や砂だけで山水を表現する庭です。石組で山や滝を表し、敷きつめた白砂に竹ぼうきなどで水の流れを描き、川を表現するのです。**室町時代**（1392〜1573）に中国から輸入した山水画の影響を受けており、多くは**禅**院の前庭として作庭されています。

Japanese gardens : *Nihon-teien*, compared to Western gardens that are laid out geometrically, are laid out placing importance on the natural view. They mainly imitate of the natural world, with heaped-up earth likened to mountains, ponds to oceans, and with rivers made by drawing water; some also incorporate a tea garden with arranged stepping stones and stools.

　In addition, there is the **dry Japanese garden** as one of representative styles of *nihon-teien*. This is a type of gardens that do not use water and express landscapes only with rocks and the sand. Hills and waterfalls are expressed by rock constructions, and rivers are expressed by making marks on spread white sand with bamboo brooms to depict water flowing. In the **Muromachi Period**(1392-1573), it was influenced by landscape painting imported from China, and many were designed as entry-way gardens for **Zen** temples.

cost: 500,000

【盆栽】
Bonsai
ぼんさい

　盆栽は鉢植えにした観賞用の草木で、日本独特の芸術の1つです。代表的なものには松が挙げられますが、そのほかさまざまな草木も育てられています。

　伸びすぎた根があれば鉢から出して切り、新しい土に植え替え、枝をこまめに剪定し、時には幹や枝に針金を巻いて成形するなどして、好みの形に仕上げていくのです。

　草木の成長に合わせて行われるため、何世代にもわたって受け継がれていくこともあります。理想の形に仕上げるには専門家でもかなりの知識と手間を必要としますが、趣味として親しまれています。日本では主に中・高年の趣味とされていますが、アメリカでは若者にも人気があります。

Potted dwarf tree : *Bonsai* are miniaturized potted plants and trees for aesthetic appreciation and are an art form unique to Japan. The **pine tree** is cited as typical, but all sorts of other plants and trees are nurtured.

　When the roots have grown too long, the plant is taken out of the pot, cut, planted in fresh dirt, the branches are diligently pruned, and wire is sometimes wrapped around the trunk and branches to shape them to the desired configuration.

　To keep this up as the trees and plants grow, they are handed down across several generations. To complete the ideal shape requires a considerable amount of knowledge and labor, even for an expert, but it has an intimate appeal as a hobby. In Japan, it is chiefly taken up as a hobby by those in middle and old age, while in the United States it is also popular among young people.

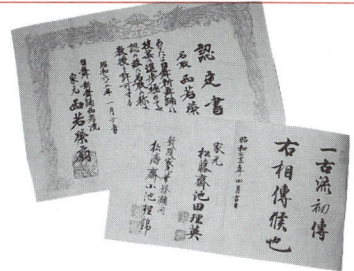

【家元】 Iemoto
いえもと

日本の古典芸能の多くは、それぞれがいくつかの流派を持っていますが、家元とはその流派の芸道を受け継いでいる、正統の家や人のことです。家元は自分の流派の芸道を守り、弟子からまたその弟子へと代々受け継がせていくのです。現在では**華道**や**茶道**、**日本舞踊**、**能**や**狂言**など多くの分野で家元制度が取り入れられています。

家元という言葉の起源は、**平安時代**（794～1185）の**雅楽**の家にあるといわれていますが、家元制度が盛んになったのは18世紀以降のことです。18世紀半ばからは家元が免許状伝授を行うようになりました。**名取**や**師匠**を介し、家元の権威が弟子たちにも継承されるようになったのです。

Head of the school : Most of Japan's classical performing arts have any number of schools, and the term *iemoto* refers to the legitimate house or person that inherits the artistic ways of those schools. The *iemoto* protects the artistic ways of his own school and has successive generations of disciples succeed to those ways. At present, the *iemoto* system is entrenched in most artistic fields such as **flower arrangement**, **tea ceremony**, **classical Japanese dance**, **Noh** and **Kyogen**.

The term *iemoto* is said to have originated in a school of **ancient court music** in the **Heian Period**(794-1185), but the *iemoto* system has flourished from the middle of eighteenth century on. From the middle of the eighteenth century, *iemoto* started to give certificates of initiate. Through **accredited master** and **master**, *iemoto* authority was passed on to disciples.

スポーツ

【相撲】
Sumō
すもう

　日本の伝統的な格闘技で、1909年に国技に制定されました。古代には農耕儀礼や神事として行われていたため、現在も儀式的な要素を多く含んでいます。相撲の試合では、まわしのみを身に付けた2人の**力士**が**土俵**に上がり、一方が**土俵**から出るか、足の裏以外の体の一部が地面につくまで戦います。日本相撲協会が**大相撲**の興業を年6回行っており、その模様はテレビやラジオでも中継されます。

　1960年代からは**大相撲**の海外巡業もしばしば行われており、『スモウ・ワールド』という英文相撲雑誌も世界各国で愛読されるなど、大相撲人気は国際的なものとなっています。また、近年は外国人**力士**の活躍も目立っています。

Sumō : This is traditional Japanese wrestling and in 1909 was established as the national sport. In ancient times, it was practiced as agricultural and Shinto rituals, so it still today includes many ceremonial elements. In a *sumō* match, two **wrestlers** wearing only a *sumō* wrestler's loincloth enter the **ring**, and they fight until one either leaves the **ring** or touches the ground with any part of his body other than the bottom of his feet. The Japan Sumō Association puts on six annual tournaments of the **professional *sumō*** per year, and these are broadcast on both television and radio.
　Since the 1960s, overseas tours of the tournaments of the **professional *sumō*** have frequently made, and have become so popular internationally that an English *sumō* magazine called "Sumō World" is avidly read in a number of countries. In addition, the accomplishments of foreign **wrestlers** recently have attracted attention.

【四股】 しこ Shiko

　力士は土俵に上がると、土を踏み固める動作を繰り返します。これは力士が下半身を鍛えるための重要な基本動作で、四股といい、稽古の前後にも繰り返し行われています。

　しかし、四股は単なる準備運動ではありません。日本には古来、大地を踏んで地の邪気を払い、正気を招き寄せるという信仰があり、力士が四股を踏むのも、地にひそむ悪霊を踏みつけるという神事に由来しているのです。

Stamp : When *sumō* wrestlers enter the **ring**, they repeat an action of stamping down the dirt. This is an important, basic action for **wrestlers** to train the lower half of the body. It is called *shiko* and is done repeatedly before and after practice.

　However, *shiko* is not simply a preparatory exercise. Since ancient times in Japan, there was the belief that stamping the earth swept away evil spirit and summoned right spirit; *sumō* **wrestlers** doing *shiko* also derived from a Shinto ritual of stamping underfoot evil spirits that lurk in the ground.

【仕切り】 しきり Shikiri

　仕切りとは力士が土俵で相対し、勝負開始前に戦う姿勢を構えることです。相撲では一瞬の立ち合いが勝負を決定するため、阿吽の呼吸が合わないときは何回でも繰り返します。入念な仕切りを繰り返し、気合いが充実したところで勝負に入るのです。かつてフランスの詩人、ジャン・コクトーは、立ち合いの阿吽の呼吸をバランスの奇跡だと絶賛したこともあります。

Toeing the mark : *Shikiri* refers to the fighting posture taken by the **wrestlers** as they face each other in the **ring**, just prior to the start of the match. In *sumō*, the brief instant of standing up to wrestle decides the match, so, when the wrestlers are not in sync with each other, they repeat their toeing the mark any number of times. They repeat *shikiri* with scrupulous care, starting the match only when they are completely ready. The French poet Jean Cocteau once praised this synchrony of toeing the mark as a miracle of balance.

【横綱】
よこづな
Yokozuna

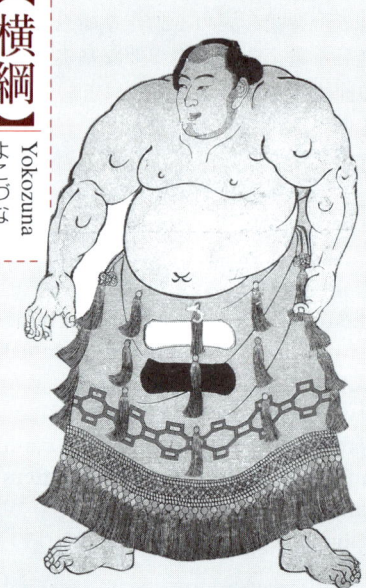

力士の地位の最高位です。横綱の**力士**が化粧まわしの上に締める縄も「横綱」といいますが、これは**しめ縄**が変化したものです。**大関**で２場所連続優勝か、それに準ずる成績を挙げた者だけが横綱になれます。200年余りの歴史を持つ**大相撲**ですが、横綱に昇進したのはたった64人（1993年８月現在）と、非常に狭き門です。1993年には米国人の曙が第64代横綱に昇進し、初の外国人横綱が誕生しました。

Grand champion : *Yoko-zuna* is the highest rank for *sumō* **wrestlers**. The rope that **wrestlers** of *yokozuna* wear on the wrestler's belt with elaborately embroidered apron also called *yokozuna* and is a modification of a **sacred Shinto rope**. Only those wrestlers who win two consecutive tournaments, or achieve similar results, as the **second highest rank** can become *yokozuna*. The **professional *sumō*** have a history of more than two hundred years, but, with only 64 wrestlers having been promoted to *yokozuna*(by August 1993), it is an exceedingly narrow gate to that rank. In 1993, Akebono, an American, was promoted as the 64th *yokozuna* and became the first foreigner to reach the top rank.

【土俵入り】
Dohyōiri
どひょういり

身の清らかさを示したり、**土俵**の神に正々堂々と戦うことを誓ったりする意味で、**大相撲**では十両以上の**力士**は取り組み前に土俵入りという儀式を行います。十両・幕内力士は番付順に**土俵**に上がり、円陣を作って行いますが、**横綱**は太刀持ちと露払いを従えて登場し、1人ずつ行います。特に**横綱**の土俵入りでは各横綱の個性が表れ、それぞれに豪華で迫力あるパフォーマンスが見られます。

Display of *sumō* wrestlers in the ring : To indicate their purity of body and to pledge to the god of the **ring** that they will fight fairly, **wrestlers** of the **professional** *sumō* ranked junior grade and above participate, before wrestling, in *dohyōiri*. The junior and senior grade wrestlers enter the **ring** in order of rank and make a circle; **grand champions**, however, are each accompannied by a **sword bearer** and a **herald** and perform the ceremony one at a time. The individual character of each **grand champion** is expressed particularly through the *dohyōiri*, in which one can see the splendor and appeal of their respective styles.

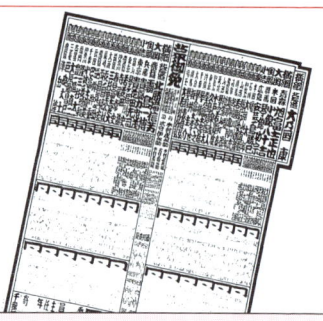

【相撲部屋】
Sumō-beya
すもうべや

大相撲では、各部屋の**力士**同士が戦って勝負を競います。そのため**力士**は必ず相撲部屋に所属し、師匠である**親方**のもとで毎日稽古します。**師匠**と弟子の強固な関係をタテ軸に成立しているのが相撲部屋で、昔の封建社会の人的結合形態と似たところがあります。番付の位が下の者は、上の者の付き人となって世話をしたり、**ちゃんこ鍋**を作ったりします。**親方**夫人である部屋の**おかみさん**は、対外交渉をしたり母親代わりになって**力士**の面倒を見たりと、大きな役割を果たしています。なお、相撲部屋に所属するのは**力士**だけではありません。**行司**や呼び出し、床山のほか、巡業での進行や力仕事をする人々などがいる部屋もあります。

Sumō **stables :** The **wrestlers** of the **professional** *sumō* from the different stables contest each other. The **wrestlers** always belong to *sumō-beya* and practice daily under *oyakata* who is a **stable master**. *Sumō-beya* form a solid vertical relationship between **master** and disciple, which resembles the situation of human relationships in the old feudal society. Those lowest on the ranking list are assigned to serve those higher up, doing such things as making the *sumō* **wrestlers' dish**. The **madam** of the stable, who is a wife of the **stable master**, fulfills a large role, carrying out negotiations with the outside and looking after the problems of the **wrestlers** as a surrogate mother. Moreover, **wrestlers** are not the only ones who belong to *sumō-beya*. There are also stables with *sumō* **referees**, callers, professional *sumō* hairdressers, and people who do promotions for provincial tours and do manual labor.

【柔道】 Jūdō
じゅうどう

　柔道は日本の代表的な格闘技の１つです。100年ほど前、嘉納治五郎が古来から伝わる武術を改良し、**講道館柔道**を創始したことが基礎となって、スポーツとしての柔道に発展したのです。相手の力と体重をうまく利用して倒すのが柔道の特徴で、技は投げ技と固め技の２つに大別されます。

　選手のしめる**帯**の色は、各人の力量を示す級位や段位を表します。例えばいちばん下の５級は白帯、初段から５段までは黒帯、９段から最高位の10段は赤帯といった具合です。柔道は第２次大戦後は欧米各地にも普及し、オリンピックの正式種目にもなっています。また、1951年創立の国際柔道連盟には152ヵ国が加盟しています（1992年８月現在）。

Judo is one of Japan's representative techniques of hand-to-hand combat. About one hundred years ago KANŌ Jigorō reshaped traditional martial arts and developed judo as a sport through the establishment of ***Kōdōkan*** **Judo**. The key point of judo is to overwhelm an opponent by taking advantage of his force and weight. Judo techniques can be roughly divided into two categories: throwing techniques and grappling techniques.

　The color of participants' **belts** shows rank which indicates physical ability. For example, those of the fifth class, the lowest rank, wear a white belt, those the first to the fifth rank wear a black belt, and those of the ninth and the tenth rank, the highest ranks, wear a red belt. After World War Ⅱ, judo spread everywhere in North America and Europe and became an official Olympic event. The International Judo Federation was founded in 1951 and currently 152 member nations(by August 1992).

【剣道】

Kendō
けんどう

剣道はフェンシングとよく似ています。もともとは武士の訓練として広まったのですが、**江戸時代**（1603～1867）中期から今のような形式になりました。剣道の試合では、2人の対戦者は 鎧（よろい）に似た防具を身につけ、**竹刀**（しない）を使って戦います。相手の頭、胴、小手のいずれかを打ったり、のどを**竹刀**で突いたりし、それが決まれば得点となります。試合の制限時間は5分で、3ポイント中2ポイントを先取した者が勝ちです。

心身を鍛えられるスポーツとして海外でもよく知られており、1970年創立の国際剣道連盟には、31ヵ国が加盟しています（1992年8月現在）。

Japanese fencing : *Kendō* is somewhat similar to fencing. It originally was propagated as a discipline for warriors and took its current form from around the middle of the **Edo Period**(1603-1867). In a *kendō* match, the two combatants wear protective outfits resembling armor(*yoroi*) and attack with **bamboo swords**. They score points by hitting their opponent's head, trunk, forearms or charging at their throat with the **bamboo sword**. The match lasts no more than five minutes and the winner is the first to score two out of three points.

Kendō is well known overseas as a sport that can discipline mind and body. The International *Kendō* Federation was founded in 1970 and currently has 31 member nations(by August 1992).

【空手】

Karate

からて

空手は中国の**拳法**と沖縄の武術とが組み合わさって完成され、**護身術**として発達してきました。武器を使わず、こぶしやひじ、足などを使って戦います。基本戦法は突き、守り、蹴りとひじうちです。

空手の試合は、「組手」と「型」の２種類に分けられます。組手試合では、有効な突きや蹴りの技を仕掛けると得点になるのですが、実際の攻撃は相手の身体に当たる寸前でやめなければなりません。型試合では、１人または団体でさまざまな技の組み合わせを披露します。このときは技の正確さや姿勢、**気合い**などが判定基準となります。空手では強さだけでなく、精神面も重視されているのです。

Karate was formed by combining Chinese **kung-fu**(*kenpō*) with *Okinawan* martial arts and developed as the **art of self-defense**. One fights not with weapons but with fists, elbows and feet. Basic tactics include the forward fist thrust, defense, kicking and the backward elbow thrust.

Karate matches are of two kinds: sparring match(*kumite*) and form competition(*kata*). Matches against an opponent are scored by launching effective thrusts and kicks, but blows must stop short of hitting the opponent's body. *Kata* matches are demonstrations of various combinations of techniques by one person or a group. Judgment standards are based on the techniques' accuracy, posture and **spirited shout**(*kiai*) displayed. Karate emphasizes not only physical strength but spiritual aspects as well.

【合気道】

Aikidō
あいきどう

合気道は、起源は古代中国にさかのぼりますが、「**気**」の概念が**神道**と結びつき、日本独自の発展をとげてきました。武器を使わない武術の1つで、相手の手足や関節をつかんでひねることによって、あまり力を使わずに、相手を倒したり押さえ込んだり、当て技をかけたりします。また、合気道特有の呼吸法を修得することによって、より技が効果的になるのです。

合気道の基本技は、老若男女を問わず無理なく修得できるようになっています。精神修養に効果的なのはもちろんですが、現在では、主に心身の鍛錬や健康法の一環として普及しています。

Aikido finds its origin in ancient China, but the concept of *ki* is connected with **Shinto** and has a peculiarly Japanese development. A martial art without weapons, aikido makes it possible to overwhelm and throw opponents by grasping and twisting their hands, feet or joints, without resorting so much to strength. Also, one's technique becomes the more efficient as one learns the special aikido art of breathing.

Fundamental aikido techniques can be learned without difficulty by old or young, male or female. It is certainly effective for one's spiritual cultivation, and at present, it is spreading principally as a link to the disciplines of mind and body and to the maintenance of good health.

note: *Ki* refers to the power that is the driving force of life.

【弓道】
Kyūdō
きゅうどう

　かつて日本では、弓は武器として使われていました。しかし**室町時代**（1392〜1573）末期以降は、武士が心身を鍛錬するために弓道を重んじるようになり、その後武道の1つとして発展を遂げました。現在の弓道は日本版アーチェリーといえるでしょう。しかし弓道では勝負よりも礼節を重んじ、無心を追求します。

　弓道の**弓**は木と竹を張り合わせたもので、長さは2メートル余りあります。竹製の矢を用い、右手に**ゆがけ**という革の手袋をはめて行います。的までの距離は、近距離で28メートル、遠距離だと60メートル以上が一般的です。

Japanese archery : Bows and arrows used to be in practical use as weapons in Japan. However, from the end of the **Muromachi Period** (1392-1573), warriors valued *kyūdō* as a discipline for mind and body and thus advanced its development as a martial art. Modern day *kyūdō* is similar to archery in the Western countries. However, *kyūdō* values manners and formality rather than victory or defeat, and pursues the detachment of mind.
　The archery's **bow** is made of laminated wood and bamboo and it is just over two meters long. It is operated by wearing an **archer's glove** on the right hand and using bamboo arrows. Generally, the distance to the target is 28 meters in a short-distance shooting and 60 meters in a long-distance shooting.

　なぎなたは日本古来の武道の１つです。もとは一騎打ちの戦闘用でしたが、次第に僧兵や医師、婦女の武器へと移行してきました。**明治時代**（1868〜1912）以降は、女子の武道として発達しました。学校教育にも取り入れられるようになりました。

　競技用の「なぎなた」の長さは２メートル余りあります。柄の部分は樫の木でできており、先端の刀の部分は竹を２枚張り合わせたものです。

　競技としてのなぎなたには、演技競技と試合競技とがあります。演技競技は服装・態度・技の良し悪しが判定の対象となり、試合競技では打突が決まると勝ちとなるのです。

Japanese halberd : *Naginata*, or long sword, has been used in Japanese martial arts since ancient times. Originally, it was used in man-to-man combat, but gradually it became the weapon of choice for warrior priests, physicians and women. From the **Meiji Period**(1868-1912) on, it was developed for use in martial arts for women. It was even introduced into the school curriculum.

The length of *naginata* used in competition is about two meters. The handle is made of oak and the tip of two layers of laminated bamboo.

There are two kinds of *naginata* competition: performance and match. Performance competition is judged on propriety of attire, attitude and technique, while victory in match play is determined by a successful **hit or lunge**.

【忍術】
にんじゅつ
Ninjutsu

忍者は兵法上の特別な技術を備え持った人々で、**戦国時代**（1467～1568）に活躍しました。もちろん、現在の日本では**忍者**の姿を見ることはできません。

彼らはひそかに敵の戦術や戦力を調べたり、兵器を破壊したり、敵のリーダーを暗殺したりする役割を担っていました。それらの役割を遂行するために城に忍び込んだり、正体を見抜かれないように変装したり、相手の目をくらませて逃げたりするのが忍術です。具体的には、水上を歩く、水中に潜む、塀を越える、音を立てずに歩く、瞬時にして消えるといった技術です。どれも「敵の虚を突く」という心理作戦が根底にあります。

The art of spycraft : *Ninja* were people provided with special techniques in the art of war and flourished in Japan's **age of warring states** (1467-1568). There are no ***ninja*** in today's Japan.

Ninja were responsible for spying on the enemy's war tactics and fighting capacity, destroying his arms and assassinating enemy leaders. *Ninjutsu* the *ninja* art of stealth meant sneaking into castles, to be in disguise to conceal the true character, deceiving the enemy's eyes for the escape, and so on, in order to execute the duties. In concrete terms, *ninja* techniques included walking on, and submerging into, water, scaling walls, walking silently and disappearing suddenly. Their every action was grounded in the psychological strategy of catching their opponents off their guards.

遊び・遊び道具

【羽根つき】
はねつき Hanetsuki

　羽根つきは**正月**に女の子がするゲームで、バドミントンに似ています。**羽子板**という、美しい絵の描かれた木製のラケットを使って、**羽根**（羽を付けた小さな玉）を打ち合うのです。**羽子板**には、布で人物の絵を刺繍したものもあり、こちらは美しい置物として人気があります。

　羽根つきには**晴れ着**を着て行い、打ち損じた人は顔を**墨**で一筆塗られるというルールもあります。**着物**姿の女の子が羽根つきに興じる姿は、かつては**正月**の風物詩の１つでした。しかし都市化が進んで遊び場が激減したり、時代の流れとともに子供の遊びのスタイルも変化したことなどから、最近ではあまり見られなくなりました。

Shuttlecock game : *Hanetsuki*, played by young girls at **New Year**, resembles badminton. A wooden racket called a *hagoita*(**battledore**), on which is painted a beautiful picture, is used to hit a **shuttlecock**— a small, rounded piece with feathers attached—back and forth. Featuring cloth-embroidered human portraits, some battledores are also popular as beautiful ornaments.

　The shuttlecock game is played in **formal attires**, and there is also a rule that one who fails to hit it must have the face marked with **India ink** by a stroke of a brush. The **kimono**-clad girl enjoying the shuttlecock game was formerly a part of **New Year**'s scenery. But in recent years one hardly sees this anymore, because places to play have sharply decreased as urbanization has advanced and children's style of playing games has changed with the changing times.

【凧揚げ】 Takoage たこあげ

　日本の凧は四角形が多く、**竹**の骨に紙を張り、表面に武士や**歌舞伎**役者の絵を描いたり文字を書いたりします。凧揚げはかつては子供の成長を祝い、将来の多幸を祈って行われていましたが、今は伝統的な**正月**の遊びとして親しまれています。凧揚げ大会は**正月**以外にも各地で行われ、1辺が数メートルから10メートル以上の大凧を揚げたり、凧同士を空中で喧嘩させたりする行事もあります。

Kite-flying : Japanese kites are usually square shaped, made with paper glued on a **bamboo** frame, and pictures of warriors or **Kabuki** actors are drawn on the surface together with Japanese writing. *Tako-age* used to be practiced to celebrate a child's growing up and to pray for the child's happiness in the future, but now it is enjoyed as a traditional **New Year**'s activity. There are regional *tako-age* tournaments, besides at **New Year**, where large kites from a few meters to 10 or more in size are flown and even kite-fighting events.

【カルタ】 Karuta

　「カルタ」という言葉は、ポルトガル語の carta が語源といわれています。カルタはトランプのような長方形の札に絵や文字が描かれています。遊ぶときは、1人が**読み札**を読み、それに合う**絵札**をほかの人が競い合って取り、最も多く取った人が勝ちとなります。代表的なものにはことわざを網羅した**いろはガルタ**や**短歌**を描いた**歌ガルタ**などがあります。現代では主として**正月**に遊びます。

Card game : The word *karuta* is said to have come from the Portuguese *carta*. *Karuta* are rectangular, like ordinary playing cards, with pictures or Japanese writing drawn on them. When playing, one player reads out a **card for reading** (*yomi-fuda*) and the other players compete to take the **picture card** (*efuda*) that matches it; the player who takes the most cards is the winner. As typical Japanese aspects of the game, there are ***iroha-garuta*** that contain the Japanese proverbs and **poem cards** (*uta-garuta*) on which the **poems in 31 syllables** known as *tanka* are written. Nowadays, the game is played principally at **New Year**.

【百人一首】
Hyakunin-isshu
ひゃくにんいっしゅ

通常は藤原定家（ふじわらのていか）の撰による『小倉百人一首』のことをさします。百人一首は**平安時代**（794〜1185）の歌人を中心に、**鎌倉時代**（1185〜1333）初期までの優れた歌人の**和歌**を1首ずつ、合わせて100首選び出したもので、**江戸時代**（1603〜1867）以後、**歌ガルタ**として広く行き渡りました。歌の内容は恋歌が43首と圧倒的に多く、次に四季の歌が32首あります。作者は男性が79人、女性が21人で、恋愛感情や自然や季節に対する想いを日本人独特の繊細な表現で表しており、古典文学の代表的作品としても名高いものとなっています。また、**正月**には欠かせない遊びの1つでもあります。

The Hundred Poems by One Hundred Poets : This generally refers to the poetry anthology entitled "**Ogura hyakunin-isshu**," compiled by FUJIWARA no Teika(Sadaie). It gathered 100 *waka* —the **classical Japanese poem**, specifically in this case Poem in 31 syllables— one each by the most outstanding poets from the **Heian Period**(794-1185) and the early years of the **Kamakura Period**(1185-1333). From the time of the **Edo Period**(1603-1867), this poetry anthology was widely spread and used as the **poem cards**. The overwhelming majority—43 selections—are love poems, followed by seasonal poems—32 selections. 79 of the poets are male, 21 female, and they express thoughts of love, nature and the seasons with a refinement unique to the Japanese people. It has become well-known as the representative work of classical Japanese literature. It's one of the essential game of **New Year**.

【すごろく】 Sugoroku

室内ゲームの１つで、**盤すごろく**と**絵すごろく**があります。前者は２人で行います。木盤に駒石を15個並べ、筒に入れた２個の賽を交互に振り出し、目の数だけ駒石を進めるもので、早く敵陣に入れた方が勝ちです。一方、後者はいくつにも区切られた絵が描かれた１枚の紙を使い、数人で遊びます。賽を１つ振り、目の数だけ「振り出し」から進み、早く「上がり」に着いた人が勝ちとなるのです。

Japanese backgammon : One of indoor games in two different forms, **board** *sugoroku* and **picture** *sugoroku*. The former is for two players. Each player lines up 15 pieces on a wooden board and throws a pair of dice by turns. Pieces are moved by the count on the dice and the player who put his pieces into the opponent's territory first wins. The latter is for several players using a piece of paper with many sections and pictures drawn on it. Each player advances from the start(*furidashi*) by the count on a die that he has thrown, and the first one to reach the goal(*agari*) is the winner.

【福笑い】 ふくわらい／Fukuwarai

正月によく行われるゲームです。**お多福**という女性の顔の輪郭を描いた紙と、眉、目、鼻、口、耳の形に切り抜いた紙片とが組み合わされたもので、１人が目隠しをして、目鼻などを輪郭の上に並べて顔を作るのです。勘に頼って行うため、出来上がりが滑稽な顔立ちになるところに福笑いの面白さがあります。

Jovial laughter game : This is a game that frequently is played at **New Year**. Pieces of paper cut in the shape of eyebrows, eyes, a nose, a mouth, and ears are to be matched with an outline drawing of a woman's face, known as the **homely woman** (*otafuku*); to play, one person is blindfolded and creates a face by placing the eyes, nose and other pieces on the outline. Because one proceeds by instinct, the comical features of the completed picture cause the jovial laughter.

【折り紙】

正方形の紙をのりやはさみを使わずに折るだけで、鳥や**金魚**、かぶとなどさまざまなものの形を表現する技法、遊戯です。日本の伝統芸術の１つですが、中でも鶴は折り紙細工の傑作として広く認められています。この鶴を千羽折り、糸でつなぎ合わせたものを**千羽鶴**といい、病気見舞いなどで早期快癒の祈りをこめて贈ります。

アメリカではオッペンハイマー主宰のザ・フレンズ・オリガミ・オブ・アメリカが有名ですが、イギリスにはブリティッシュ・オリガミ・ソサエティがあり、イタリア、ベルギー、オランダなどにも折り紙協会があります。今や、折り紙は各国で広く愛好されるようになっています。

The art of paper folding : *Origami* is an amusement and a skill of folding square paper without using paste or scissors to shape things such as birds, **goldfish** and helmets. It is a traditional Japanese art, and in particular the crane is widely recognized as the masterpiece of origami. 1,000 folded cranes linked together by thread is called *senbazuru*(**One Thousand Cranes**) and is made and given to a sick person with the wish for a speedy recovery upon visiting him.

In the United States, Oppenheimer's The Friends ORIGAMI of America is well-known, and in the United Kingdom there is the British ORIGAMI Society. There are *origami* societies also in other countries such as Italy, Belgium, and Holland. Today, *origami* has come to be widely enjoyed in numerous countries.

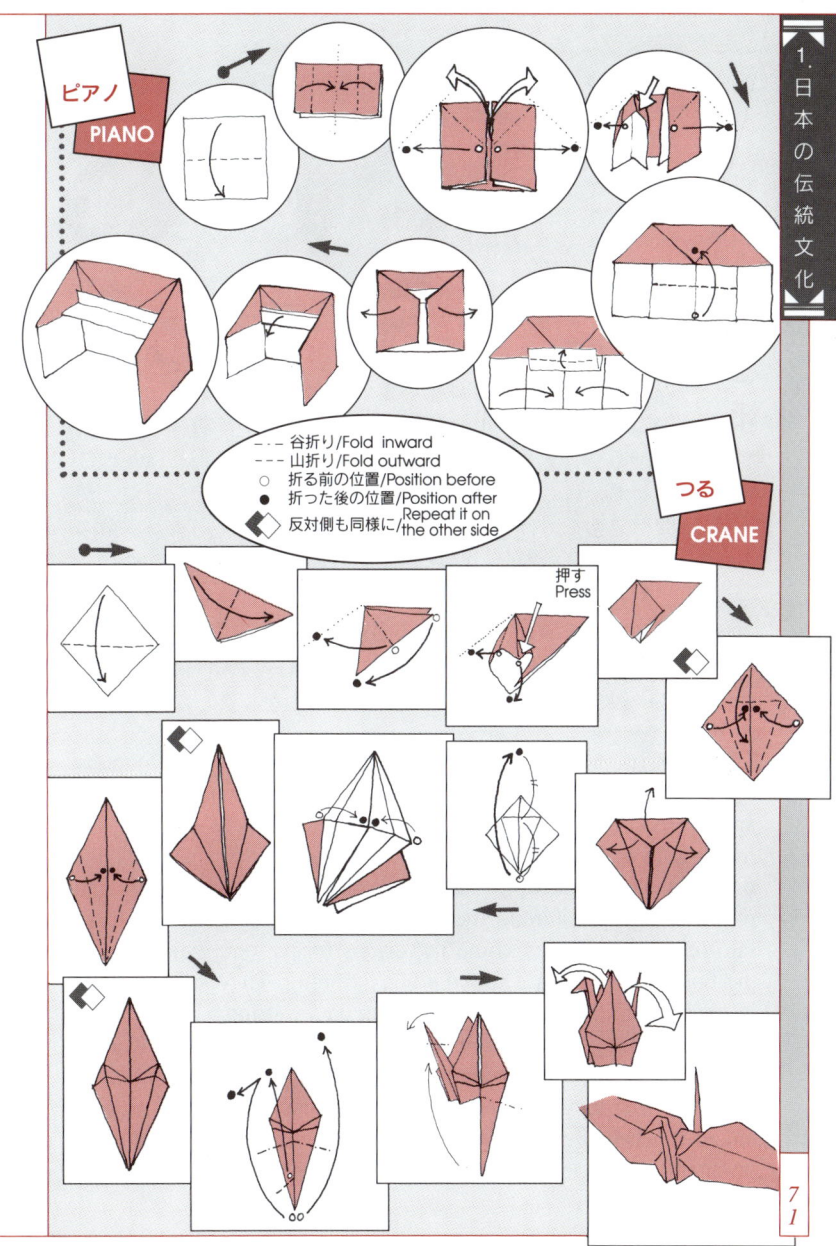

ピアノ
PIANO

--- 谷折り/Fold inward
--- 山折り/Fold outward
○ 折る前の位置/Position before
● 折った後の位置/Position after
◇ 反対側も同様に/Repeat it on the other side

つる
CRANE

押す
Press

7
1

【こま】 Koma

　こまは、何世紀もの間、子供に最も人気のある遊び道具の1つでした。多くは丸い木製の胴に心棒を貫き、これを中心として回転させます。素材は木のほかに**竹**、貝、鉄などがあり、手やひもで回転させ、単独で回したりほかのこまとぶつけたりして遊びます。形はさまざまで、胴に穴が開けてあって回すと音が出るものもあります。また、糸の上を渡らせるなど、伝統的な曲芸にもよく使われます。

　もとは中国から朝鮮半島の高麗経由で8世紀に伝来したもので、これが「こま」の名前の由来ともなっています。初めは宮廷や貴族の遊びでしたが、**江戸時代**（1603〜1867）に一般に広まり、次第に子供の遊びとなりました。

Tops : *Koma* for centuries have been one of the most popular playthings for children. Most are round and made of wood and pierced through the middle with a rod that is the axis for rotating. In addition to wood, they are made of other materials like **bamboo**, shells and iron; they are rotated by hand and string and played with by spinning them separately and by bumping them into other *koma*. They come in various forms; one with holes in the body even makes a sound when spinning. They are also used in traditional feat, such as sliding them on the string.

They originally came from China, by way of Koma in the Korean Peninsula, in the eighth century, and that is the source of the name *koma*. At first they were a game for court people and the nobility, but in the **Edo Period**(1603-1867) they became widespread and gradually came to stay as a game for children.

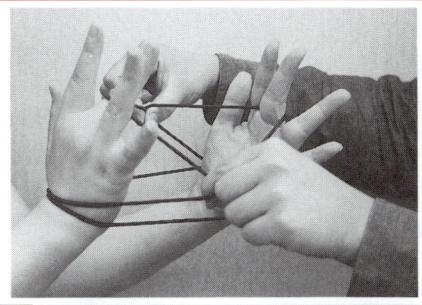

【あやとり】Ayatori

あやとりは女の子の伝統的な遊びで、輪にした糸を両手首や指先にかけて橋、琴、川などのさまざまな形を作り出していきます。

1人で両手の指で操作しながら作り出すやり方と、2人で受け渡しながら互いにやりとりをし、形を変えていくやり方とがあります。外国でも、あやとりに類する遊びは各地で見られます。

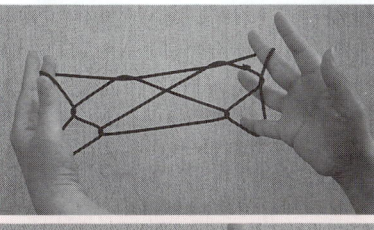

（上：ABOVE／橋：bridge）
（下：BELOW／熊手：bamboo rakes →p.50)

Cat's cradle : *Ayatori* is a traditional game for girls. A string tied in a loop is held by the wrists or fingertips of both hands and made into various shapes like a bridge, *koto*, or river.

One person alone can play by manipulating the fingers of both hands, and two persons can change the shapes by passing them back and forth to each other in various styles of holding the string. Games similar to *ayatori* can be seen in many parts of the world.

【竹馬】
Takeuma
たけうま

　２本の竹ざおにそれぞれ適当な高さの足掛かりを付けたものを馬になぞらえて乗り、竹の上の部分を握って歩行する子供の遊び道具です。古くは葉のついた**竹**を適当な長さに切り、その根元の方に手綱代わりのひもを付けたものを馬に見立て、またがって遊んでいました。これが変化して後の竹馬となったのです。今ではあまり見られなくなりましたが、子供のバランス感覚を養うために授業の一環として取り入れている学校もあります。また、北欧では夏至の日の行事の１つとして、竹馬と同じような木製の馬遊びが行われています。

Stilts : *Takeuma* is a set of two bamboo(*take*) poles with footrests attached which children use as playthings by climbing on them as on a horse(*uma*), grasping the top part of the bamboo poles and walking around. In the past, they would cut leafy **bamboo** to an appropriate length, tie a string to the roots in place of reins and play by mounting this as if it were a horse. After some modifications, this became *takeuma*. It's rarely seen in these days, but there are schools which incorporate *takeuma* into their curriculum for the purpose of cultivating the children's sense of balance. In addition, as an event for the summer solstice in Northern Europe, there is a game with a wooden horse similar to *takeuma*.

【おはじき】 Ohajiki

主に女の子の遊び道具で、昔は巻き貝や小石を使って
いましたが、今では色とりどりの**陶器**やガラス、プラス
チックなどでできたおはじきを使います。これらを床に
まき散らし、おはじきとおはじきの間を指で区切った後
ではじき当て、当たったら自分のものになります。多く
取った方が勝ちです。指ではじいて遊ぶことから「おは
じき」という名前がつきました。

Marbles : *Ohajiki* is basically a plaything for little girls. In
the past, they used roll shells and pebbles, but now they
use variously colored **ceramic**, glass or
plastic *ohajiki*. These are scattered on
the floor, and, after dividing them by
finger, the ones you aim at and hit are
yours. The person who takes the most
wins. The name *ohajiki* came from
playing by snapping or flicking(*hajiku*)
with the fingers.

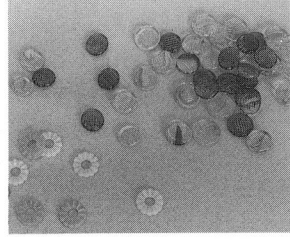

【お手玉】 Otedama おてだま

布製の小さな袋に小豆や小石、**米**などを入れたもので、
女の子の遊びに使います。5、7、9個がそれぞれセット
になっていて、その中の1つを大きく、または目立つよう
に色を変えて作り、親玉とします。歌を歌いながら1つを
空中に投げ、その間に下にまいた数個のお手玉を取りさば
いたり、数個のお手玉を両手で交互に投げ、落ちないよう
に受けることを繰り返したりして遊びます。

Beanbags : *Otedama* is a small bag made of cloth and filled
with small beans, pebbles, **rice** and the like, used in a game
for young girls. It comes as a set of either five, seven, or nine
beanbags, one of which, larger and conspicuously colored
different from the others, is the chief bag(*oyadama*). One plays by
tossing up a bag, then singing and manipulating one or more bags
on the ground in a certain way while the tossed bag is in midair, or
by juggling them.

【けん玉】
Kendama
けんだま

木の棒の一端をとがらせ、もう一端は皿形にし、穴を開けた球を糸で結びつけた木製の玩具です。球を皿の部分にのせたり、柄の先に刺したりして遊ぶもので、同じような遊びはヨーロッパにもありますが、日本では愛好者の間でけん玉選手権も行われています。**大正時代**（1912〜1926）からは柄が十字形になり、皿の部分が３つになりました。

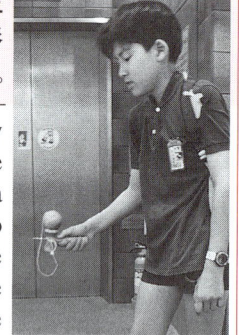

Cup and ball : *Kendama* is a wooden toy consisting of a wooden stick with one end sharpened, the other end shaped like a dish, and a ball with a hole in it connected to the stick by string. The object is to balance the ball on the dish part and to stick it on the sharp end of the stick. There is a similar game in Europe, as well, but there are even kendama championships held in Japan. Since the **Taisho Period**(1912-1926) the shaft has been cross-shaped and has three dish parts in total.

【鬼ごっこ・隠れんぼ】
おにごっこ／Onigokko・かくれんぼ／Kakurenbo

子供たちの戸外の遊びです。鬼ごっこは**じゃんけん**で**鬼**になる人を決め、その**鬼**がほかの人を追いかけて捕まえたら、捕まった人が次の**鬼**になるというものです。隠れんぼも**じゃんけん**で**鬼**を決め、その**鬼**が目をつぶり、数を数えている間にみんな物陰などに隠れます。数え終わると**鬼**は隠れている子供たちを探します。どちらも日本の子供たちの最もポピュラーな遊びです。

Tag, Hide-and-seek : These are outdoor games for children. In *onigokko*, the person who is **it**(*oni*[meaning demon or ogre]) is decided by the **game of scissors-paper-stone**(*janken*), and when the one who is **it** chases and catches another person, the person caught becomes **it** next. In *kakurenbo* the one who is **it** is also decided by *janken*, and, while that person counts with eyes closed, the others all go and hide. When finish counting, the one who is **it** starts looking for the children who are hiding. Both are very popular games for Japanese children.

【じゃんけん】Janken

じゃんけんは、順番を決めたり、ちょっとした勝負をつけたりするときに行うゲームで、「じゃんけんぽん」と言いながら、同時に手を出すのです。握りこぶし（グー）は「石」、２本指（チョキ）は「はさみ」、開いた手（パー）は「紙」を意味します。石ははさみに、はさみは紙に、紙は石に勝つことができます。全員が同じものを出すか、３種類がすべて出たときは「あいこでしょ」と言って、勝負がつくまで繰り返し行います。

Game of scissors-paper-stone is played to decide things like order of participation or victory or defeat in trifling games. While saying "*jankenpon*," players put one hand forward in a fist—stone(*gū*)—or with two fingers protruding— scissors(*choki*) —or with all fingers completely open—paper(*pā*). Victory is determined with stone breaking scissors, scissors cutting paper, or paper covering stone.

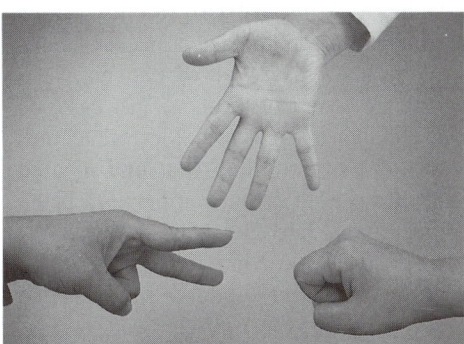

When everybody puts forward the same shape, or when all the three kinds of shape is put forward, they keep on playing, saying "it's a tie"(*aikodesho*) until the winner is decided.

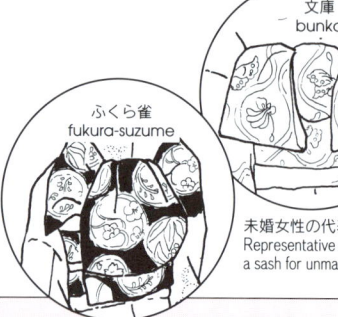

文庫
bunko

ふくら雀
fukura-suzume

未婚女性の代表的帯結び
Representative styles of fastening
a sash for unmarried women

衣生活

【着物】 Kimono きもの

　一般に、着物は特別な儀式やパーティーなどの際に着ることが多く、日常的にはほとんど洋服を着ます。しかし最近は、着物の美やファッション性が見直されてきています。

　着物の礼装にはいくつかあります。未婚女性の第一礼装は**振袖**で、一般の着物より袖が長めです。また、既婚女性の第一礼装は**5つ紋**の付いた**黒留袖**ですが、既婚・未婚の区別のない礼装もあります。一方、男性の改まった和装としては、既婚・未婚の別なく、**羽織はかま**を着用します。

　着物のときは**帯**を結び、靴下の代わりに**足袋**をはき、外出時には**草履**をはくというのが基本です。

Kimono are generally worn for such occasions as special ceremonies and parties, while Western clothes are almost always worn for daily activities. However, recently the beauty and fashionableness of kimono are being revaluated.

　There are several kinds of ceremonial kimono. The prime ceremonial kimono for unmarried women is **long-sleeved kimono**,　which sleeves are than a regular kimono. In addition, the prime ceremonial kimono for married women are **black fixed-sleeved kimono**; it has **five family crests**. And there are ceremonial kimono that make no distinction between married and unmarried women. Meanwhile, men wear the ceremonial clothes of **Japanese half-coat and pleated loose-fitting trousers**, which make no distinction between being married and unmarried, as their formal Japanese-style garments.

　It is a standard to fasten a **sash** over kimono, to wear **Japanese socks**(*tabi*) instead of socks, and to wear **Japanese sandals**(*zori*) when going out.

【振袖】ふりそで Furisode

未婚女性の第一礼装

Long-sleeved kimono : The prime ceremonial cloth for unmarried women.

【日本髪】にほんがみ／Nihongami

未婚女性は、**着物**を着るときは主に島田髷に結います。

Japanese coiffure : Single women generally arrange their hair in the Shimada coiffure when they wear **kimono**.

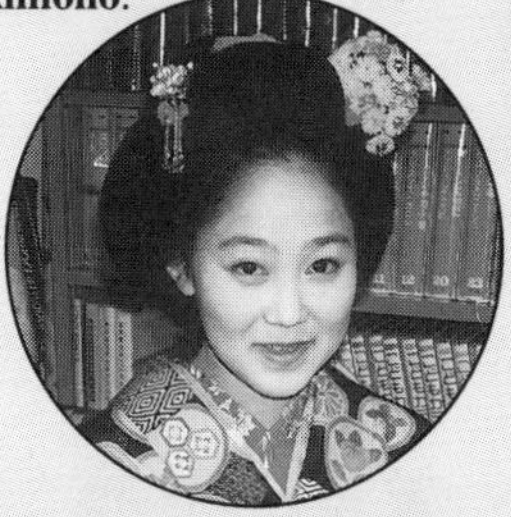

【帯揚げ】おびあげ／Obiage

帯の結び目が下がらないように結びます。

Sash bustle : It is tied to prevent a knot of a **sash** from sliding down.

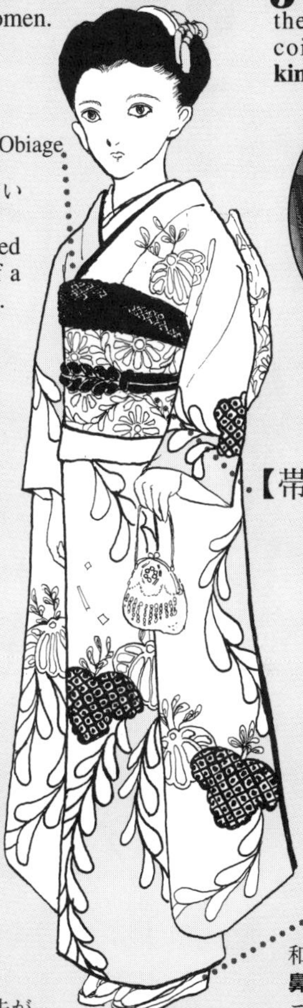

【帯締め】おびじめ／Obijime

帯が解けないように、結んだ**帯**の上に締めます。代わりに**帯留め**を用いることもあります。

Sash band : It is fastened over a tied **sash** so that the **sash** will not be undone. It can be substituted by a **sash clip**.

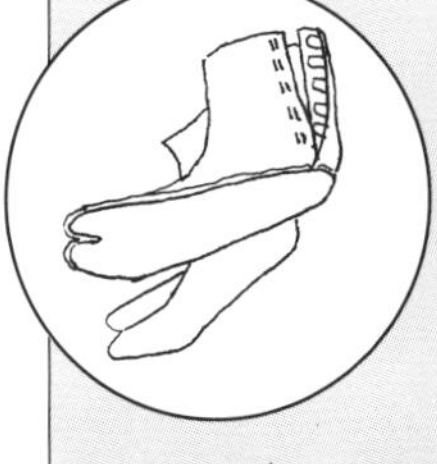

【草履】ぞうり／Zōri

和装用の履物で、底は平らで**鼻緒**があります。主に革やビニールなどでできています。

Japanese sandals : A traditional footwear for the use with a **kimono**. It has a flat sole and a **clog thong**, and which is chiefly made of leather or vinyl.

【足袋】たび／Tabi

和装用の靴下です。足先が、親指と他の４本の指とに分かれています。

Japanese socks : Socks used when wearing a kimono. The toes are separated into a part for a big toe and a part for the other four toes.

【和装小物】わそうこもの／Wasō-komono Accessories for kimono

帯留め / Obidome
/Sash clips

くし / Kushi
/Combs

かんざし / Kanzashi
/Ornamental
hairpins

バッグ／Baggu
/Handbags

【お太鼓】おたいこ／Otaiko

最も一般的な帯結びの1つで、年輩の
人から若い人まで結ぶことができます。

Drum knot fastening : One of the
most popular styles to fasten a
sash and can be worn by old and
young alike.

桐たんす
Paulownia-wood chest

既婚女性の第一礼装

Black fixed-sleeved kimono :
The prime ceremonial cloth
for married women.

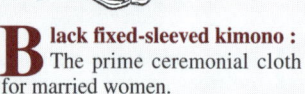

【黒留袖】くろとめそで
Kuro-tomesode

【羽織】はおり／Haori

着物の上にはおるもので、5つ紋が付いています。

Japanese half-coat : A jacket to wear over a **kimono**, properly adorned with **five family crests**.

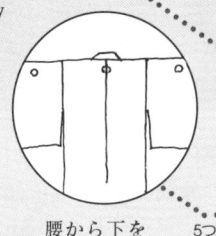

5つ紋

【羽織はかま】はおりはかま Haori-hakama

Japanese half-coat and pleated loose-fitting trousers : The ceremonial clothes for men.

男性の礼装

【はかま】Hakama

腰から下を覆うゆったりとした衣服で、**着物**の上から着用します。

Pleated loose-fitting trousers : They loosely cover the lower half of the body and are worn over a **kimono**.

【草履】ぞうり／Zōri

男性用の草履は、主に灯心草やいぐさで編んであります。

Japanese sandals : *Zōri* for men are mainly woven with **rush**.

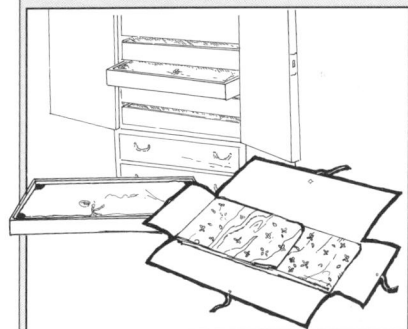

着物をしまうときは紙に包み、虫や湿気を防ぐため、**桐たんす**に収納します。

Storing of kimono : Kimono are wrapped in paper and stored in a **paulownia-wood chest** to be protected against insects and humidity.

【着物の収納】きもののしゅうのう／Kimono no shūnō

【浴衣】
ゆかた
Yukata

浴衣は湯上がりや夏季に着る木綿の**着物**で、裏地はありません。**振袖**など礼装の**着物**に対し、浴衣は気どりのないふだん着です。素肌の上に着ることもでき、ふつうは**足袋**もはかず、素足で**下駄**をはきます。ことに暑い夏の夕方、ひと風呂浴びた後に着る浴衣の着心地は格別で、見た目にもさわやかで涼しげに感じられます。

夏祭りや**花火大会**、**盆踊り**などでは浴衣姿の人も多く見られ、夏の風物詩の１つになっています。また、多くの旅館やホテルには浴衣が用意されており、ねまき代わりに着ることもできます。

Informal cotton kimono : *Yukata* are cotton **kimono** without lining, which are worn after taking a bath and in the summertime. In contrast to ceremonial **kimono**, like the **long-sleeved kimono**, *yukata* are ordinary, unassuming clothing. They can be worn next to the skin, and it is usual to wear **wooden clogs** without **Japanese socks** when wearing kimono. *Yukata* are comfortable to wear, especially on summer evenigs after taking a bath; they are refreshing and cool even to look at.

Lots of people in *yukata* are seen at summer festivals, **fireworks displays**, and the **Bon Festival dance**; *yukata* on such occasions constitute a poetic summer scene. In addition, *yukata* are set out in most inns and hotels, and they can be worn in place of pajamas.

【下駄】｜げた／Geta 草履に比べ、カジュアルな和装用の履物です。２枚の歯の付いた木製の台に、鼻緒がすげられています。

Wooden clogs : Compared to **Japanese sandals**, *geta* are footwear worn with casual Japanese-style attire. **Clog thongs** are tied to a wooden base under which two wooden supports are attached.

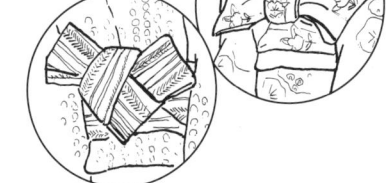

【浴衣の帯結び】｜ゆかたのおびむすび／Yukata no obi-musubi
Examples of how to tie the **sash** for the **informal cotton kimono**.

食生活

【米】
Kome
こめ

　日本人は稲作民族であり、2千年以上前から稲から取れる米を主食として生活してきました。従って、米は日本の農業の中で最も重要な作物であり、日本文化の基底には米に関係したものが多いのです。米から**酒**を作り、もち米から**餅**を作り、**せんべいや団子**も作ります。おめでたいときには**赤飯**を食べ、または神に供えます。ピクニックなどには**おむすび**を持って行くし、腐らないように酢を混ぜてさまざまな種類の**すし**を作ります。また、米を収穫した後の稲の茎は「ワラ」として、履物の**わらじ**や**蓑**などを作り、屋根をふく材料にも利用されていました。

Rice : The Japanese are a rice-cultivating people who have lived for more than 2,000 years with rice as their staple food. Accordingly, rice is Japan's most important agricultural product, and many aspects basic to Japanese culture are related to rice. *Sake*, **rice cakes**, **rice crackers**, and **dumplings** are all made from rice. On auspicious occasions, Japanese eat **rice boiled together with red beans**, which they also serve as an offering to divinities. Japanese bring **rice balls** along on picnics, and mix the rice with vinegar so that it won't spoil and make various kinds of **sushi**. The Japanese also used the stems from the harvested rice plants as straw to make **straw sandals** and **straw raincoats** and even as material to make thatched roofs.

【魚】
Sakana
さかな

　日本列島は海に囲まれているため海産物が豊富に採れ、特に魚類は日本人の食生活に欠かせません。新鮮な魚が入手できるため生のまま食べる料理─刺身やすしなどは人気のある料理です。そのほかに焼いたり煮たりする調理法が盛んで、西洋料理のように蒸したり揚げたりする料理は多くありません。また、魚は文化とも深く関係しています。鯛は1匹をまるごと焼くと縁起が良いとされ、結婚式などでは必ず出されますし、海老は尾が曲がっているため腰が曲がるほど長生きすることにたとえられて、やはり縁起が良いとされています。

Fish : The **Japanese archipelago**, encircled by the sea, abounds in marine products. Fish in particular is essential to the Japanese diet. Because fresh fish is easily obtainable, dishes that are eaten raw, like *sashimi* and **sushi**, are popular. In addition, grilled or boiled cooking is widespread, but steamed or fried dishes as in Western cooking, are not numerous. Fish is deeply related to Japanese culture. When a **sea bream** is grilled whole, it is considered good luck and is invariably served on such occasions as **weddings**. And **lobstar or prawn** too is considered good luck, because, in a figurative sense, the more its tail is curved and its back bent, the longer one's life.

【麺類】Menrui めんるい

　伝統的な麺類としては**うどん**と**そば**の2種類があります。**うどん**は小麦粉を原料とし、主に京都や大阪を含む西側に盛んです。**そば**は寒くても土地がやせていても比較的栽培しやすい植物で、その実からそば粉を作り、練ってから細く切って食べます。主に東京を含む東側で好まれます。それぞれ温かい汁に入れてさまざまな具と共に調理します。夏は冷たい汁につけて食べます。最近は中華料理の麺類の一種である**ラーメン**が、日本的な調理法で急速に日本人の味覚に浸透しています。特に即席**ラーメン**はわずか数十年で国民的な愛好を得ました。これは今や「ヌードルスープ」として世界中で販売されています。

Noodles : There are two kinds of traditional noodles; *udon* and *soba*. *Udon* is made of wheat flour and is widespread principally in Western Japan, including Kyoto and Osaka. *Soba*(buckwheat) comes from a plant relatively easy to cultivate even when the weather is cold or the soil has worn thin; the grain of this plant is made into *soba* flour, then kneaded, finely cut, and cooked for eating. It is relished principally in Eastern Japan, including Tokyo. Both dishes are prepared in a hot soup together with various ingredients. In summer, the noodles can be dipped in a cool broth and eaten. In recent year, a Chinese brand of noodle known as *rāmen*, when prepared Japanese style, has rapidly permeated the Japanese sense of taste. Instant *rāmen* in particular in only a few decades has captured the national fancy. It is now sold all over the world as a kind of "Japanese noodle soup."

【丼物】
Donburimono
どんぶりもの

日本料理はふつうご飯を小さな**茶碗**に盛り、**おかず**はほかの皿などに盛られて食卓に出されますが、丼物は**茶碗**より大きな丼にご飯を入れ、上にさまざまな具をのせたもので、これ１つで食事を済ますことができます。代表的な具は、**天ぷら、とんかつ、うなぎ**、鶏肉、卵、まぐろ**刺身**などです。都会では最近丼物専門店が多くなり、メニューも豊富です。牛肉を調理して丼物にした「**牛丼**」の店は、アメリカやヨーロッパにも進出しています。

Bowl of rice with a topping : Japanese cuisine usually comes with rice in **rice bowls**(*chawan*) and **side dishes** served on other plates. With *donburi-mono*, however rice is served in a porcelain bowl, larger than ***chawan***, with various kinds of ingredients on top, and this constitutes a complete meal. Typical ingredients include **Japanese fried food**, **pork cutlets**, boild **eel**, chicken, egg, and tuna *sashimi*. Recently in cities, shops specializing in *donburi-mono* have increased and their menus are rich in a variety of dishes. Shops featuring "**gyū-don**," which is a *donburi* prepared with beef have even extended their business to the United States and Europe.

【鍋料理】
Naberyōri
なべりょうり

　日本文化は「和の文化」ともいわれ、仲間同士の和を大事にします。その和を確認するために仲間が集まって**酒を**飲み、食事をするのはその文化の型の１つですが、そんな集まりに鍋料理は適しています。鍋の中に汁と具を入れて温め、それを囲んで４〜５人が適当に鍋の中から具と汁を自分の食器に取って食べます。仲間意識が持て、話もはずみます。具も汁もさまざまな種類があり、家庭の数と同じだけ味や作り方の種類があるとさえいえます。代表的な具としては**魚**、貝類、あらゆる野菜、肉類などで、汁は**味噌**や**醤油**などで味付けされます。

Cookpot dishes: Japanese culture, which can be called "a **culture of harmony**," places importance on harmony among friends. One cultural form for confirming harmony involves friends getting together to drink **sake** and eat, and *naberyōri* is appropriate for such gatherings. Soup stock and ingredients are put in a pot and heated; four or five persons sit around it, put soup and ingredients from the pot into their own bowls and eat. This enhances the bond of friendship and stimulates the discussion. There are all sorts of ingredients and soup stocks, as many flavors and ways of preparing, in fact, as there are households. Typical ingredients include **fish**, shellfish, a variety of vegetables and meats, and soup stocks are seasoned by **soy bean paste** or **soy sauce**.

【すき焼き】
すきやき／Sukiyaki

肉を使った現代日本の代表的な料理の１つです。日本人には**仏教**の教えにより伝統的に獣肉食を嫌悪する習慣がありました。しかし、**明治時代**(1868〜1912)に西洋料理が日本に入って肉を食べることがタブーではなくなり、このすき焼きも盛んになりました。牛肉と野菜や**豆腐**を鉄鍋に入れて**醤油**と砂糖の味付けで温め、生卵につけて食べます。

Sukiyaki : This is a typical contemporary Japanese dish featuring beef. There was the Japanese cultural belief, following **Buddhist** teaching, that eating meat was traditionally considered repugnant. However, in the **Meiji Period**(1868-1912), when Western cooking came into Japan and eating meat ceased to be a taboo, *sukiyaki* became popular. Beef, vegetables and **tofu** are put into an iron pot, seasoned with **soy sauce** and sugar, heated, then dipped in a raw, beaten egg and eaten.

しゃぶしゃぶ
Shabushabu

この名称は、この料理の特徴を良く表しています。極めて薄い肉を沸騰したお湯につけて左右に軽く振るときに出る音が日本人には「しゃぶしゃぶ」と聞こえるのです。極上質の牛肉を１〜２ミリに切って皿に並べ、食べるときに一片を沸騰したお湯につけると３〜４秒で肉の色が変わります。これを**醤油**ベースのたれやゴマだれにつけて食べます。

Shabushabu : The name well expresses the distinctive aspect of this dish. The Japanese hear the sound of lightly swishing the very thinly sliced beef in boiling water, then taking it out, as "shabushabu." Very high-grade beef is sliced no thicker than one to two millimeters and laid out on a plate. To eat, one slice is put into the boiling water for three to four seconds until the color of the meat changes. This is then dipped into a sauce based on **soy sauce** or ponnded sesame dressing and eaten.

【天ぷら】 Tenpura てんぷら

現代日本の代表的な料理の１つ。**魚**や貝、野菜などに小麦粉を水で溶いた衣を付けて、熱した植物油の中に入れて揚げ、専用のつゆにつけて食べます。小麦粉を直接付けて揚げるフライと違って、さっぱりとした味が特徴。材料もバラエティーに富み、店でも家庭でも、その場で作りながら食べる方法が最もおいしく食べられます。天ぷら丼（天丼）は庶民的な人気メニューです。

Japanese fried food : This is a typical modern Japanese dish. **Fish**, shellfish, vegetables and the like, are dipped into the batter of wheat flour dissolved in water, fried in hot cooking oil, dipped in a special broth, and eaten. Its special characteristic is a light taste, distinct from food that is directly coated in wheat flour and fried. The ingredients are rich in their variety, and the tastiest way to eat them is on the spot while preparing them, whether at a restaurant or at home. *Tenpura donburi* (or *ten-don*) is a widely popular menu item.

【刺身】 Sashimi さしみ

日本料理の特徴の１つは、材料をなるべく新鮮なまま料理に生かすということです。その代表的な料理がこの刺身だといっていいでしょう。たとえばフランス料理だと材料を必ず加工しますが、これとは対照的といえます。刺身は、生の**魚**を適当な大きさに切り、**醤油**をつけて食べます。この料理は、いかに優れた材料を見分け料理するかが板前の腕の巧拙を分けるのです。

Slices of raw fish : A distinctive characteristic of Japanese cuisine is to enliven dishes with ingredients that are as fresh as possible. *Sashimi* is typical of such dishes. This is in contrast to French cuisine, for example, in which the ingredients are invariably processed. *Sashimi* is raw **fish**, cut in appropriate sizes,

which are dipped in **soy sauce** and eaten. For this dish, how to select and cook high-quality ingredients determines the proficiency of the cook's skill.

【懐石料理】

Kaiseki-ryōri
かいせきりょうり

懐石とは、禅僧が懐を温めるために抱いた熱い石のこと。小さな石では十分体を温めることができないように、この料理も量が少なくて十分に空腹を満たすことはできません。主に茶の湯（茶道）で、茶を出す前に出す簡単な食事のこと。茶道は仏教の禅の精神を基本としているため簡素を旨としています。従ってこの料理も、基本的には獣肉を排し、菜食が中心となっています。しかし、料理屋で出す懐石料理は仏教精神とは離れ、簡素よりもその味を競うことに終始しているようです。

Tea lunch : *Kaiseki* refers to a heated stone that a Zen priest holds to warm the chest. Just as a small stone cannot sufficiently warm the body, neither can this cuisine, with its small amount of food, sufficiently satisfy an empty stomach. It is mainly the simple meal served before having **tea** at a **tea ceremony**. The art of the **tea ceremony**, based on the spirit of **Zen Buddhism**, aims at simplicity. Accordingly, this cuisine also excludes meat and centers on a vegetable diet. However, the *kaiseki ryōri* served at restaurants is removed from the spirit of **Buddhism** and, instead of simplicity, only appears to have a rivalry of flavors all the time.

【すし】
Sushi

　日本の代表的な料理の1つ。もともとは腐敗を防ぐための魚の漬物のことでしたが、**江戸時代**(1603〜1867)に酢を使うようになり、ご飯を一緒にして食べるようになりました。しかし江戸（今の東京）では江戸湾で取れた新鮮な魚の生の切身をのせ、手で握ってすしを作りました。これが「江戸前ずし」で、現在世界中で日本のすしといっているものはこのことです。実際は、日本中にさまざまな種類のすしがあり、その地域の食文化を形成しています。関西では「押しずし」といって、手で握るのではなく木の箱の中に酢を混ぜたご飯を入れ魚の切身などをのせ、上から押しつけて固く締めて作ります。

Sushi : A typical Japanese cuisine. Originally, it referred to fish pickled to be preserved from spoiling, but in the **Edo Period**(1603-1867) vinegar came to be used in the preparation, and they were put together with boiled rice for eating. However, in Edo (present-day Tokyo), sushi was made by laying slices of raw fish, freshly caught in Edo Bay, on rice and rolling it by hand. That "*Edomae-zushi*"(Edo-style sushi), is what is known throughout the world as Japanese sushi. In fact, throughout Japan there are many different kinds of sushi shaping a region's food culture. In Kansai, so-called "*oshi-zushi*"(pressed sushi) is not rolled by hand, but instead, rice mixed with vinegar is put into a wooden container, with slices of fish on it, and pressed from the top to shut tightly.

【梅干し】 Umeboshi うめぼし

梅の実を塩漬けにした上で日光にさらしたもの。酸っぱみが強く味覚を刺激して唾液を多く分泌させるため、食糧事情の悪かった時期は、便利な保存食品として人気がありました。これさえ1粒あれば、ご飯とともに十分おいしく1食分を食べることができました。今でも**おむすび**や**弁当**には欠かせない日本人の基本食品です。

Pickled plums : These are **plums** pickled in salt and exposed to the sun for drying. Since the tartness strongly stimulates the sense of taste and causes saliva to flow, this was popular as a convenient preserved food in those times when there were food shortagese. Even just one of these pickled plums made a sufficiently tasty meal with rice. Today, it is still a basic food item, essential for **rice balls** and **lunches**, for the Japanese.

【おむすび】 Omusubi(Onigiri)

ご飯を両の手のひらで握ったもの。**おにぎり**ともいいます。普通は三角形か丸形で、中に**梅干し**や焼いた魚肉などを入れ、回りに**のり**を巻くのが普通です。遠足やハイキングなどの外出の際には、アメリカ人のサンドイッチのように最もポピュラーな携行食品です。都会のコンビニエンスストアでは、独身者向けの人気食品の1つとなっています。

Rice balls : These are made by rolling rice in the palms of the hands. They are also called *onigiri*. Usually, they are made into triangular or round shapes with a **pickled plum** or fish in the middle and wrapped with **laver** on the outside. Like sandwiches for the Americans, they are the most popular item for carrying along when on outings or hiking. In urban convenience stores, they have become popular food items for single men and women.

【赤飯】
Sekihan
せきはん

　赤いご飯のこと。もともと米作が日本に伝わった当時は赤い米が主でした。その後次第に白い米が一般化し、赤い米は生産されなくなりました。そのため、小豆をもち米に混ぜて赤い米のご飯を作りました。祝事の際にはこの赤飯を供えたり食したりしました。現在でも赤飯は祭りや身内に祝い事があったとき（例えば子供が誕生したとき、結婚式のときなど）に食べたり神に供えたりします。

Rice boiled together with red beans : *Sekihan* literally means red rice. When rice cultivation was originally brought to Japan, it was mainly red **rice**. Gradually, as white **rice** was popularized, red **rice** was stopped being produced, and instead began to be prepared by mixing red beans to glutinous rice. This red rice boiled together with red beans was dedicated and eaten on ceremonial occasions. Even today, for **festivals** and felicitous occasions with relatives(for example, when babies are born or for **weddings**), *sekihan* is eaten and dedicated to the divinities.

【餅】
Mochi
もち

　米には大きく分けると、炊いて食する一般的なものと、もち米とがあります。もち米は、蒸した後に杵でついてペースト状にして餅となります。正月には必ず餅を焼いたり雑煮に入れたりして食べます。日本人にとっては米と同様に餅も最も古い食べ物であり、赤飯と同じように赤い餅を白い餅と共に祝い事に食べたり神に供えたりします。このように、赤と白は日本人にとってめでたい色の組み合わせなのです。

Rice cakes : Roughly divided, there are two kinds of rice; the regular kind that is boiled to eat and glutinous rice. Glutinous rice becomes *mochi* after it is steamed and pound into a paste with a **wooden pestle**. At **New Year**, *mochi* is invariably grilled or put into **soup with rice cakes and vegetables** and eaten. For the Japanese, *mochi* is, along with rice, the oldest food, and like **rice boiled together with red beans**, red *mochi* is eaten together with white *mochi* on ceremonial occasions and dedicated to the divinities. Thus, red and white make an auspicious color combination for the Japanese.

【豆腐】 Tofu とうふ

大豆を原料にしたゼリー状の食品。タンパク質に富み、そのまま**醤油**をつけて食べることもできますが、いろいろな料理の材料にも使われ、きわめて応用性に富んだ食品です。現在では健康食品としても脚光を浴び、日本人の長寿の原因の1つであると指摘されることもあります。アメリカなどでは健康食として、「豆腐ステーキ」がレストランのメニューにも出現しています。

Bean curd : Tofu is a jelly-like food, made from soybeans. Rich in protein, it can be eaten as it is with **soy sauce**, while it is also used as an ingredient in various dishes, being a food with abundant applications. At present it is highlighted as healthfood and has even been indicated as a reason for the long life expectancy of the Japanese people. In the United States and other countries, "tofu steak" has appeared as healthfood on restaurant menus.

【納豆】 Nattō なっとう

大豆を煮てわらなどで作った筒に入れ、納豆菌を繁殖させて作ります。大豆が発酵して糸を引き、粘り気があります。日本独特の食品で、**日本列島**のおもに東側で食され、朝食の人気メニューの1つですが、関西ではあまり好まれません。しかし最近はバランスの取れた健康食品として人気もあり、関西でも徐々に食べる人が増えています。

Fermented soybeans : *Nattō* is made by cooking soybeans and putting them into a pipe made from straw to allow the *nattō* fungus to propagate. The soybeans ferment and rope are sticky. A food peculiar to Japan, it is a popular breakfast item eaten mainly in the eastern part of the **Japan Islands**; it is not really liked in the western part. However, recently it is popular as healthfood for a balanced diet, and numbers of people who eat it are gradually increasing even in the western part.

【おでん】Oden

鍋料理の一種。魚のすり味をさまざまに加工して鍋に入れ、大根、昆布、卵などを加えて煮込んだ冬の代表的な料理。家庭でもよく料理しますが、都市では屋台のおでん屋が人々に親しまれています。冬には、サラリーマンが屋台でおでんを食べながら燗をつけた酒を飲む姿が目立ちます。最近はコンビニエンスストアでも温めて売っています。

Japanese hotchpotch : This is one kind of **cookpot dishes**. It is a typical wintertime dish in which various kinds of minced **fish** are processed and put in the pot, and Japanese radishes, kelp, eggs and the like are added and cooked. It is often prepared in the

home, but in cities people are fond of *oden* at **street stalls**. In winter, white-collar workers drinking warmed **sake** while eating *oden* at **street stalls** are conspicuous. In recent years, *oden* can be bought, warmed up, even at convenience stores.

【焼き鳥】Yakitori やきとり

鶏肉を使った日本風バーベキューです。飲み屋や屋台で酒を飲むときには最も大衆的な料理です。鶏肉とねぎを交互に串に通して焼き、醤油ベースのタレや塩で味をつけるのが代表的です。牛肉がサーロインやテンダーロインなどに分かれているように鶏肉も、もも肉、手羽肉、胸肉などに分かれます。仕事の後に「焼き鳥で1杯」は、サラリーマンの合言葉ともいえるほど人気があります。

Grilled chicken : This is Japanese-style barbecue using chicken. It is the most popular dish when drinking **sake** in bars or **street stalls.** Typically, pieces of chicken and Welsh onions are alternately stuck on a skewer, grilled and flavored with a **soy souce** based sauce or salt. Just as beef is divided into parts like sirloin and tenderloin, chicken too is divided into thigh, wing, breast and so on. To "drink over *yakitori*" after work is so popular that it can be said to be the office worker's password.

【海苔】のり Nori

　日本では海産物が豊富に採れます。のりも海草の一種で、岩に苔状に付着したものです。**江戸時代**(1603〜1867)以降、のりを紙状に薄く作る技術が開発されてから一般化しました。**すしやおむすび**には欠かせぬ材料で、料理するときは火にあぶってから使います。細かく刻んだり、小さく切ったりしていろいろな料理の材料として使われています。あぶった後、**醤油**をつけてご飯と共に食べることもできます。

Laver : In Japan, marine products are abundantly taken from the sea. *Nori* is one kind of seaweed, which adheres to rocks in a mossy form. From the **Edo Period**(1603-1867) on, *nori* was popularized after a technique was developed to make it paper thin.

It is an indispensable ingredient for **sushi** and **rice balls** and is used after first drying it over fire. Chopped finely or cut in small pieces, it is used as an ingredient for various dishes. After being dried, it can also be dipped in **soy sauce** and eaten with rice.

【漬物】つけもの Tsukemono

　漬物は、乾燥法と並んで人類最古の食品加工法で作ったものです。日本ではおもに野菜が対象になりますが、塩を混ぜる方法とぬかにつける方法があります。ぬかは米を精製するときに出る**米**の外側の粉で、ビタミンB₁が多く含まれています。キュウリや白菜、ナスなどはおしんことして、和食にはなくてはならない副食です。

Pickled vegetables : *Tsukemono*, together with methods of drying food, is produced by a means of processing food that is as old as the human race. In Japan, mainly vegetables are prepared as *tsukemono* either by mixing with salt or by dipping in rice bran. Rice bran is the powder produced of the outer coat of **rice** when refining it and is rich in vitamin B_1. Cucumbers, Chinese cabbages or eggplants as pickled vegetables are necessary ingredients of Japanese food.

【和菓子】Wagashi わがし

日本固有の菓子の総称です。大きく分類すれば干菓子と生菓子の2つに分けられます。特に茶の湯の席で出される和菓子は、茶の味を引き立てるための味を考えて作られ、また色や形状も、見るだけでも鑑賞に耐え得るような芸術的なものが発達しました。餅や砂糖を材料にし、甘味を主体にしながら歯触りや舌触りにも気を配って作られます。

Japanese confectionery : *Wagashi* is a general term for characteristically Japanese confectionery, which can be divided into two large categories, dry and unbaked confections. In particular, *wagashi* served on the occasion of the **tea ceremony** are made keeping in mind flavors that will bring out the taste of the **tea**, and the artistic aspects of color and shape are developed so that they can be appreciated visually as well. *Wagashi* are mostly made to be sweet, using **rice cakes** and sugar as ingredients, and also with close attention to their texture against the teeth and tongue.

【せんべい】Senbei

日本の菓子の中でも最もポピュラーなものです。もち米や小麦粉を原料にして、7～8センチ程度の丸や四角の形に薄く伸ばすか型に入れるかして焼き、醤油をつけて焼いたり、ゴマや塩を混ぜたりして味をつけます。江戸時代（1603～1867）に完成し、日本全国にいろいろな種類があります。餅を薄く切って乾かしたものは「かきもち」といって、せんべいの一種に数えられます。

Rice crackers : These are the most popular Japanese confectionery. They are made from glutinous rice and wheat flour. The dough is streched thinly into circles or squares of about seven to eight centimeters, or put into molds, then baked; taste is supplied by baking it with **soy sauce** applied or by mixing it with

sesame and salt. *Senbei* were perfected in the **Edo Period**(1603-1867) and there are various kinds throughout Japan. Thinly-cut, dried **rice cake** called *kakimochi* is considered one kind of *senbei*.

【酒】
さけ
Sake

　米と水で作った醸造酒で、日本古来のアルコール飲料です。温めて飲むことができるので酔いが早く回り、冬には体が温まります。良い酒は、冷やして飲むと上質のワインと似た味がします。そのためヨーロッパのワイン品評会に出品され、賞を獲得する酒もあります。大量生産して全国販売している酒もありますが、全国各地にその土地の酒造工場があり、米や水の質、あるいは醸造法の違いによってそれぞれ独特の味を作り出しています。これを「地酒」といい、最近の日本酒ブームの主役となっています。アルコール濃度は15％程度で比較的飲みやすいため、女性の愛好家も増えています。

Rice wine : Brewed with **rice** and water, this is a Japanese alcoholic beverage since ancient times. Because it can be drunk warmed up, intoxication comes on more quickly and in winter it warms the body. When drunk cold, good sake has a taste similar to fine quality wine. As a result, there are some kinds of sake that have won prizes when submitted for exhibition at European wine competitions. Some kinds of sake are mass-produced and sold throughout Japan, however, there are local sake breweries in every region across the country, which make their respective characteristic tastes based on the quality of **rice** and water and differences in brewing processes. This kind of sake is called *"jizake"* (locally brewed sake), and has played the main role in the recent sake boom. With the alcohol concentration of around 15%, it is comparatively easy to drink, resulting in increasing numbers of female fans.

【焼酎】
Shōchū
しょうちゅう

酒が醸造酒であるのに対し、焼酎は蒸留酒です。蒸留の技術は11世紀にアラビアで開発され、東洋には13世紀に伝わりました。原料は麦・米・とうもろこし・さつまいもなどが主で、アルコール濃度は高く30〜45％ぐらい。酒ほど人気はありませんが、西日本では各地に独特の焼酎があり、沖縄の「泡盛」は最も有名です。焼酎を使って自家用に梅やリンゴの果実酒を作ることは法律で許されています。

Low-class distilled spirits : In contrast to **sake**, which is brewed, *shōchū* is distilled liquor. The technique of distilling was developed in Arabia in the eleventh century and brought to the East in the thirteenth century. The raw materials are mainly wheat, **rice**, corn and sweet potatoes, and the alcohol concentration is high at about 30 to 45%. It is not as popular as **sake**, but in Western Japan each region has its own *shōchū*, the most famous being "*awamori*" from Okinawa. The law allows the use of *shōchū* to make **plum** or apple liquor for home consumption.

【甘酒・白酒】
あまざけ・しろざけ／Amazake,Shirozake

白色の濃厚な酒を白酒といいます。日本酒とは製法が異なり、蒸したもち米と米麹にみりんや焼酎を混ぜて作ります。アルコール飲料としては一般的ではなく、甘さがあるため、多くはひな祭りなどの特別な日に、主に女性や子供が飲みます。一方甘酒も味は甘く、主に正月や祭りなどに神社で出されたり、寒い冬に家庭で飲んだりします。こちらは米粥に麹を混ぜて醸造したものです。

Sweet sake, white sake : White, concentrated **sake** is called *shirozake*. The manufacturing process is different from regular sake; it is made by blending a sweet kind of sake and **low-class distilled spirits** with steamed glutinous rice and rice malt. It is not a regular alcoholic beverage; with its sweetness, it is mostly drunk by women and girls on special days like the **Doll's Festival**. Meanwhile, *amazake* also has a sweet taste and is served mainly at **Shinto shrines** for **New Year**'s and other **festivals**, and is also drunk in homes in the cold winter. This sake is brewed by blending malted rice with rice gruel.

【茶】
ちゃ Cha

　茶は東南アジアの温・熱帯地方が原産。日本語のchaは英語やフランス語の tea、thé などと同じ語源を持っています。イギリス人が紅茶を生活の一部としているのと同様、日本でも茶は生活に欠かすことができません。午後3時は「おやつ」の時間といって、お菓子とお茶をいただくのが昔からの日本人の習慣です。しかし一方では、そのような茶の日常性を断ち切って、**禅**の精神を取り入れながら精神を修養するという**茶道**が**安土桃山時代**（1573〜1603）に成立し、現在も盛んに行われています。もともと日本茶は**仏教**の**僧**が薬用に用いていたことからも分かるように、ビタミンが多く含まれ、健康にも大変よいとされています。

Green tea : *Cha* was originally produced in the temperate, tropical regions of Southeast Asia. The Japanese word *cha* has the same derivation as, for example, the English word "tea" and the French word "thé". In the same way as the British people make black tea part of their daily lives, in Japan too *cha* is indispensable in people's lives. A long-standing Japanese custom is to have "refreshment time" at three in the afternoon to partake of sweets and *cha*. Meanwhile, however, the **tea ceremony**, for which the tea is quite different from the *cha* used daily and which improves one's character by taking in the spirit of **Zen**, was developed in the **Azuchi-Momoyama Period**(1573-1603) and is widely practiced still today. As made evident by that **Buddhist priests** originally used Japanese *cha* for medicinal purposes, it is known to include a lot of vitamins and is considered to be very good for the health.

【醬油】
Shōyu
しょうゆ

醬油は大豆を主原料とする日本固有の調味料の一種です。英語の soy は、日本語の「しょうゆ」から派生した語です。独特の香りを持つ褐色の液汁であるこの優れた調味料は、日本の多くの料理になくてはならぬものです。従って、日本人の味覚の基本をなしているとさえいえるでしょう。醬油がなければ、私たちは**すき焼き**も**すし**も**刺身**も食べられません。煮物の味付けもできません。

最近はアメリカをはじめ西洋諸国でも売られ、ステーキなどの味付けにも使われています。「照り焼きステーキ」は醬油ベースのたれをつけて焼いたものです。

Soy sauce is a unique Japanese condiment made from soy beans. The English word "soy" derives from the Japanese word *shōyu*. This outstanding condiment, a brown liquid with a peculiar smell, is essential for most Japanese cooking. Accordingly, one can say that it constitutes the basis of the Japanese people's sense of taste. Without soy sauce, the Japanese can't eat *sukiyaki*, **sushi**, or *sashimi* or even season any of their cooking.

Soy sauce recently has sold well in the U.S. and other Western countries, and has been used as seasoning for steak and other foods. "*Teriyaki* steak" is grilled with a sauce based on soy sauce.

【味噌】
Miso
みそ

　味噌も**醤油**と同じく大豆を原料としています。茶色がほとんどでペースト状の調味料です。多くの日本人は朝食に**味噌汁**を飲みます。さまざまな具、例えば**豆腐**や**わかめ**や野菜類を入れ、最後にこの味噌を溶かし温いスープにします。スープ以外の利用法としては、**ラーメン**に入れたり**おむすび**につけたり、あるいはさまざまな**鍋料理**の味付けに使ったりします。また、この中に魚や肉を入れておくと長期間腐らずになおかつおいしい味がつきます。

　味噌も日本人にはなくてはならない大切な調味料です。最近は、特に**味噌汁**は栄養のバランスのよくとれた健康食として高く評価されています。

Soy bean paste : Like **soy sauce**, *miso* is made from soy beans. It is a paste-like condiment mostly in a brown color. Many Japanese have ***miso* soup** for breakfast. The hot soup is made by adding several ingredients to broth, for example, **tofu**, **seaweeds**, or vegetables, then stirring in the soy bean paste. In addition to soup, it is used as seasoning for ***rāmen***(a Chinese brand of noodle), **rice balls**, and all kinds of **cookpot dishes**. Fish or meat pickled in this *miso* keep for a long time and, yet with enhanced taste.

　Soy bean paste is also an important condiment that is indispensable to the Japanese people. Recently, ***miso* soup** in particular has been valued as a health food that contributes to a balanced diet.

【料亭】
Ryōtei
りょうてい

日本料理専門のレストランといえます。高級料亭は伝統的な日本建築の建物に**日本庭園**を備え、部屋はほとんど個室であり、料理も店が用意したコースが中心です。**芸者を**呼ぶこともできます。伝統と格式を重んじ、なじみ客の紹介や予約がなくては入れません。最高級料理店ですから、料金が高いので個人ではあまり利用せず、主に会社の接待や、政治家や団体の会合に使われます。

Traditional Japanese-style restaurants : These are restaurants specializing in Japanese cuisine. High-class *ryōtei* are buildings constructed with traditional Japanese architecture and furnished with a **Japanese garden**, the rooms are mostly private and the cuisine is mainly prix fixe. *Geisha* can be called in. Great importance is attached to tradition and status; without an introduction and reservations by familiar customers, one cannot get in. They are very exclusive and expensive restaurants, so individuals rarely use them. They are mainly used by companies with expense accounts and by politicians and other groups for meetings.

【居酒屋】
Izakaya
いざかや

日本式のパブといっていいでしょう。酒は**日本酒**や**焼酎**、またはビールが中心で、食べ物は**焼き鳥**や**刺身**など魚類が多く、冬は**鍋料理**や**おでん**などの温かいものが加わるのが一般的です。入口には赤いちょうちんが下がっていることが多いので、別名「赤ちょうちん」とも呼ばれます。都会では会社帰りのサラリーマンが同僚や友人同士で飲むことが多いのですが、最近はOLも増えてきました。

Japanese pubs : These can probably be called Japanese-style pubs. The liquor is mainly **sake**, **low-class distilled spirits**, and of course beer, and the food is mostly **grilled chicken** and different kinds of fish, like *sashimi*; generally in winter, **cookpot dishes** and warm ones like **Japanese hotchpotch** are added. Red lanterns often hang at the entrance, so *izakaya* are also known by another name— "red lantern." In cities, white-collar workers on their way home from work often stop there to drink with colleagues and friends, and recently working women, too, have been stopping in more and more.

【屋台】
やたい
Yatai

車が付いているので、人が引いて移動できる屋根付きの料理屋、とでもいえるでしょう。繁華街の通りや駅前に出店することが多く、種類は**ラーメン**、**おでん**、**焼き鳥**などが主です。たいていは酒類を出してくれるので移動式飲み屋ともいえます。他には、小さな家の形に作った持ち運び可能な台として、祭礼のときに物を売ったりして使うものも意味します。

Street stalls : Since these are on wheels so that a person can pull, they can be described as mobile restaurants with roof attached. Most of them are set up on busy streets and in front of stations, and they specialize in the kind of food they serve—mainly, *rāmen*(a Chinese brand of noodle), **Japanese hotchpotch** or **grilled chicken**. They usually serve alcoholic drinks, so they can also be called as mobile pubs. In addition, the term also refers to transportable stalls in the shape of a small house, used for selling things at festivals.

【甘味】
かんみ
Kanmi

甘味とは甘い食べ物全般を指しますが、主に日本独特の甘い菓子やデザート類を意味します。甘味類を出す店を甘味処とか甘味喫茶といい、あんみつ、みつまめ、ようかん、**団子**などがメニューに並んでいます。あんみつは、サイの目に切った寒天に蜜をかけ、あんをのせたもので、日本の甘味類の代表的な味です。和製以外のメニューとしてはアイスクリームやパフェなどに人気があります。

Kanmi means any sort of food with a sweet taste, but it mainly points out sweets and deserts peculiar to Japan. Places that serve *kanmi* is called *kanmi* spots or *kanmi* parlors. Their menus consist of *anmitsu*, *mitsumame*(similar to anmitsu but it contains beans instead of bean jam), sweet bean jelly, **dumplings**, and the like. *Anmitsu* is agar* sliced into dice with syrup poured on and topped with bean jam, and is a typical example of Japanese *kanmi*. Popular sweets besides Japanese ones are ice creams and parfaits.

*a gelatinlike product of certain seaweeds.

住生活

an openwork of a transom

【日本家屋】
Nihon-kaoku
にほんかおく

伝統的な日本家屋は、基本的には木と紙でできています。部屋は地面から20〜30センチ高く、板張りの床の上に畳が敷いてあり、仕切りにはふすまや障子が使われています。これらは木枠に紙を張ったものです。家の内と外は厳しく分けられ、靴をはいたまま室内に入ることは決してできません。

ふすま/Paper sliding doors

Japanese houses : Traditional *nihon-kaoku* basically are made of wood and paper. Rooms are raised 20 to 30 cm above the ground, **flooring rush mats** cover floors of wooden boarding, and **paper sliding doors** and **sliding paper screens** are used as partitions. These are paper glued on wooden frames. Inside and outside are strictly separated; one never goes inside with shoes on.

【欄間】らんま／Ranma

　部屋と部屋の仕切りの上部に、通風・採光目的で設けられたもので、ふつうは格子や透かし彫りの装飾が施されています。

Transoms : These are built above the partitions between rooms for ventilation and lighting and ordinarily are done with decorative lattices and openwork.

床の間/Alcoves

障子/Sliding paper screens

畳/Flooring rush mats

【床の間】とこのま Tokonoma

　床の間は、和室の壁面に設けられた、**一畳**か半畳程度の部分で、**掛軸**や**生け花**を飾る場所です。床は板張りで、周囲より一段高くなっているのがふつうです。古くは神を拝むための場所だったのですが、**室町時代**（1392〜1573）から**安土桃山時代**（1573〜1603）にかけて造り付けとなり、座敷の装飾的性質を持つものになりました。しかし最近の集合住宅には、床の間のない間取りも多く見られます。

Alcoves : *Tokonoma* is about the size of about one or a half *tatami* **mat** and is set into a wall of a Japanese-style room. It is the place to put up **scrolls** or display **flower arrangements**. Its floor is made of wood and is a step higher than the rest of the room. In the past, it was a place where divinities were worshipped, but from the **Muromachi**(1392-1573) and the **Azuchi - Momoyama Period**(1573-1603) on it became a standard built-in feature with a decorative purpose. Recently, however in the average residence, there are many floor plans without *tokonoma*.

【畳】たたみ Tatami

　畳は**平安時代**（794〜1185）から使われていましたが、当時は人が座る場所にだけ敷いており、部屋中に敷くようになったのは**室町時代**（1392〜1573）からです。畳の台は乾燥したわらを重ねて縫ってあり、その上に**いぐさ**で編んだ 畳 表 をかぶせてあります。畳1枚は約90センチ×180センチで、和室の広さは畳の枚数で表されます。なお、畳の縁を踏むと傷みが早いため、踏まないのがマナーです。

Flooring rush mats : *Tatami* have been used since the **Heian Period**(794-1185), when they were laid out only for sitting. From the time of the **Muromachi Period**(1392-1573), they were used to cover the whole floor. A *tatami* mat is made of straw bundled in layers which are stitched together, and the surface is covered with tightly woven **rushes**. One *tatami* mat measures about 90 × 180 cm(about 3' × 6'), and the size of a Japanese room is expressed by its number of *tatami* mats. It is worthy of note that Japanese customarily avoid stepping on the edge of a *tatami* mat, because that will hasten its wear and tear.

【布団】
ふとん
Futon

布団は日本の寝具で、**敷き布団**と**掛け布団**とがあります。中には綿や羽毛が詰められています。ベッドのマットレスにあたるのが**敷き布団**で、その上にシーツを敷きます。毛布などと一緒に上に掛けるのが**掛け布団**です。日本は湿気が多いので、天気のいい日には布団を日に当てて乾燥させます。布団は、使わないときは畳んで**押し入れ**にしまっておけるので、日本の狭い部屋には合理的な寝具なのです。

Thick bedquilts : There are two kinds of *futon*; **quiltlike mattress** and **quilts to be covered with**. *Futon* are filled with cotton or feathers. **Quiltlike mattress**, like a bed mattress, are covered by sheets, while **quilts to be covered with** are used as coverings with blankets. Since Japan is quite humid, *futon* are hung out on nice days to air in the sun. *Futon* which can be put in a **closet** when not being used are practical bedding for small Japanese rooms.

【座布団】
ざぶとん
Zabuton

座布団は日本版クッションで、**畳**の上に座るときに使うものです。四角い形をしていて、ちょうど1人が座れるくらいの大きさです。中にはふつう綿が詰められています。

座布団の覆いは、さまざまな模様や絵を描いた布でできていますが、夏になると**いぐさ**などで編まれた、さらっとした感触で、風通しのいいものが好まれます。

Japanese cushions : *Zabuton* are Japanese-made cushions used when sitting on **flooring rush mats**. Square in shape, they are just large enough for one person. They are usually filled with cotton.

Coverings of *zabuton* are finished in cloth with all sorts of patterns and pictures, but in summer, a kind of coverings prefered is woven with **rushes** which is cool to the touch and creates good ventilation.

【正座】Seiza せいざ

正座は、畳の上に座るときの正式な座り方で、**茶の湯**の席など、正式な場では必ず正座をすることになっています。両足を折り畳んでかかとの上に腰をのせるので、慣れていない人には、長時間の正座はつらく感じられるでしょう。しかし、正座をすると、頭から背骨にかけての体の中心線が床と垂直になるので、安定したよい姿勢が保てるのです。畳に座るときには体にいい座り方なのです。

Sitting straight : *Seiza* is the proper way to sit on **tatami** mats and is always practiced on such formal occasions as **tea ceremony**. Since the legs are folded under so that the body rests on the heels, people who are not accustomed to it probably feel that doing *seiza* for a long time is painful. However, when doing *seiza* the central line of the body from the head down the spine is perpendicular to the floor, so one can maintain a well-balanced posture. When sitting on **tatami** mats, it is good for the body to sit that way.

【あぐら】Agura

正座に対し、リラックスした座り方があぐらです。両足を前に出してから、三角形になるように組んで座ることを「あぐらをかく」といいます。男性はよくこの座り方をしますが、女性にとっては行儀の悪い座り方です。女性がリラックスして座るときは、ひざを開かず**正座**していた足をそのまま横に流して座るのがふつうです。

Sitting cross-legged : In contrast to **sitting straight**, the relaxed way of sitting is *agura*. Starting with legs out straight and folding them in like triangles is called "sitting cross-legged." Men often sit this way, but it is ill-mannered for women to do so. Relaxed sitting posture for women is generally to maintain the **sitting straight** with knees together but with the feet just off to the side.

【障子】Shōji しょうじ

障子は、長方形の木の枠の中に、細い木を**格子**にしてはめ込み、それに**和紙**を張った引き戸です。部屋の出入口や間仕切り、あるいは窓に取り付けて使います。採光を考慮しているため、障子を閉めていても、**和紙**を通して柔らかい光が差し込んできます。典型的な**日本家屋**には必ず見られるものですが、住居が洋風化するにつれて、少なくなってきています。

Sliding paper screens : *Shōji* are sliding doors with fine wood **latticework** built into a rectangular wooden frame and pasted with **Japanese paper**. They serve as entry and exit for rooms, are used as room partitions, and can be installed in windows. With respect to lighting, even when *shōji* are closed, soft light flows through the **Japanese paper.** They are invariably seen in typical **Japanese houses** but are becoming scarce as more residences become westernized.

【ふすま】Fusuma

ふすまは、**畳**の部屋を仕切ったり、**押し入れ**の戸として使ったりします。裏表には、**和紙**の下張りの上に厚い紙が張られ、この紙の上に美しい模様や絵が描かれているので、インテリアとしても優れています。部屋の雰囲気を変えるには、このふすま紙を張り替えればいいのです。**障子**と違って採光は考えられていません。間仕切りとしての機能とデザインの美しさが、ふすまの特徴でしょう。

Paper sliding doors : *Fusuma* are used to partition **flooring rush mats** rooms and as **closet** doors. A thick paper is glued on top of a **Japanese paper** lining. The beautiful designs and pictures painted on this paper create a superb room interior. In order to change the atmosphere of a room, one only has to change the paper. Unlike *shōji*, lighting is not taken into consideration. *Fusuma* principally function as room partitions and as beautiful works of art.

【かわら】Kawara

　かわらは**日本家屋**の屋根に使われるもので、7世紀ごろに中国から伝わりました。現在は粘土やセメントを主な原料としています。かわらを使った屋根は「かわらぶき」といいます。使用する箇所に応じて、さまざまな形のものがあります。**鬼がわら**は主に**鬼**の形をしており、魔よけの意味で用いられています。

Roofing tile : *Kawara* are tiles used on the roofs of **Japanese houses**. They were brought from China in the seventh century. Today they are made principally with clay and cement. Roofs made of *kawara* tiles are called "***kawarabuki***." They come in all sorts of shapes, depending on the location where they are used. **Tiles with the figure of ogres** usually are done in the form of **ogres** and are used as charms against bad luck.

【風鈴】Fūrin　ふうりん

　風鈴は、ガラスや金属、**陶器**でできた小さな鈴で、主に夏の間、家の軒先などに釣り下げます。鈴の下方には、**短冊**とよばれる長方形の紙片が付いており、ここには日本の古い詩や歌が書かれています。**短冊**が風を受けると鈴が鳴ります。湿気が多くてむし暑い日本の夏ですが、風鈴が風に搖れる音は、日本人にとっては一服の清涼剤なのです。

Wind-bells : *Fūrin* are small bells made of glass, metal or **ceramic** which are hung from the eaves of houses chiefly in summer. A rectangular strip of paper which is called *tanzaku* is hung from a clapper, and ancient Japanese poems or verses are written on it. When the *tanzaku* catches the breeze, the bell chimes. In the hot, humid Japanese summer, the sound of the *fūrin* vibrating in the breeze is, for the Japanese, a puff of coolness.

【こたつ】Kotatsu

こたつは、日本人の「畳の上に座る生活」にマッチした暖房器具です。木製のテーブルを布団で覆い、中に火のついた炭が入っている陶器を入れておきます。すると内部が温まるので、腰まで布団で覆って座ると体が温まります。現在では炭ではなく、テーブルの裏面にある電気ヒーターで温めます。西洋の暖炉のように、日本では冬に、このこたつを囲んで家族がくつろぐのです。

Heater with a thick quilt : *Kotatsu* is a heating apparatus that fits the Japanese "lifestyle of sitting on **flooring rush mats**." A low wooden table is covered with a thick quilt and underneath is placed a **ceramic** container with burning **charcoal**. This makes it warm underneath, so when sitting covered to the  waist with the thick quilt the body warms up. Today, it is done not with **charcoal** but with an electric heater beneath the table. As with the Western fireplace, the family in Japan relaxes around the *kotatsu* in winter.

【火鉢】Hibachi ひばち

火鉢は日本古来の暖房器具です。陶器や木、金属でできています。中に灰を入れて炭火をおこし、手をかざして温めたり、部屋を暖めたりします。灰の中に、五徳という輪状の台を置き、上にやかんをのせると、お湯を沸かすこともできます。しかし、生活様式の変化などにより、現在の一般家庭からはほとんど姿を消してしまっています。

Braziers : *Hibachi* are ancient Japanese heating devices, made of ceramic, wood or metal. Ashes are laid in, a charcoal fire is kindled, hands held out to it are warmed, and it warms the room. It can also be used to boil water, by putting a brass kettle on a **ring-shaped support with a tripod** in the ashes. However, as lifestyles change,  this apparatus has almost completely disappeared from the average contemporary family household.

【いろり】 Irori

いろりは煙突のない暖炉に似ています。部屋の中央の床を四角く掘り、**まき**を燃料にして、そこで火をたくのです。大きさは、90センチ四方か180センチ四方です。中央には、天井から**自在かぎ**というかぎがつるされ、鍋や**鉄びん**を下げることもできます。昔はいろりを囲んで食事をするなど、一家だんらんの場でしたが、今では、田舎に古くからある農家などでしか見られません。

Sunken hearths : *Irori* resemble fireplaces without chimney. A square hole is dug in the middle of a room, and fire is kindled with **firewood** as fuel. Its size is either 90 or 180 cm on each side. In the center, a **pot hanger** is suspended from the ceiling, from which cookpots or **iron kettles** are hung. In the past, the whole family would gather around the *irori* to eat and do other things, but nowadays this only happens in the countryside in old farming households.

【そろばん】 Soroban

そろばんは計算に使う道具で、中国から伝わりました。5個ないし7個の玉をさした棒が何本も長方形の枠の中にはめ込んであり、その玉を動かして計算します。現在は電卓に押され気味ですが、そろばんを学習すると暗算に強くなることから、そろばん塾も多数存在しています。また、そろばんの検定試験もあります。

Abacuses : *Soroban* are instruments used for calculation. They were brought from China. Several slender poles running through five or seven round pieces are inserted into a rectangular frame. The round pieces are moved to do the calculations. Nowadays, its place seemes to be taken over by calculators, but learning *soroban* strengthens the ability to calculate mentally, so there are a lot of private *soroban* schools. There is even a license examination of *soroban*.

【うちわ】 Uchiwa

うちわは細く割った**竹**を広げて骨組みにし、紙を張ったもので、千年以上も前に中国から伝わりました。暑い夏に、あおいで風を送り、涼を得ます。店名や商品名をうちわに刷り込んで、宣伝用に使うこともあります。**浴衣**を着てうちわであおぐ姿は、夏の風物詩の1つとなっています。

Round fans : *Uchiwa* have frameworks of thinly split, spread-out **bamboo** on which paper is glued, and were brought into Japan from China more than 1,000 years ago. In the hot summer, fanning creates breezes and refreshment. They are also used for advertising by stenciling on store names and product names. The sight of a person wearing an **informal cotton kimono** and fanning oneself with an *uchiwa* is a typical Japanese summer scene.

【扇子】 Sensu せんす

扇子は折りたたみ式の**うちわ**といえます。**うちわ**が中国伝来であるのに対し、扇子は日本で発明されました。あおいで風を起こし、涼をとるのに使われるほか、**日本舞踊**や**落語**には欠かせない小道具でもあります。扇子を広げた形は、次第に栄えていくことを象徴する「**末広がり**」であるため、祝い事の小道具や、記念品に使われたりもします。

Folding fans : *Sensu* can be said to be collapsible *uchiwa*. While *uchiwa* came from China, *sensu* originated in Japan. In addition to being used to create breezes and refreshment, *sensu* are indispensable props for **classical Japanese dance** and for **comic storytelling**. Because the shape of the unfolded fan is "**broadening toward the end**," symbolizing rising prosperity, it is also used as prop for celebrations or as a memento.

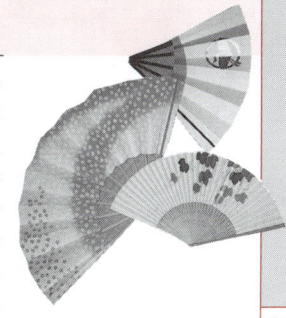

【箸】 Hashi はし

箸は、食事をするときに食物をはさむ2本の棒で、古代中国から伝わりました。日本では、食事のときはほとんど箸を使います。**漆**を塗った木や**竹**、またはプラスチック製のものが多いのですが、中には象牙製の高級品もあります。来客用、あるいは飲食店で出される箸は、**割り箸**という使い捨ての白木の箸です。幼少時に両親から箸の使い方を習うため、大部分の日本人は箸を上手に使えるのです。

Chopsticks(*hashi*) are two sticks that hold food between them when one eats. They were brought from ancient China. In Japan, *hashi* are almost always used when eating. Most are made of wood or **bamboo** painted with **lacquer** or of plastic, but there are also high-class ones with the inside made of ivory. *Hashi* put out for visitors or in restaurants are **half-split chopsticks**; made of

unfinished wood, they are to be used and thrown away. Most Japanese are skillful at using *hashi*, because they learned how from their parents during childhood.

【風呂敷】 Furoshiki ふろしき

風呂敷は、スカーフに似た正方形の布で、物を包んで持ち運ぶときに使います。材質は絹や綿です。**江戸時代**(1603〜1867)、**銭湯**へ持って行く下着や、銭湯で脱いだ着物を包むのに使われたため「『風呂』敷」とよばれるようになりました。包むときは、真ん中に物を置いて、後は対角線上の隅を結びます。

Wrapping cloths : *Furoshiki* are square cloths resembling scarves and are used to wrap and carry things. They are made of silk or

cotton. In the **Edo Period**(1603-1867), they came to be called "*furoshiki*"('bath' wrapping cloths) because they were used to wrap one's underclothes when going to the **public bath** or to wrap one's clothes while there. When wrapping, the object is placed in the middle and the opposite corners are tied together.

【たんす】 Tansu

　たんすは、衣類や小道具を収納する木製の家具です。伝統的な日本のたんすは、収納しやすいように引き出しと引き戸を組み合わせてあり、角が傷まないように金具で補強されているものもあります。現在では、服をハンガーで収納できるよう開き戸を組み合わせた「洋だんす」が普及しています。**和服**用には、衣類を湿気から守る**桐たんす**が重宝されています。

Bureau, chest : *Tansu* are furniture made of wood and are for keeping clothing or small objects. The traditional Japanese *tansu* has easy-to-use drawers and sliding doors and the corners are strengthened with metal to guard against damage. Nowadays "Western-style *tansu*," in which clothes are kept on hangers and doors pull open, are widely used. For **Japanese-style garments**, **paulownia-wood chests** that protect clothing from humidity are highly valued.

【のれん】 Noren

　のれんは、日本の商店の軒先にかかっている短い布です。禅寺が防寒用に用いた垂れ幕に端を発し、**江戸時代**（1603〜1867）以降は、商家が屋号などを入れて商業用に使うようになりました。あるいはまた、店の象徴として、営業権や信用を意味する言葉としても使われます。開店するときは「のれんを出す」、支店を出すときは「のれんを分ける」のように言うのです。

Shop curtains : *Noren* are short cloth curtains hung on the entrances to Japanese shops. Beginning with the scraps of cloth on hanging screens used in Zen temples to ward off cold, merchant houses since the **Edo Period**(1603-1867) have put their names on *noren* and used them in business. The word "*noren*," is also used to signify good will and credit of a shop, as its symbol. In opening a shop, one is said "to hang out the *noren*" and when establishing branch stores, the saying is "to divide the *noren*."

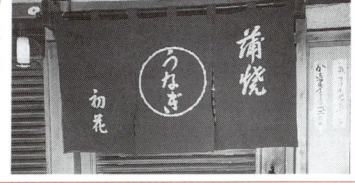

【風呂】
Furo
ふろ

　日本では風呂に入るとき、体は浴槽の外で洗い、汚れを落としてから浴槽につかります。通常、家族全員が入り終わるまで浴槽の湯は替えないので、きれいに使います。40〜50年前までは木製の浴槽が一般的でしたが、現在はほとんどがタイル、合成樹脂やステンレスで作られています。

　寒い冬は風呂で体を温め、湿度の高い夏は汗が乾きにくいため、風呂で汗を流します。日本の生活に風呂は欠かせません。1日の疲れをいやすにも風呂は最適です。今では日本の大部分の家庭に風呂があり、さまざまな種類の入浴剤も発売されているので、好みの入浴剤を入れて楽しむ人も多くなっています。

Japanese bath : In taking a Japanese *furo*, one enters the bathtub only after first washing off outside the tub. Generally, the whole family uses the same tub of hot water, so they keep it clean. Until 40 or 50 years ago *furo* made of wood were common, but now they are almost all made of tile, plastic or stainless steel.

In the cold winter the *furo* warms the body and in the highly humid summer it washes away the constant stream of perspiration. The *furo* is indispensable to Japanese life. It is the optimum cure for a day's fatigue. Because today the majority of Japanese homes have *furo* and all manner of bathing remedies are being sold, the number of people is increasing who enjoy their baths by adding their favorite bathing remedy to the water.

【炭】
Sumi
すみ

　日本は山岳地帯が国土の60％以上を占め、その山々は森林で覆われています。従って木を使った文化が発達しました。炭もその１つでしょう。1960年以降の**高度成長期**の前までは、炭はまきや石炭とともに日本の主要な暖房燃料であり、炭を使った文化は千年以上続いたのです。**奈良時代**（710～784）には鉄を鋳造するのにも炭が熱源となりました。**茶の湯**で湯を沸かすにも炭が必要だし、**火鉢**や**こたつ**にも炭が必要です。

　今ではガスや電気が炭に取って代わっています。しかし**焼き鳥**はガスで焼くより炭で焼く方がおいしいし、**茶の湯**には今でも炭が必要だ、というわけで、炭文化は細々ながら現在も続いています。

Charcoal : The mountainous regions in Japan comprise more than 60% of the land and are covered with forests. As a result, a culture using wood developed. *Sumi* also is a part of this. Prior to the **period of high growth of economy** after 1960, *sumi*, together with **firewood** and coal, was Japan's main fuel for heating, and culture using *sumi* had continued for more than 1,000 years. In the **Nara Period**(710-784), *sumi* became the energy source for casting iron. *Sumi* was necessary to boil water for the **tea ceremony**, and also necessary for **braziers** and **heaters with thick quilts**. Now, gas and electricity have replaced *sumi*. However, **grilled chicken** tastes better if grilled with *sumi* instead of gas, and for the **tea ceremony** even now *sumi* is necessary—which means that the *sumi* culture, though barely, still continues.

【和紙】
わし
Washi

　紙の製法は7世紀初頭、中国から朝鮮を経て日本に伝わり、日本独自の発展を遂げました。和紙には、手すきのものと、機械すきのものとがあります。前者は**コウゾ**など木の皮を原料とする**半紙**や美濃紙などで、後者は故紙や木材パルプなどを原料とする**障子紙**などです。

　現代生活において、和紙を使う機会はそう多くはありませんが、和紙には丈夫さや渋さ、温かさなど、洋紙にはないよさがあります。そのような持ち味を生かして、和紙を使った便箋や封筒、ランプシェードなども発売されています。

Japanese paper : The process of making paper was brought to Japan from China through Korea at the beginning of the seventh century and had a characteristic Japanese development. *Washi* can be made by hand or by machine. The former is **common Japanese writing paper** or *mino* paper which are made of the bark of trees, like **paper mulberry**, and the latter is ***shōji* paper**, for example, which is made from used paper and wood pulp.

 In contemporary life, there are not so many opportunities to use *washi*, but it has merits, such as durability, subdued and comfortable quality in its color and textile, not found in Western paper. Making the most of such characteristics, items made of *washi*, like letter-writing pads, envelops and even lampshades are being sold.

【家紋】
Kamon
かもん

　家紋は、家々によって定められた紋です。日本の家紋は約1万2千種類あるといわれていますが、その多くには、魔よけのはたらきを持つ、縁起のいい植物が用いられています。たとえば天皇家の**菊**の紋は、**菊**が薬草で、魔よけになるとされたことから作られたものです。そのほかに文字や動物を図案化したものも多くあります。

　家紋の起源は**平安時代**（794〜1185）前期、持ち主を区別するために貴族の牛車に付けられた印でした。その後武士にも普及し、戦争の際の旗印に用いられたのをはじめ、多くのものに印されるようになりました。以後庶民にも普及し、現在は日本中のほとんどの家が家紋を持っています。

Family crest : *Kamon* is a crest fixed for each family. It is said that there are about 12,000 kinds of *kamon* in Japan, most of which depicting auspicious plants that possess talismanic power against evil. For example, the **chrysanthemum** crest of the Imperial Family was created because the **chrysanthemum** is a medicinal plant and a talisman against evil. In addition, there are many crests that are designed after letter of characters and animals.

　Kamon originated in the early years of the **Heian Period**(794-1185) as emblems on the cow carriages of the nobility to distinguish among the owners. After that, they spread to warriors and were used to mark many kinds of objects, beginning with flag emblems in time of war. Later, they spread to the masses also; today virtually every family throughout Japan has a *kamon*.

宗教

文化庁「宗教年鑑」1992年版
Agency for Cultural Affairs
"The Religion Yearbook"
1992 edition

【宗教の信者の数】 Shūkyō no shinja no kazu しゅうきょうのしんじゃのかず

　日本人が信仰する宗教は神道と仏教とに大別されます。しかし現代日本では、「結婚式は神式で、葬式は仏式で」というように、神道も仏教も信仰するというよりは、生活の中に深く根を下ろした「習慣」という側面が強くなってきました。

The number of people who believe in religion : Religion in Japan can roughly be divided into **Shinto** and **Buddhism**. However, in contemporary Japan, both **Shinto** and **Buddhism** are becoming more like a deeply rooted "custom" practiced in daily life ragher than object of faith, as observed in the general practice of "a **wedding** with Shinto rites and a **funeral** with Buddhist rites."

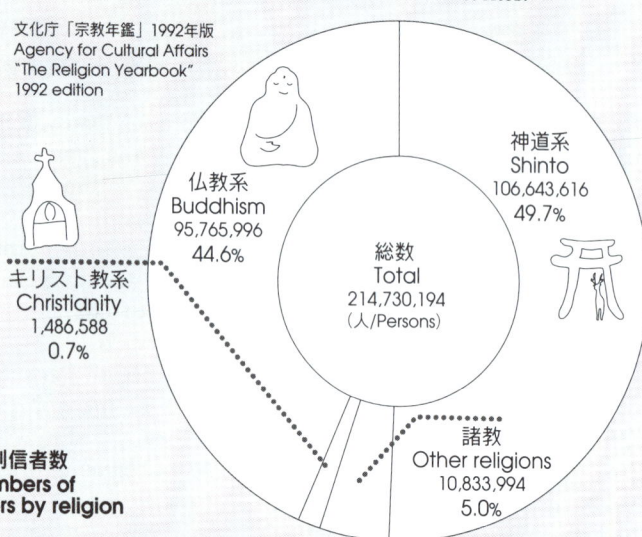

仏教系
Buddhism
95,765,996
44.6%

神道系
Shinto
106,643,616
49.7%

キリスト教系
Christianity
1,486,588
0.7%

総数
Total
214,730,194
（人/Persons）

諸教
Other religions
10,833,994
5.0%

◎宗教別信者数
The numbers of believers by religion

…各宗教団体が自発的に提出する数字が収録されている。
…It contains data provided voluntarily by each religious organization.

【神道】
Shintō
しんとう

　神道は日本古来の宗教であり、日本人の自然観と先祖崇拝の念がその中核をなしています。地上の森羅万象は神々によって生み出され、神々の司るところとされ、すべての自然には神が宿るとされます。山や木は御神体となることが多く、**鳥居**や**しめ縄**でそこが神域であることを表します。普通は**神社**を建てそこに神が宿る御神体を安置します。神道は日本人の感性の基礎をなしていますが、現在の日本人は、神道に信仰心を抱くというより文化的アイデンティティーを感じる人が大部分だといえるでしょう。

　神道は一方で、**天皇制**を宗教的に支えたものであり、今でも天皇家の宗教として古いしきたりを残しています。

Shinto, literally meaning the way of the gods, is the Japanese religion from the ancient times, centering on the ideas of Japanese intimacy with nature and ancestor worship. All things on earth were brought forth and ruled over by the gods who reside throughout all nature. Mountains and trees often become objects of worship, and **Shrine archways** and **sacred Shinto rope** mark sacred areas. Ordinarily, **shrines** are built there, and objects of worship in which a god or gods reside are enshrined. Shinto constitutes the foundation of the sensibility of the Japanese people, but most present-day Japanese, rather than placing faith in Shinto, feel their cultural identity through it.

　Shinto meanwhile supported the **Emperor system** in a religious sense, and even now its ancient customary practices remain as the religion of the Imperial Family.

【神社】
Jinja
じんじゃ

神社は**神道**の神をまつった建物です。入口には神域を示す**鳥居**があり、神をまつった本殿（神殿）といくつかの付属の施設から成つています。神社の本殿は高床式になつており、屋根は一般に茅や檜（ひのき）の皮でふいてあります。

正月はどの神社も**初詣**の参拝客でにぎわいます。そのほかに、赤ちゃんが生まれたときお**宮参り**に行つたり、**七五三**を祝つて参拝したり、祈願するためにお参りをしたりと、たとえ**神道**の信者ではなくても、神社は日本人にとつて縁（ゆかり）の深い場所なのです。

Shinto shrines are buildings where **Shinto** deities are enshrined. At the entrances are **Shinto shrine archways** indicating the shrine precincts, then come the main sanctuary and other facilities. The floor of the main building is elevated and roofs are generally thatched with cogon grasses and Japanese cypress bark.

The Shinto shrine is a place of deep affinity for the Japanese people, even for those who are not **Shinto** believers, as being observed at **New Year**, when virtually all Shinto shrines are thronged with worshippers for the **first temple or shrine visit of the New Year**. In addition, they visit the shrines on such occations as **newborn infant's shrine visit**, to cerebrate the **gala day for children of three, five and seven years of age**, and to offer prayers.

【神主】かんぬし Kannushi

　神主は、**神社**で神事に仕える人です。供え物をしたり、祝詞をあげたりして、神に仕えます。参拝に来た人々に**お祓い**をしたり、**結婚式**をとり行ったりします。

　一方、**神社**の経営にかかわることも神主の仕事です。**おみくじ**や**お守り**、**縁起物**の売上や**さい銭**の計算などは、すべて神主の監督下で行われるのです。

Shinto priests : *Kannushi* are Shinto priests who minister at **Shinto shrines**. They serve the divinities by making offerings and reciting a **Shinto prayer**. They also perform the **Shinto purification** for people who come to worship and execute **weddings**.

Meanwhile, Shinto priests' work also involves **shrine** administration. Management, for example, of sales of **written oracles**, **talismans**, and **good luck charms**, and accounting of **money offerings**, all come under the direction of the Shinto priests.

【鳥居】とりい Torii

　鳥居は**神社**の参道の入口にあり、神のいる聖域であることを表す**神道**のシンボルとなっています。もとは雄鳥を**神社**に奉納するときの止まり木でした。2本の柱の上に2本の横木が取り付けられています。日本全国どこにでも見られます。鳥居を見たら、その奥には**神社**か、神の宿る**ほこら**があると考えていいでしょう。

Shinto shrine archways : *Torii* are archways at the approaches to **Shinto shrines** and have become symbols of **Shinto**, indicating a sacred place where divinities dwell. Originally, they were perches for roosters offered to **shrines**. Two crosspieces are set on top of two upright pillars. These are everywhere in Japan. On seeing a *torii*, one can expect to find on the other side a **Shinto shrine** or a **small shrine**.

【おみくじ】Omikuji

　おみくじは、**神社**や**寺**に祈願して物事の吉凶を占うためのくじです。総合的な運勢には大吉・中吉・吉・小吉・凶などがあり、ほかに学問、商売、縁談、勝負事など、いろいろな項目ごとに運勢が記されています。

　正月には多くの人が初詣に行き、おみくじを引くのを楽しみにしています。しかし、本当に自分の運勢を知るためにおみくじを引くというよりは、軽い遊び感覚で引くことの方が多いようです。おみくじは細長い紙に運勢が書かれているので、読んだあとはふつう木に結びつけ、祈願の成就を願います。

Written oracles : *Omikuji* are written oracles, obtained by drawing lots in which the good or bad luck of events is indicated when going to pray to **Shinto shrines** or **Buddhist temples**. One's overall fortune can range from outstanding to average to bad, covering various aspects of life such as academics, business, marriage proposals, and victory or defeat.

At **New Year** most people visit shrines, and enjoy drawing *omikuji*. However, rather than for the purpose of actually learning about their fortunes, most people seem to draw them with a sense of playfulness. *Omikuji* are written on long narrow paper and usually are tied to trees after being read in hopes that their prayers will be answered.

【お守り】
Omamori
おまもり

　お守りは、幸運を呼び入れ、邪悪を追い払うといわれているもので、小さな木片や紙片に神の名や祈願文、寺社名などが書き込まれています。ふつうは**神社**や**寺**で売っています。その**ご利益**は、交通安全、合格、商売繁盛、無病息災、安産など、さまざまです。

　お守りには、お守り袋に入れて身につけたり、車の中につるしたりするものと、家の中に置いたり、柱や門戸に貼りつけたりするものとがあります。旅に出たり危険な仕事をしなければならない家族や恋人に贈って、安全や健康を祈ることも、一般に行われています。

Talismans : *Omamori* are said to summon good fortune and expel evil, so divinities' names or prayers or temple and shrine names are written on pieces of wood or scraps of paper. These are usually sold at **Shinto shrines** and **Buddhist temple**. **Answers to prayers** include traffic safety, success in passing a school's entrance exam, business prosperity, good health and easy child delivery.

　Omamori are put in pouches and kept on one's person, hung in cars, placed in the home or attached to pillars or gates. It is a common practice to present them to members of family or a lover who are leaving for travel or doing dangerous work, and pray for their safety and health.

【さい銭】
Saisen
さいせん

　さい銭は、**神社**や**寺**に参拝したときに捧げるお金です。たいていの寺社には**さい銭箱**があり、参拝客はそこに随意の金額のさい銭を投げ入れて祈願をしたり、あるいは祈願成就のお礼をしたりします。似た言葉に「喜んで捨てる」という意味の「喜捨」があります。これは寺社や困っている人に進んで金銭を差し上げるという意味で、必ずしも**さい銭箱**に入れるものではありません。

Money offerings : *Saisen* are offerings of money made when worshipping at **Shinto shrines** or **Buddhist temples**. Usually, there is an **offertory box**, where worshippers pray, tossing in any amount of money they wish, or else they offer money as thanks for prayers that have been answered. There is a similar word "*kisha*"(charitable donation), which means to "happily abandon." It means offering of money to temples and shrines or people in trouble, and that money is not neccessarily given through an **offertory box**.

【絵馬】
Ema
えま

　絵馬は、上部が屋根の形をした板に馬などの絵が描かれたもので、願をかけるときや、願い事がかなったときに寺社に奉納します。特に受験の合格祈願に多く使われます。古代日本には、願い事をするとき馬を献上する風習がありましたが、後に、馬の絵の描かれた絵馬を奉納するように変わったのです。現在は馬以外の絵のものもあります。

Votive pictures : *Ema* are pictures of horses drawn on wood, the upper part of which has a roof, and presented to temples and shrines when making vows or when one's prayer is answered offering prayers. 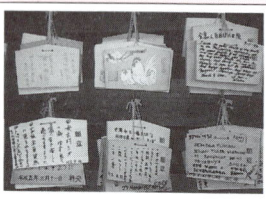 They are mostly used in praying for success in passing entrance exams. In ancient Japan, there was the practice of presenting horses when praying for something, but this later changed to offering votive pictures of horses. At present, there are other pictures besides horses.

【宮参り】 みやまいり／Miyamairi

赤ちゃんが生まれて30日ほどたったとき、初めて**神社**に連れて行ってお参りすることを、宮参りといいます。

かつて宮参りは、赤ちゃんが**神社**の**氏子**となり、社会の一員となるための最初の手続きとして、重要な行事でした。しかし、現在では形式的に祝うという色合いが強くなっているようです。

Newborn infant's shrine visit : About thirty days after a child is born, it is taken to a **Shinto shrine** for its first shrine visit. This is called *miyamairi*.

Miyamairi used to be an important event by which the child became a **parishioner** of a **Shinto shrine** as its first step toward becoming a member of society. However, to say, it tends to be practiced only formally.

【しめ縄】 しめなわ／Shimenawa

神聖な場所をほかと区別するために張る縄で、しめ縄の「しめ」とは禁忌を意味します。しめ縄は**神社**の社殿や**鳥居**に張られているほか、家庭の**神棚**にも見られ、**正月**の**しめ飾り**もこのしめ縄にいろいろな**縁起物**を付けて作ったものです。また、**相撲の横綱**が締める「横綱」も、このしめ縄が変化したものです。

Sacred Shinto rope : This is a rope hung out to distinguish sacred places from the rest; the *shime* of *shimenawa* means "taboo". In addition to being hung in the main building at **Shinto shrines** and on **Shinto shrine archways**, *shimenawa* are seen on **Shinto family altars**, and the **New Year sacred straw festoon** is made by attaching various **good luck charms** to the *shimenawa*. And the belt or "sideways rope"(a literal translation of *yokozuna* which means the grand champion) worn by the **grand champion** in **sumō** is another form of the *shimenawa*.

【お祓い】Oharai
おはらい

神道では、本性は善である人間に罪を犯させるのは穢れ（けが）だとされています。だれでも知らないうちに穢れが身に付いてしまい、それがたまると罪や災いが起こるから、時にはお祓いをして穢れを清めねばならないとされてきました。お祓いにはいろいろあります。自分で塩をまいたり、手や口を水で清めたりするほか、**神社**で**神主**に御幣（こへい）を振ってもらい、災難や穢れを取り払ってもらうこともあります。

Shinto purification : In **Shinto**, a sin committed by man, whose nature is good, is considered to be caused by impurity. Since anybody, without knowing it, can acquire impurity, and sins and misfortunes occur if it accumulates. Receiving *oharai* from time to time has been thought necessary to cleanse the impurities. There are various kinds of *oharai*. For example, in addition to sprinkling salt or cleaning one's hands or mouth with water, which can be done by oneself, calamity and impurity are also exorcised by having **Shinto priests** wave in a sweeping motion a sacred staff with cut paper at **shrines**.

【厄年】Yakudoshi
やくどし

厄年とは、災難に遭ったり健康を害したりするおそれが多いので、注意しなければならないとされる年齢です。年齢に1を加えた歳で、男性は25歳、42歳、60歳、女性は19歳、33歳です。男性の42歳、女性の33歳は特に悪い年とされ、「大厄（たいやく）」とよばれます。迷信の1つかもしれませんが、これらの年齢が実際に健康上、仕事上の転機に当たることも多いため、**神社**に厄払いに行く人もいます。

Unlucky age : With *yakudoshi* there is a big chance of encountering misfortune or injuring one's health, so it is an age when one must be careful. This happens when men turn 25, 42 and 60, and women 19 and 33, in the *yakudoshi* measurement. One's *yakudoshi* is measured by adding one to the actual age. The ages of 42 for men and 33 for women are considered to be particularly bad years, and are called "great calamity." This may be just a superstition, but, because there have been many occasions when these ages actually have corresponded to turning points in people's health or jobs, there are those who go to **Shinto shrines** for exorcism.

【神棚】 Kamidana かみだな

神棚は、家の中で**神符**（しんぷ）（**神社**からいただくお札、お守り）をまつってある棚で、多くは**鴨居**の上にあります。木製で屋根と階段があり、中央に**神符**を納めるのです。**酒**や食べ物、ろうそくなどを供え、神棚の前で家内安全や商売繁盛を祈ることもあります。近年までたいていの家では神棚をまつっていたものですが、最近は少なくなりました。

Shinto family altars : *Kamidana* are altars, generally installed in the home above the **lintel**, where **charms and amulets** from **Shinto shrines** are enshrined at. The altars are made of wood with roofs and steps, and the **charms and amulets** are put in the center. Occasionally, **sake**, food and candles are offered, and people prayed for family safety and business prosperity in front of the *kamidana*. Until not long ago, most homes had *kamidana*, but recently they have decreased in number.

【仏壇】 Butsudan ぶつだん

仏壇は、仏像や位牌を安置して礼拝するための壇で、一般には家庭に置かれた**仏教**の祭壇を指します。中央に仏像や仏画、あるいは先祖の位牌を収めます。ほかに燭台・香炉・鈴（りん）などの仏具を置き、朝晩線香をあげて拝むのです。仏壇は家庭における先祖**供養**の場といえるでしょう。

Buddhist family altars : *Butsudan* are altars for enshrining and worshipping Buddhist images and mortuary tablets, and the term generally refers to **Buddhist** altars placed in the home. A Buddhist image or picture, or else ancestral tablets are placed in its center. In addition, Buddhist altar equipments, like candlesticks, incense burners and bells, are set up, and incense is burned while offering prayers in the morning and evening. *Butsudan* can probably be called the place in the home for ancestors' **memorial services**.

【仏教】
Bukkyō
ぶっきょう

　仏教が日本に伝わったのは6世紀の半ばでした。その後当時の政治権力闘争の中で仏教擁護派が勝利を収め、国家の保護の下で各地に寺院が作られ、全国に広められることとなりました。**鎌倉時代**（1185〜1333）には、仏教は新たな指導者が何人も現われて思想的深化が図られ、弱者を救済する立場を鮮明にさせました。**禅宗**はやはり**鎌倉時代**に中国で学んだ**僧**によって日本にもたらされ、主に武士の宗教として栄えました。現在、日本では仏教を背景に持つ文化が民衆の生活に深く根を下ろし、**神道**とともに日本人の精神文化を形成しています。また、近代に至っても絶えず仏教の新しい宗派が起こり、信者を獲得しています。

Buddhism : *Bukkyō* came to Japan in the middle of the sixth century. Supporters of *bukkyō* subsequently won a victory in the political power struggles of the time; building temples in every area under government patronage, it spread throughout the country. In the **Kamakura Period**(1185-1333), as a number of new leaders appeared and deepened its philosophy, *bukkyō* made clear its position of saving the weak. The **Zen Buddhism** was brought to Japan in the **Kamakura Period** by **priests** who studied in China, and it flourished principally as the religion of samurai. At present, a culture in Japan that has *bukkyō* as its backdrop has laid roots deeply in the lives of the people and, together with **Shinto**, forms the spiritual culture of the Japanese people. Also, even today new sects of *bukkyō* keep emerging and gaining believers.

平等院鳳凰堂
Byōdōin hōōdō
in Kyoto

【寺】 Tera てら

寺は、**僧**や**尼**が居住して修行や仏事などを行うところで、仏像が安置されています。入口には山門があり、本堂、講堂、塔、鐘楼などから成つています。屋根はほとんどがかわらぶきです。また、日本人の墓のほとんどは寺の敷地内にあります。

人々は、**盆**や**彼岸**には先祖の**墓参り**のために寺へ行き、死者の命日には親戚中が集まり、寺で**僧**にお経をあげてもらいます。一方、京都や奈良には、千年以上もの歴史を持ち、現在では観光名所にも数えられる寺がいくつもありますが、そのような寺へは建物や仏像を拝観する目的で出かけるのです。

Buddhist temples are where **priests** and **nuns** reside to practice ascetic exercises and Buddhist ceremony, and Buddhist images are enshrined. At the entrances are two-story temple gates, then come buildings such as the main temple, an auditorium, a pagoda, a bell tower. Almost all the roofs are tiled. Most graves are set within the temple site in Japan.

People go to temples during the **Bon Festival** and **equinoctial week** to **visit the graves** of their ancestors, and relatives gather on the anniversaries of the dead and have **priests** recite sutras in the temple. On the other hand, there are numerous temples in Kyoto and Nara that have more than 1,000 years of history and have been identified as places of sightseeing interest. People visit such temples for the pleasure of appreciating the structures and the Buddhist images.

【僧、お坊さん】

そう、おぼうさん／Sō, Obō-san

僧は出家して仏門に入った人で、ふつう髪を剃り、袈裟を着用します。滝に打たれたりする荒行による精神修養を続ける場合もありますが、僧の多くは任意に結婚もしています。大部分が**寺**に住み込みで修行し、墓を維持したり、**寺**で行われる法要で読経したりしますが、**葬式**や一部の法要などの際は家庭に出向いて読経します。

Buddhist priests : *Sō* are persons who renounce the world and enter the priesthood. They usually shave their heads and wear a Buddhist priest's stole. There are occasions when spiritual cultivation is continued through rigorous austerities, like being pelted by a waterfall, but most priests are also married at their choice. The majority reside in **temples** where they practice ascetic disciplines, maintain graves, and chant Buddhist sutras for memorial services held at their **temples**. They also go to chant sutras in homes for **funerals** and for some private memorial services.

【数珠】

じゅず／Juzu

数珠は、仏を拝むときに手にかけたり、数珠を繰って**念仏**の回数を数えたりします。カトリックにおけるロザリオと似ています。仏様を礼拝するときや、亡くなった人の霊前にお参りするときなども、数珠を手にかけます。数珠の珠はふつう108個ありますが、これは**仏教**における**百八の煩悩**を除くためといわれています。

Buddhisst rosaries : *Juzu* are held in the hands when praying to Buddha or the dead, or for counting the number of times **Buddhist prayers** are recited by handling the beads. It is similar to the Catholic rosary. *Juzu* are held in the hands when worshipping Buddha and also when paying respects to the spirits of the dead upon visiting their graves. There are usually 108 *juzu* beads which are said to remove the **108 worldly desires** cited in the **Buddhist** teaching.

【禅宗】 Zenshū ぜんしゅう

禅宗は**仏教**の宗派の１つです。6世紀前半にインドの**達磨**が中国に伝えたもので、日本へは**鎌倉時代**（1185～1333）に**栄西**や**道元**が中国から伝えました。武士道をはじめ、**茶道**など伝統文化や日本人の生活全般において、**禅**は強い影響を与えてきました。禅の教えでは、真理は言語表現を超越しているため、座禅を組み、心を鎮める修業によってのみ悟りが体得されるといわれています。

Zen sect : *Zenshū* is one sect of **Buddhism**. In the first half of the sixth century, Indian **Bodhidharma** introduced Zen to China, and in the **Kamakura Period**(1185-1333) people like **Eisai** and **Dōgen** brought it from China to Japan. **Zen** has rendered a strong influence on the way of the warrior, as well as the traditional culture like the **tea ceremony**, and on every aspect of the lives of the Japanese people. Because truth, according to the **Zen** teaching, goes beyond verbal expression, enlightenment can be realized only through sitting in meditation and training in calming the self.

【初詣】 Hatsumōde はつもうで

初詣とは、新年に初めて寺社へお参りすることです。日本では、特に**仏教**や**神道**の信者でなくても、**正月**にはその年の健康や幸せを祈るために寺社にお参りに行くという習慣があります。初詣の際は**さい銭**を捧げ、**おみくじ**をひいたり、**縁起物**を買ったりします。有名な寺社は大変な人出になり、テレビのニュースでも必ず放映されます。

First temple or shrine visit of the New Year : *Hatsumōde* is the first visit to a Buddhist temple or Shinto shrine in a new year. There is the custom in Japan of making visits to temples or shrines at **New Year**, even if people are not **Buddhist** or **Shinto** believers, in order to pray for health and happiness in the new year. On the occasion of *hatsumōde*, people give **money offerings**, draw lots for **written oracles**, and buy **good luck charms**. The crowds at famous temples and shrines are huge and are always broadcast on television newscasts.

right : Buddhist family altar
left : Shinto family altar

【神仏習合】
Shinbutsu-shūgō
しんぶつしゅうごう

　日本では昔から、外来の**仏教**と民俗宗教である**神道**が、時には合成されたりして共存してきました。**仏教**は有神教ではなく、一方**神道**は自然崇拝を主としているため、合成されても矛盾が生じなかったのです。これを神仏習合といいます。6世紀の**仏教**伝来以降、**仏教寺院**の建設を**神社**が補助するなど、この傾向は長く続きました。

　日本が近代国家として発足するとき（1868年）に政府が**神道**強化の方針をとったため神仏習合が禁止されたこともありましたが、現在でも、同一家庭内に**仏壇**と**神棚**の両方が置かれていたり、**結婚式**は神式で挙げるのに**葬式**は仏式で行うといったことが、ごくふつうに行われています。

Shinto-Buddhist synthesis : In Japan long ago, **Buddhism**, which came from abroad, and **Shinto**, which is a folk religion, occasionally came together in a synthesis. Because **Buddhism** is not a theistic doctrine and **Shinto** principally worships nature, there were no contradictions in synthesizing them. This is called *shinbutsu-shūgō*. This tendency continued for a long time after **Buddhism** was introduced in the sixth century as seen in **Shinto shrines** supporting in building **Buddhist temples** .

　When Japan began to function as a modern nation state in 1868, *shinbutsu-shūgō* was prohibited because the government set a policy of strengthening **Shinto**. But now, it is quite commonly practiced to set up both **Buddhist family altars** and **Shinto family altars** in the same house, or to have **weddings** with Shinto rituals and **funerals** with Buddhist rituals.

【道祖神】 Dōsojin どうそじん

道祖神とは、悪霊を防いで通行人を保護したり、旅の安全を守ったりする神で、道端や道の分かれ目に立てられています。神体は石造りで、主に「道祖神」などの文字が彫られたり、男女の姿が浮き彫りになっていたりします。もともとは村の内と外を区別し、悪霊などの侵入を防ぐ村の守り神とされていたようですが、今では男女の縁結びの神だとか、子供と親しむ優しい神だともいわれています。

Traveler's guardian deities : *Dōsojin* are deities that defend against evil spirits, protecting travelers and maintaining safety on trips. They are set up at roadsides and crossroads. They are shaped out of stone, usually with the characters for "*dōsojin*" carved into the stone and the figures of both sexes carved in relief. Originally, they were used to mark village boundaries and were apparently taken to be deities that protected villages against the invasion of evil spirits. Now they are regarded as deities that arrange to make a couple or else as gentle deities with an affinity for children.

【地蔵菩薩】 じぞうぼさつ／Jizō-bosatsu

釈迦が亡くなった後、弥勒菩薩が出現するまでの間、この世の生き物すべてを救うとされています。日本では特に高さ１メートル前後の地蔵の石像が、境界神として町や村の境や辻に建てられています。子供が死ぬと死後の魂を救済するともいわれ、子供の交通事故現場に建てられることもあります。今も多くの人に敬愛され、親しみをこめて「お地蔵さん」と呼ばれます。

Guardian deity : *Jizō-bosatsu* is thought to relieve all living things in the world, from when **Buddha** has died until the **Benevolent Bodhisattva** appears. In Japan, stone *jizō* statues, usually about one meter high, are erected as boundary gods at the boundaries of towns and villages and at crossroads. *Jizō* are said to rescue the spirits of children when they die and have even been erected at the actual spot where traffic accidents with children have occurred. Most people today feel a closeness to *jizō*, fondly calling them "*o-jizō-san*(dear *jizō*)".

【縁日】 Ennichi えんにち

縁日は特定の神仏に縁のある日で、その日に寺社に参拝すると特別な利益があるといわれています。大勢の人が集まりますが、その多くは宗教的背景は特に意識せず、立ち並ぶ露店を楽しみにやってくる人々です。昔懐かしい食べ物や玩具、ゲームの店が軒を並べ、とりわけ夏の夜は、夕涼みを兼ねて浴衣姿で縁日に繰り出す人も多く、夏ならではの独特の雰囲気が味わえます。

Fairs : *Ennichi* are the days connected to certain Shinto or Buddhist deities. It is said that there will be special returns to the prayers offered on these days at shrines or temples of those deities. A crowd of people gather on these occasions, but most have no particular consciousness of the religious background and come to enjoy the lines of street stalls. *Ennichi* feature shops with nostalgic foods, toys and games. Especially on summer evening *ennichi*, many people sally forth in **informal cotton kimonos** partly for enjoying the cool evening breeze and create the distinctive atmosphere only seen in summer.

【酉の市】 とりのいち／Torinoichi

酉の市は、11月の特定の日に神社で行われる祭りで、「お酉様」とも呼ばれます。本来は、開運・商売繁盛の神をまつる鷲神社の祭りでしたが、現在はほかの神社でも行われています。酉の日は11月に2回か3回あり、順に「一の酉、二の酉、三の酉」といいます。その日は神社の境内に、縁起物の熊手などを売る露店がたくさん出店されます。

Festival of the rooster : *Torinoichi* is a festival that occurs at **Shinto shrines** on set days in November and is also called "Honorable Rooster"(*otorisama*). Originally, it was a festival at Ōtori Jinja that celebrated the gods of luck and business prosperity, but now it occurs at other shrines too. Festival days occur two or three times in November and are known as the "First Rooster," "Second Rooster," and "Third Rooster" in order. On these days, lots of street stalls selling **bamboo rakes** as **good luck charms**, and the like are set up in the **shrine** compound.

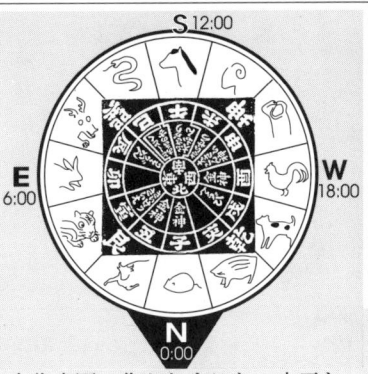

【十干十二支】 Jikkan-Jūnishi じっかんじゅうにし

　十干十二支とは時間と空間を秩序づける方法で、古代中国で作られました。十干と呼ばれる10個の記号と、十二支と呼ばれる12個の記号を、単独または組み合わせて日付や年、月、時刻、方位を表します。十干と十二支を合わせて干支ともいいますが、今では主に十二支のみをさして干支と呼び、その記号には子、丑、寅、卯、辰、巳、午、未、申、酉、戌、亥の12種類の動物が当てられています。「戌年の生まれ」というように年齢を表したり、年賀状にその年を表す動物を描いたりします。なお、60歳になると、10進法である十干と12進法である十二支が一巡して元の年に還ることから、還暦として祝う習慣があります。

The ten calendar signs and the twelve horary signs : *Jikkan-jūnishi* are a method of placing order on time and space and were created in ancient China. The ten signs called *jikkan* and the twelve signs called *jūnishi*, independently or in combination, express dates, years, months, times and directions. The combination of *jikkan* and *jūnishi* is also called the **sexagenary cycle**(*eto*), but now the term *eto* chiefly refers only to *jūnishi*, the signs of which correspond to twelve kinds of animals–rat, ox, tiger, hare, dragon, serpent, horse, sheep, monkey, rooster, dog, boar. Saying, "I was born in the year of the dog," expresses one's age, and the animal expressing that year is drawn on **New Year's cards**. Moreover, there is the custom of celebrating one's **60th birthday**, for the conbinations of *jikkan*, on the decimal scale, and *jūnishi*, on the duodecimal scale, complete a full cycle and return to the original combination of the year when one was born.

【陰陽道】
On'yōdō
おんようどう

　陰陽道とは、自然現象を解き明かすことによって人間の吉凶を判断し災厄を避ける方術で、中国から伝来しました。天文学や暦法と密接な結び付きがあり、さまざまな**祭り**や祓（はらえ）が行われます。日本では**平安時代**（794〜1185）に最も盛んになり、陰陽道の影響から、方位にまで吉凶を意識するようになりました。その後さらに、大安や仏滅などのように日に吉凶を設けるようになりました。**結婚式**には万事に凶であるとされる仏滅の日を避け、万事良しとされる大安の日を選んだり、**葬式**は友を引くとされる友引の日を避けて行うなど、現代生活においてもその考えが生きているものも多くあるのです。

Divination by the principles of Yin and Yang : *On'yōdō* is an art brought from China that interprets natural phenomena to pass judgement of good or bad fortune on man to avoid calamity. It is closely related to astronomy and the calendar, and all sorts of **festivals** and Shinto purification rituals are performed for it. At its height in Japan during the **Heian Period**(794-1185), *On'yodo* came to have so much impact on people that they became conscious of good or bad fortune, even with directions. Moreover, later, people had come to assign good or bad fortune to days, such as "the lucky days" and "the most unlucky days". This way of thinking is prevalent in contemporary life, in avoiding, for example, "the most unlucky days" for **weddings**, and choosing instead "the lucky days". In the same way, "the trail days" are avoided for **funerals**, for they mean to trail a friend(into death).

【キリスト教】
Kirisutokyō
きりすときょう

キリスト教は1549年に伝来し、カトリック教会のイエズス会士、フランシスコ・ザビエルが布教を始めました。16世紀末には時の最高権力者**豊臣秀吉**が封建制度の確立の妨げになるとして厳しく弾圧し、第2次世界大戦中には外来宗教として排撃されたりした歴史もありました。現在はもちろん**憲法**で宗教の自由が認められています。キリスト教信者の割合は**仏教**系に比べるとごく少ないものの、一定の社会的地位を築き、さまざまな活動をしています。特に教育面では、幼稚園から**大学**までキリスト教に基づいた教育を行っている私立学校も多く、また文学では**遠藤周作**などの世界的に知られたクリスチャンの小説家もいます。

Christianity : *Kirisutokyō* was transmitted to Japan in 1549 when the Jesuit priest Francis Xavier began his missionary work. In its history in Japan, Christianity underwent severe pressure brought by **TOYOTOMI Hideyoshi**, the most powerful man in the late sixteenth century, as an obstacle to the establishment of feudalism, it was denounced during the Second World War as a foreign religion. At present, freedom of religion, of course, is recognized by the **constitution**. The proportion of Christian believers, compared to **Buddhists**, is quite small, but they have built up a definite social standing with various kinds of activities. Especially in the area of education, there are a lot of private schools, from kindergartens to **universities**, that base their education on *Kirisutokyō*. In addition, in literature there are Christian novelists, like **ENDŌ Shūsaku**, who are internationally known.

【だるま】
Daruma

　だるまは、南インドに生まれ中国に渡った**禅宗**の始祖**達磨の座禅**姿を表した、手足のない人形です。**達磨**は９年もの間、石の上で座禅を組んで瞑想し続けたために足が萎え、歩くことができなくなったと言われています。

　だるまの多くは張り子細工で、顔以外は赤く塗られています。底は重く、起き上がりこぼしになっています。倒しても元通りに起き上がるため、開運の**縁起物**の１つとされています。ふつう目は白く、願いがかなったときに目玉を描き入れる、という習わしがあります。

Bodhidharma dolls : *Daruma* are dolls without hands and feet representing the **sitting meditation**(*zazen*) posture of **Bodhidharma**, founder of the **Zen sect**, who was born in southern India and crossed over to China. **Bodhidharma**'s legs were said to be paralyzed because he meditated continuously on top of a rock for some nine years with his legs crossed, and he became unable to walk.

Most *daruma* are made of papier-mâché and, except for the face,

are painted red. The bottom is heavy and works as a tumbler. Because it bounces back to its original position when it's pushed over, it serves as a **good luck charm**. There is the custom of painting in the eyes, which are usually white, when a wish has been fulfilled.

【七福神】 Shichifukujin しちふくじん

七福神は、福をもたらす7人の神です。**仏教**や**神道**、**道教**などの神や聖人から成るもので、よく宝船に乗った姿で描かれます。かつて中国の故事に7人の聖者の話があったのに倣（なら）い、日本でも縁起のよい7人の神を集めて信仰するようになったといわれています。

七福神が広まったのは**室町時代**（1392〜1573）ごろからですが、現在でも、七福神ゆかりの寺社で長寿や家内安全を祈ったり、商家が商売繁盛を願って七福神の絵を飾ったりすることがあります。

The seven gods of good luck : *Shichifukujin* are the seven gods that bring good luck. They consist of gods and holy persons of **Buddhism**, **Shintoism** and **Taoism** and are often drawn riding in a treasure ship. It has been said that in Japan, imitating a historical story of seven holy men in ancient China, people put together seven gods of good luck and became to believe in them.

Shichifukujin became widely known in the **Muromachi Period** (1338-1573). Nowadays, at temples and shrines with *shichifukujin* connections, people pray for long life and family well-being, and merchants, hoping for business success, display *shichifukujin* pictures.

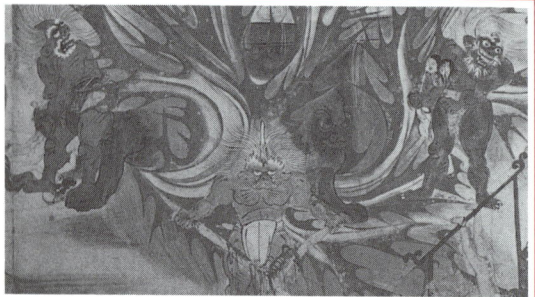

【鬼】
おに
Oni

鬼とは、想像上の悪の象徴です。712年に成立した『古事記』にその原形が示されたのをはじめとして、数多くの日本の歴史書や民話などに登場しています。

時代の変遷とともに**陰陽道**や**仏教**の影響を受け、鬼はさまざまな形態を持つようになりました。一般には人の形をしていて角や牙があり、裸で腰に虎の皮をまとい、恐ろしい顔かたちをした怪力のあるものとして描かれています。

節分の**豆まき**はこの「鬼」を追い出し、福を招くために行います。**鬼**ごっこで人を捕まえる役も「鬼」といいますし、無慈悲な人を鬼にたとえたりと、現代生活の中でも「鬼」という言葉は比喩的によく使われています。

Ogres : *Oni* are imaginary symbols of evil. Their original form was first delineated in "**Kojiki**"(the Record of Ancient Matters), completed in 712 A.D., and they have since appeared in many historical writings and in folktales.

As generations passed, the notion of *oni* was influenced by *on'yōdō* (**divination by the principles of Yin and Yang**) and **Buddhism**, and they took on a variety of forms. Generally, they are depicted as humans with horns and fangs, as naked but for tiger skin around their haunches, and as beings of herculean strength with fearsome facial features.

The **bean scattering** at the **eve of the first day of spring** is carried out to drive these *oni* out of home, and to invite good fortune in. The word *oni* is often used metaphorically in everyday life; for example, in **tag**, the one who is "it" is called *oni* and ruthless people are often compared to *oni*.

2. 現代日本人の生活様式

日本人の精神

【幽玄】
Yūgen
ゆうげん

　ことばの意味には表れなくても、あるいは目には定かに見えなくても、それ故にこそその奥に人間が感じることが可能な美の世界、これが幽玄です。これは、**余情**を重んじ省略をよしとする日本人の心情の根底に流れている情緒のひとつです。このような情緒は、用いることばの種類や数が限られた中ですべてを表現しなければならなかった短詩形の成立過程にも関係があります。つまり余情を大事にする幽玄の美は、少しのことばで多くのことを考えることが可能なところに成立する美です。従ってすべてを言わずとも相手に通じる、同質の文化を共有する共同体の中でこそ可能となった美の世界であるともいえるでしょう。

The subtle and profound : What is neither apparent in the meanings of words nor clearly visible to the eyes is, for these very reason, the aesthetic world that man can sense behind it all: This is *yūgen*. It is one of the emotions flowing in the depths of the Japanese feelings that value **suggestiveness** and encourage brevity. This kind of deep emotion is related to the process of shaping a short poetic style which tries to express everything using limited kinds and numbers of words. That is to say, the beauty of *yūgen,* which values suggestiveness, is an aesthetic quality that takes shape where only a few words can awaken many thoughts. Therefore, it can be said to be an aesthetic world made possible only in a community sharing a homogeneous culture, where people communicate without saying everything.

【わび・さび】 Wabi, Sabi

　わびもさびも、日本の伝統的な芸術、なかでも**茶道や俳句**などが目指す究極の美的境地を意味しています。両方ともある種の寂寥感が根底にあり、簡略をよしとし、華美を嫌うという点が共通しています。わびは、静かに澄んで落ち着いた様子を表すもので、主に茶道を大成した**千利休**が追求した境地です。さびは枯れて渋みがあることを意味し、**芭蕉**の**俳句**の理想的境地とされました。彼らは、利害やわずらわしい人間関係から自由となって、自然と一体となった美を追求したのです。

Subtle taste, elegant simplicity : *Wabi* and *sabi* are the highest aesthetic values aimed at by traditional Japanese arts, particularly the **tea ceremony** and **poems in seventeen syllables**. The two values have at bottom common qualities such as a sense of quiet sadness at the bottom, encouragement of simplicity and rejection of gaudiness. *Wabi* expresses a way of being quietly clear and calm, a state mainly pursued by **Sen-no-Rikyū** who perfected the art of the **tea ceremony**. *Sabi* means having well-seasoned, refined simplicity, an ideal state in **Bashō**'s **poems in seventeen syllables**. Both men sought the beauty that is one with nature, free from worldly concerns and annoying human relations.

【無常】 Mujō
むじょう

　無常とは**仏教**の最も大事な世界観の１つで、すべて生あるものは必ず死に、変化しないものはない、という生々流転の認識です。日本では古くから文学の主要なテーマとなり、中世の『**平家物語**』『**方丈記**』『**徒然草**』や**江戸時代**（1603～1867）の芭蕉の『**奥の細道**』など、日本の有名な作品の基調をなしています。

　『**平家物語**』では「……盛者必衰のことわりを表す。おごれるものは久しからず……」と強大な勢力を誇った最初の武士集団、平家が滅亡した物語を語り、『**方丈記**』では「行く川の流れは絶えずしてしかももとの水にあらず……」と、エッセイの冒頭を無常観から始めています。

Transiency is one of the most important views of the world in **Buddhism**; it refers to the notion of the transmigration of souls, which holds that every single life inevitably dies and everything is under constant change. Since ancient times it has been a chief subject of literature in Japan, and has formed the underlying tone of such famous Japanese works as the "**Tale of Heike**," the "**Ten-Foot-Square Hut**," and the "**Essays in Idleness**," in the midieval times, and the "**Narrow Road to the Deep North**" by **Bashō** in the **Edo Period**(1603-1867).

The "**Tale of Heike**" tells the story of the fall of Heike, the first clan of warriors that have enjoyed strong power: "....(Buddhist teaching) reveals the law that the prosperous must decay, and pride goes before a fall....". And in the "**Ten-Foot-Square Hut,**" the essay begins with a view of the world as transient: "Ceaselessly the river flows, and yet the water is never the same."

【間】
ま
Ma

　間とは時間的休止、あるいは空間的な空白を意味しますが、単なる空白ではありません。伝統的な日本の芸術、特に**能**、**歌舞伎**などの演劇、踊り、音楽、話芸あるいは絵画などを実践したり批評したりする際のキーワードともなり得る概念です。この間はリズムと呼吸とに大きく関連し、もともと音楽の概念であったものが他の芸術分野に転用されたものです。演劇では余韻を残すために台詞や動作の間におく不動の姿勢となり、音楽では演奏者の解釈次第によって間の取り方が違います。絵画では、何も描かない余白の部分が全体に与える効果が重要です。このように、何もない無が全体の動きや表現に大きな影響を与えるのです。

Interval in time or space : *Ma* means an interval in time or space, but it is not simply a blank. It is a concept that can even be the key word when practicing or commenting on traditional Japanese art, especially theater such as **Noh** and **Kabuki,** dance, music, storytelling, and painting. This *ma* is closely connected to rhythm and breathing, and is originally a concept from music that was applied to other fields of art. In theater, it is realized by a kind of stillness inserted in spoken lines or between actions to leave suggestiveness, and in music, *ma* is realized in different ways according to a performer's interpretation. In painting, the effect of empty space on the whole is important. Thus, the void containing nothing considerably affects the movement and expression of the whole.

【恩】
On
おん

　恩とは、人から受けた恩恵に対して、社会的、心理的な義務を負うことをいいます。武家社会で主君が従者に土地を与えたことに語源があります。日本の社会は、封建社会を脱してからまだ120年ぐらいの歴史しかありません。基本的には今でも**縦社会**といえます。そのため、目上の者は目下の者の面倒を公私にわたり見ることが多く、その代わり、目下の者は目上の者に恩を感じて敬意を払い、忠誠を尽くす、という傾向があります。人から受けた恩を忘れることは、倫理上許されません。ただし、他の伝統的日本の心情と考えられるものと同じく、徐々にそのような傾向は薄れつつあることもまた事実です。

Debt of gratitude : *On* is the social and psychological obligation taken on with favors received from others. The word derives from warrior society when lords granted land to followers. Japanese society has a history of only about 120 years since shedding its feudal system. At present it is still fundamentally a **vertical society**, which values strict orders and strong relationships among people of different ranks. Socially superior people often take care of their subordinates in both social and personal matters, and, in return, the subordinates, feeling *on* toward their superiors, incline to pay them respect and render them loyalty. To forget the *on* received from others is morally inexcusable. However, this kind of sentiment, as well as others considered to be traditional Japanese feelings, is gradually diminishing.

【義理①】
ぎり Giri

　日本的な情念・倫理の概念は、英語に正確に翻訳することは大変困難です。義理も英語に同じ概念はありません。封建社会の中で形成された義理の概念は、主従、親子、夫婦、兄弟、朋友、（時には敵や取引先）という人間関係の中で最も重視される規範であり、しいていえばこれらの関係の中で**恩**を受けた相手を思いやりいたわり、時には自己を犠牲にしてまで相手の幸せを実現する決意のことです。

　具体的な社会的慣習となって現れる義理は、例えば便り（**年賀状**など）、**贈答**（**歳暮**、**中元**など）などですが、主体的に行動する場合は、相手が窮地に陥っているときに自己の不利益を顧みず助力することを意味します。

Moral obligation/1 : It is quite difficult to precisely translate concepts of Japanese emotions and morals. *Giri*, too, does not have an equivalent concept in English. The concept of *giri*, which was formed in the feudal society, is the most valued standard in human relationships: Master-subordinate, parent-child, husband-wife, brothers and sisters, friends, and sometimes even enemies and business connections. If pressed to define it, *giri* involves caring for others from whom one has received a **debt of gratitude** and a determination to realize their happiness, sometimes even by self-sacrificing.

　Examples of *giri* expressed in concrete social customs are letters (such as **New Year's cards**) and **gift**(such as **year-end presents** and **midyear presents**); however, in acting voluntarily, it means to support a person, to whom one feels *giri,* without paying attention to one's disadvantage when that person is in a difficult situation.

【義理②】
ぎり Giri

　この義理が企業社会などで発揮されるときは、もともと封建的な人間関係に基づいた倫理であるため、企業の原理である合理性に反してまで、上司や取引先に尽くすこともありうるのです。これは欧米の経済活動の原理には反するため、日本の経済活動を批判する理由ともなるのです。しかし合理性が単に自己の利益のみを追求しがちであるのに対し、義理のような人間関係重視の行動原理は、ビジネス社会の中に相互扶助の概念を導入するという効果もあります。ただし、日本では反近代・反合理主義の民族主義者の中にはやくざも多いため、義理が暴力によって表現されるという場合もあり、これは批判されるべきです。

Moral obligation/2 : When this *giri* is manifested in the world of business, because it is essentially moral based on a feudalistic human relationships, it means to serve one's superiors and clients, even to the point of going against the rationality that is a business principle. It goes against the principles of Western economic activity, and has become a reason for critizing Japanese economic activity. However, compared to the rationality, according to which man tends to pursue only individual benefit, a behaviorial principle like *giri*, which place importance on human relationships, works to a good effect by introducing the concept of mutual support to the world of business. On the other hand, since there are many *yakuza* among the anti-modern and anti-rational nationalists in Japan, there are cases in which *giri* is expressed in a form of violence, which should be denounced.

【人情】
Ninjō
にんじょう

　人情とは、ふつうには親子や恋人同士や友人知人などの間に通いあう愛、同情、憐れみ、友情などの人間的な感情をいいますが、日本社会ではもう少し特殊な意味を持っています。人情は**義理**と対比されることが多く、**義理**が人に受けた恩義に報いるという人間関係の規範であるのに対し、人情は他人に対する感情の自然な発露です。「人情に厚い」といえば優しく思いやりがある人を指しますが、同時に**義理**を欠いては社会の成員として一人前とは見なされません。結局、**義理**と人情は、伝統的に日本の庶民社会の人間関係を律する2大要素でした。もちろん現代社会にも脈々として受け継がれています。

Humane feelings : *Ninjō* corresponds to various human feelings such as love, sympathy, compassion, and friendship, between parent and child, lovers, friends, and so on; yet, it has a somewhat more special meaning in Japanese society. *Ninjō* is often compared to **moral obligation** in that, while **moral obligation** is a principle of human relations that advocates returning debts of gratitude received from others, *ninjō* is a spontaneous expression of feeling toward others. The phrase, "being warm in *ninjō*" points out someone kind and thoughtful, but, at the same time, keeping up with **moral obligation** is necessary to be considered a member of society. In short, **moral obligation** and *ninjō* were the two major rules traditionally applied to human relations among the common people in Japan. Both are certainly inherited by contemporary society as well.

【恥】
はじ
Haji

　恥の意識は日本人の精神の中核をなすといわれていま
す。これは社会人類学者ルース・ベネディクトが、西洋の
「罪の文化」に対して日本を「恥の文化」と規定したこと
から広がった認識です。西洋では罪という絶対的な倫理基
準が人々の行動原理をなしていますが、日本では内的な原
理ではなく、外的な恥という感情が行動を律しているとい
うわけです。このような単純化にはさまざまな批判があり
ます。西洋人にも日本人と同じ意味での恥の意識はあるし、
日本人にも内的な道徳律がある、というわけです。しかし
日本人が恥を重視するのは確かです。特に封建時代の武士
にとっては、人前で恥をかくことは死に価したのです。

Shame : The sense of shame is said to form the core of the Japanese mentality. This is a concept that spread when the anthropologist Ruth Benedict classified Japanese culture as a "shame culture," as oppose to the Western "guilt culture". According to this classification, in Western countries, the absolute moral standard of guilt forms a principle of people's behavior, but, in Japan, behavior is not ruled by an inner principle but an external feeling of shame. There are various criticisms against this kind of simplification. For example, Western people, too, have a sense of shame like the Japanese, and the Japanese also have an inner moral principle. Nevertheless, it is true that the Japanese place importance on the sense of shame. Particularly for *samurai* in the feudal period, being put to shame in public was as good as being dead.

【根回し】
Nemawashi
ねまわし

何かを決める際に、混乱を避けて皆の合意をあらかじめ取り付けておくための技術を根回しといいます。このことばの本来の意味は、木を移動させる際に根をあらかじめ切りつめておき、移植を容易にすることでした。

異なる意見を持った者同士がいきなり会議に集まれば、なかなか意見の一致をみることはできません。しかし根回しをし、あらかじめ意見を調整しておけば、会議で無駄な時間を浪費することなく結論へと至ることができるのです。しかしこれが政治の場で行われるときには、国民には見えないところで政策が決定される恐れがあり、民主主義的ではないという批判もあります。

Prior consultation : A technique to avoid confusion and gain consent from everyone in advance when making a decision is called *nemawashi*. The original meaning of the word is to cut roots short before moving a tree, so that the tree can be easily moved.

If people with different opinions suddenly hold a meeting, they can hardly reach an agreement. But if *nemawashi* is practiced and opinions are adjusted beforehand, conclusions can be reached in meetings without wasting time. However, when *nemawashi* is practiced in politics, there is the fear that policies are not made in front of the people's eyes; thus, some criticize *nemawashi* as not being democratic.

【本音と建前】
Honne to tatemae
ほんねとたてまえ

　狭い共同体の中で、その構成員同士が平和に仲良く暮らさなければならないという、日本の地理的歴史的な条件は、人間関係のありかたにも大きく影響を与えています。例えば、本音を言えば相手を傷つけたり怒らせたりするときは、建前を言うことで、共同体の平和を保つことができます。これは皆と違う本音は控えて、建前に順応するという習慣を生み、自分の意見をなかなか言わないという日本人への批判を生む元ともなったようです。しかしほとんどの日本人は自己主張より和を尊ぶために本音を控えているといえます。国際社会では通用しないそのような態度はしかし、日本の国際化とともに徐々に変わってきつつあります。

Honest feelings and official stance : The geographical and historical situation of Japan, in which the people have had to live together in small communities peacefully and harmoniously, has worked a strong influence on human relationships. For example, when expressing honest feelings might hurt or offend others, official stance is expressed instead to keep peace in a community. This produced a custom of avoiding mention of honest feelings that are different from others and adjusting to official stance, and provided the reason for criticizing the Japanese people for hardly expressing their opinions. However, most Japanese refrain from expressing honest feelings because they value *wa*, a sense of harmony and togetherness, more than self-expression; yet, this kind of attitude is not accepted in the world community of nations, and has been gradually changing as Japan internationalizes.

社会生活

　贈り物への返礼のことをお返しといいます。日本では人間関係を円満に保つために、品物を贈り、お返しをするという儀礼的習慣が今でも根強く残っています。贈り物にもお返しにも、いつ、どのようにすべきかの大まかな基準があります。慶事・弔事のときや、**中元・歳暮**の時期には進物が贈られ、贈られた側も慣例に従ってお返しをします。

　このように物を贈り、それにお返しをすることで人間関係が確認されるのです。贈り物をもらっておきながらお返しをしなかったり、贈るべきときに贈り物を贈らなかったりすると、**義理**を欠いたとみなされます。

Return gift : Giving a gift in return is called *okaeshi*. In Japan the courtesy custom of exchanging gifts remains strongly entrenched to preserve the harmony of human relationships. There are general standards of when and how both to give gifts and give them in return. Gifts are sent for auspicious events, at times of mourning, at the **midyear** and at the **year-end**; and those to whom gifts have been sent, in accordance with customary practice, do *okaeshi*.

By giving gifts and doing *okaeshi* in this way, human relationships are confirmed. A person receiving gifts without doing *okaeshi* and not sending gifts when they should be sent is regarded as being ignorant of **moral obligation**.

【中元】ちゅうげん Chūgen

　古くは**道教**の祭事でしたが、同じ時期にある**仏教**の盂蘭盆会や、1年を前半・後半に分ける日本人の考え方の影響を受けて、祖先を供養し、半年間の無事を祝う行事となりました。霊に供えたものを後で親戚などで分け合った習慣が、現在の儀礼的な贈答習慣へと変化したのです。従って、現在の中元は、7月の初旬から15日にかけて、個人や会社が世話になった人に送る**進物**のことを主に意味します。

Midyear present : Long ago a **Taoist** ritual, *chūgen* took on the influence of the **Buddhist** *Bon* Festival, which was held around the same time, as well as the Japanese way of thinking in dividing the year into two halves, and it became an event for honoring ancestors and celebrating the safety of the first half of the year. The custom of afterwards sharing with relatives and others items, first offered up to spirits of the dead, changed into the current custom of courteously exchanging gifts. Consequently, *chūgen* today principally refers to **gifts** that individuals and businesses send from early in July to July 15th to people to whom they are indebted.

【歳暮】せいぼ Seibo

　12月の中旬に贈られる**進物**のことです。1年の半ばに贈る**中元**に比べ、1年を通して世話になったことへのお礼という意味があるので、**中元**よりも多少高額なものが贈られます。12月に入るとデパートなどは**進物**を買う人々で混雑し始めますが、その活気あるにぎわいは、近づきつつある新年を実感させる年末の風物詩ともなっています。なお普通は丁寧な意を表わす接頭語「お」をつけてお歳暮といいます。

Year-end present : This is a **gift** sent in the middle of December. Compared with the midyear *chūgen* gift, this one signifies gratitude for kindnesses throughout the year, so it costs somewhat more than *chūgen*. Early in December department stores begin to get crowded with people buying **gifts**, and that hustle and bustle is a part of the year-end scenery that gives a real sense of the approaching new year. Usually, people say *oseibo*, adding the prefix *o* to express politeness.

【年賀状】 Nengajō ねんがじょう

新年のあいさつのために出す書状で、その年の干支にあたる動物の絵を添えることが多く、元旦に届くように送ります。官製のお年玉付き年賀はがきは、抽選で賞品が当たるので人気があります。ビジネス上の年賀状は印刷した文面で済ますことも多いのですが、個人の年賀状は工夫をこらしたものも多く見られます。懐かしい友人から年賀状が届くこともあり、書くのも受け取るのも楽しいものです。

New Year's card : This is a card sent as a greeting for the new year. It usually has a picture of an animal appropriately corresponding with that year's **sexagenary cycle**(*eto*) and is sent so that it arrives on **New Year's Day**. Government post cards indicating a **New Year's gift** are popular, because the prize is awarded by lottery. Most business *nengajō* come complete with the printed contents, while writing one's own *nengajō* can tax one's ingenuity. *Nengajō* arrive from old friends; it is a pleasure both to write such cards and to receive them.

【暑中見舞い】 しょちゅうみまい／Shochū-mimai

暑中見舞いは7月15日ごろから立秋の8月8日ごろまでに送る、あいさつのはがきです。立秋を過ぎて送る場合は、残暑見舞いといいます。日本の夏は高温多湿で体力を消耗しやすく、体調を崩すことが多いので、その時期に親しい人と安否を確かめあったことからできた習慣です。

現在ではビジネスの関係者などにも送る儀礼的なものになっていますが、年賀状ほど盛んではありません。

Postcard asking after one's health in the summer : *Shochū-mimai* is a postcard sent to greet someone from around July 15th until **the setting in of fall** around August 8th. If it is sent after that, it is called a **postcard asking after one's health in the lingering summer**. The Japanese summer with its high heat and humidity frequently saps the body's strength and destroys its tone, so this is a custom that emerged from ascertaining the well-being of close friends at such a time.

Nowadays, it has become a courtesy to send these cards even to business acquaintances, but they are not as common as **New Year's cards**.

【お年玉】Otoshidama おとしだま

お年玉は、正月に、両親やあいさつに訪れた親戚などが子供に与えるお金です。元は正月に神に捧げた餅などを、改めて神から賜わったものとして各自に分け与えたことから生まれた習慣だといわれています。近年では子供の数の減少とともに、1人当たりに与えるお年玉の金額が高額化しています。この時期には出費の多い両親が、子供にお金を借りたくなったとしても不思議ではないほどです。

New Year's gift : *Otoshidama* is money given at **New Year** to children by parents and relatives who come to visit. Originally, it was said to be a custom born from sharing **rice cakes** dedicated to the deities at **New Year** as something bestowed anew by the deities. In recent years, along with the reduced number of children, the amount of *otoshidama* money given to one child is increasing. So much that it is not so strange for parents with a lot of expenses at this season to want to make a loan of the money to their children.

【へそくり】Hesokuri

もともとは「へそ（糸を巻きつけたもの）」を「繰る（巻き取る）」ことで貯めた金という意味で、封建社会の家父長制の下で家計にタッチできなかった主婦が、内職でわずかに得られた、自由にできる金銭のことでした。現在では、倹約してこっそり貯めた小額の金を意味し、「へそくり」から「へそ」を連想するためか、悲壮感よりはむしろ明るいニュアンスを持つ言葉となっています。

Secret savings : Originally, this meant money saved by "spinning"(*kuru*) the "reel"(*heso*) and it referred to the free spending money that housewives, who under the feudal society's patriarchal system could not touch the family finances, barely earned with side jobs. At present, it means a small amount of money secretly saved by frugal means, and, perhaps because the word *heso* of *hesokuri* also means the navel besides the reel, it is regarded as a word with a comical nuance rather than with a tragic feeling.

【ボーナス】 Bōnasu

もともとは臨時賞与でしたが、現在では多くの企業・官公庁で夏期と年末に定期的に支給されています。生活給であるとする考え方と余剰利益の分配であるという2つの考え方があり、景気動向や各企業の収益によって、また労働組合との力関係によって支給額は変動します。これの支給を前提とした各種ローンの返済計画が組まれることも多く、年末にはお**歳暮**を買う資金ともなります。

Bonus : The bonus was originally a special award, but now most businesses and government and public agencies provide it at the established times of summer and year end. There are two ways of thinking about this, whether to see it as a part of living wage or as a distribution of excess profit; the bonus amount fluctuates depending on economic trends, business earnings, and the power relationship with labor unions. Most loan repayment plans are made with the bonus in mind, and it is also used at year's end to buy **year-end gifts**.

【忘年会】 Bōnenkai ぼうねんかい

忘年会とは、その年の苦労や嫌なことを酒を飲んで忘れてしまう会という意味で、12月に行う宴会です。元は家族や親戚、知人などが集まって行っていましたが、現在では職場や交遊のグループを単位として、**居酒屋**やレストランなどで、時には**カラオケ**も交えにぎやかに楽しみます。なお、新年に入ると**新年会**と呼ばれる宴会が行われますが、どちらも普通の宴会で、特別な儀式などはありません。

Year-end party : *Bōnenkai* means a party occurring in December to drink sake and forget that year's hard labor and unpleasantnesses. Originally, it took place as a gathering for family, relatives and friends, but now groups from the workplace and groups of people, sharing the same taste or interest in amusement, go as units to **Japanese pubs** and restaurants and sometimes even to *karaoke* to celebrate together in lively enjoyment. In addition, just after the new year, a party called the **New Year party** takes place. Both are regular parties with no special ceremonies.

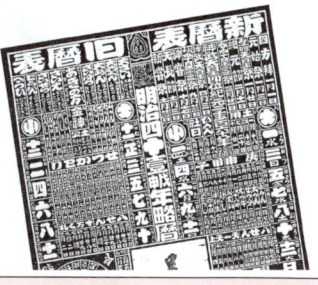

【暦】
Koyomi
こよみ

1872年に現在の**太陽暦**が採用されるまで、日本では太陰太陽暦に基づいた生活をしていました。これは月の満ち欠けを主としながら太陽がもたらす四季を合わせて作成した暦で、一般に旧暦といっています。このため旧暦時代と現在とではほぼ1カ月のずれが生じるので、今でも**正月**や**盆**などの行事は旧暦に基づいて行っている地方もあります。また四季の移り変わりを暦上に現わすのに、**立春**、夏至、小寒などの24節があり、これを目安に日本人は装いを変えたり季節を迎える準備をしたりします。日に吉凶を定める六曜は、縁起の良い日悪い日が6日ごとに繰り返され、日本人はこれによって**結婚式**や**葬式**の日取りを決めるのです。

Calendars : Until the current **solar calendar** was adopted in 1872, life in Japan was based on the "lunar solar calendar." While this is a calendar created principally on the phases of the moon, it aligns the four seasons brought by the sun and is generally called the old calendar. Thus, between the era of the old calendar and now there is a difference of nearly one month, and some regions still carry out such events as those of **New Year** and the **Bon Festival** based on the old calendar. Also, to express the changes of seasons on the calendar, there are 24 divisions such as the **first day of spring**, summer solstice and the period of the second severest cold, based on these, the Japanese change attire and prepare to greet the seasons. The cycle of the six days with their assigned good or bad fortune is repeated every six days, and the Japanese people set dates for **weddings** and **funerals** in accordance with them.

【印鑑】
Inkan
いんかん

　印鑑は、直径1～2センチ、長さ5～6センチほどの円筒状のものの底面に、名前の**漢字**をデザイン化して彫り込んだものです。材質は木が普通ですが、象牙や水晶も使用します。底面に朱肉をつけて書類に押します。

　欧米では本人のサインが重要視されますが、日本では印鑑がそれに代わります。公的文書で、意思確認と本人の同一性の証明とされる**実印**は、役所に登録されています。その重要性のために象徴的な意味合いが生じ、大きさにこだわったり、高級な材質のものを作ったりする人も少なくありません。一方、これとは別に、略式の用途に使われる印鑑もあり、それらは**認印**と呼ばれます。

Seal : *Inkan* is a small cylindrical object, 1~2 cm in diameter and 5~6 cm in length, with one's name in stylized **Chinese characters** carved into the surface of one end. It is usually made of wood but ivory and crystal are also used. One sticks the carved surface into a red ink pad, then presses it on paper.

In Europe and North America, a person's signature is regarded as important, but in Japan the *inkan* is in place of the signature. One's **registered legal seal** is proof for public documents, confirming a person's intentions and identity, and is recorded at city hall. Because of its importance, it has a symbolic meaning, and there are many persons who pay close attention to its size and who have it made out of high-quality material. Meanwhile, apart from this, there are *inkan* for informal use called **personal seals** or **signets**.

【名刺】
Meishi
めいし

　名刺には氏名、会社名、役職名、会社の住所と電話番号などが印刷されています。日本ではビジネス上の人間関係は、互いの名刺を交換することから始まります。

　連絡を取りたいときに便利な上、相手の会社や所属と地位を確認するのにも欠かせません。最近ではそれをもとにデータ・ベースを作成するためのパソコン・ソフトもあり、趣味などの個人情報もインプットできます。

　かつて名刺は画一的なデザインのものが多かったのですが、最近では個性をアピールするために、紙の質や色、レイアウトなどにさまざまな意匠を凝らした名刺も使われるようになっています。

Business cards : On a *meishi*, one's full name, company name, job title, company address, phone number and so on are printed. Business intercourses in Japan begin with the exchange of bussiness cards.

Besides their convenience when one wants to make contact, they are indispensable for confirming the other party's company, position and rank. Recently, there are even computer software to create data bases from the information on *meishi*, and personal information such as hobby can be input .

In the past, most *meishi* came in a standard design, but recently, to enhance individual appeal, *meishi* with all sorts of elaborate designs on quality paper, in color and layout have come to be used.

a tatami maker

【住環境】
Jūkankyō
じゅうかんきょう

　日本の伝統的な家屋は木で作られていて、室内は地上30センチ～40センチほど高く、**畳**が敷いてあります。高温多湿の夏季に適した構造を持っています。1960年代までは、鉄筋コンクリート建ての高層住宅はごく限られた地域にしかありませんでした。しかし、人口の都市集中と、狭い土地を活用するためには**団地**という高層住宅群を作らざるをえなくなり、現在では民間のものも含めた高層住宅が全国各地に見られます。木造住宅と違い、高層住宅は密閉されているため、夏は冷房が必須の設備となりました。室内の構造も畳部屋と床とが半々になり、畳部屋が少なくなるとともに、日本の伝統的な習慣もすたれつつあります。

Living environment : Traditional Japanese houses are made of wood, with floors raised 30-40 cm off the ground and covered with **flooring rush mats**. They have a structure that fits the hot, humid summer season. Until the 1960s, high-rise apartments built with ferro-concrete were limited to only a few areas. However, groups of high-rise apartments, known as *danchi*, had to be built for the concentration of population in cities and for making the most of limited land; at present, high-rise apartments, including those that have been privately built, can be seen all over the country. In contrast to wooden houses, high-rise apartments are tightly sealed, so air conditioning has become indispensable equipment. The numbers of rooms with **flooring rush mats** and rooms with floors are half and half; as rooms with **flooring rush mats** become more and more scarce, traditional Japanese customs are also starting to fade away.

【住宅事情（国内）】Jūtaku-jijō じゅうたくじじょう

　日本の住宅と一口にいっても、都市部と地方とでは大きく事情が異なります。例として、東京都と富山県、そして全国平均を比較してみましょう。

Housing situation(domestic) : The housing situation varies largely from urban to local regions. Let's compare, for example, Tokyo, Toyama Prefecture, and the national average.

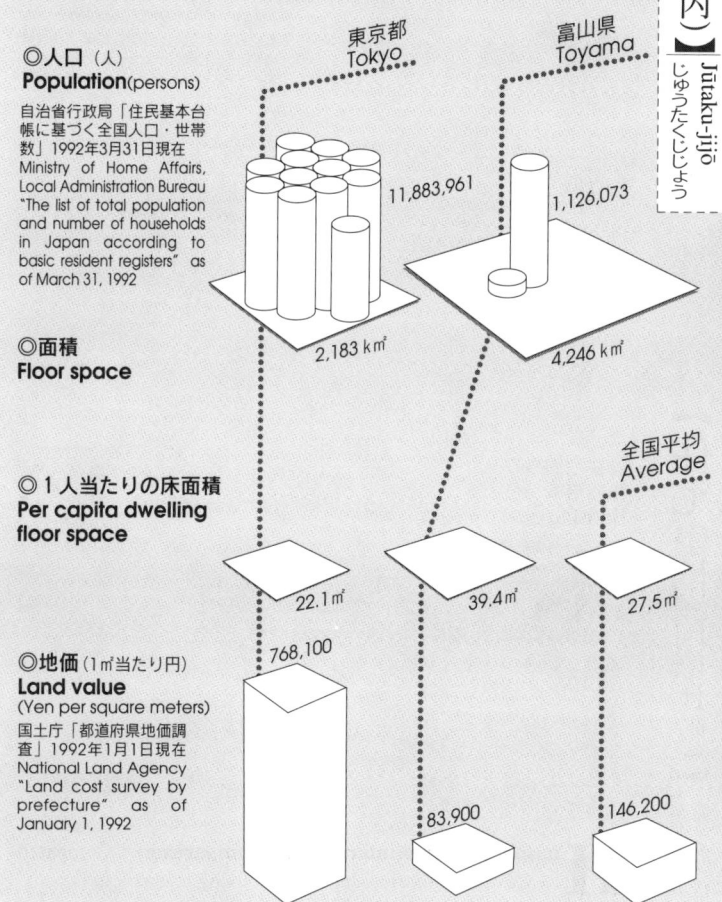

◎人口（人）
Population(persons)

自治省行政局「住民基本台帳に基づく全国人口・世帯数」1992年3月31日現在
Ministry of Home Affairs, Local Administration Bureau "The list of total population and number of households in Japan according to basic resident registers" as of March 31, 1992

東京都 Tokyo　11,883,961
富山県 Toyama　1,126,073
2,183 k㎡　4,246 k㎡

◎面積
Floor space

◎1人当たりの床面積
Per capita dwelling floor space

全国平均 Average

22.1㎡　39.4㎡　27.5㎡

◎地価（1㎡当たり円）
Land value
(Yen per square meters)

国土庁「都道府県地価調査」1992年1月1日現在
National Land Agency "Land cost survey by prefecture" as of January 1, 1992

768,100　83,900　146,200

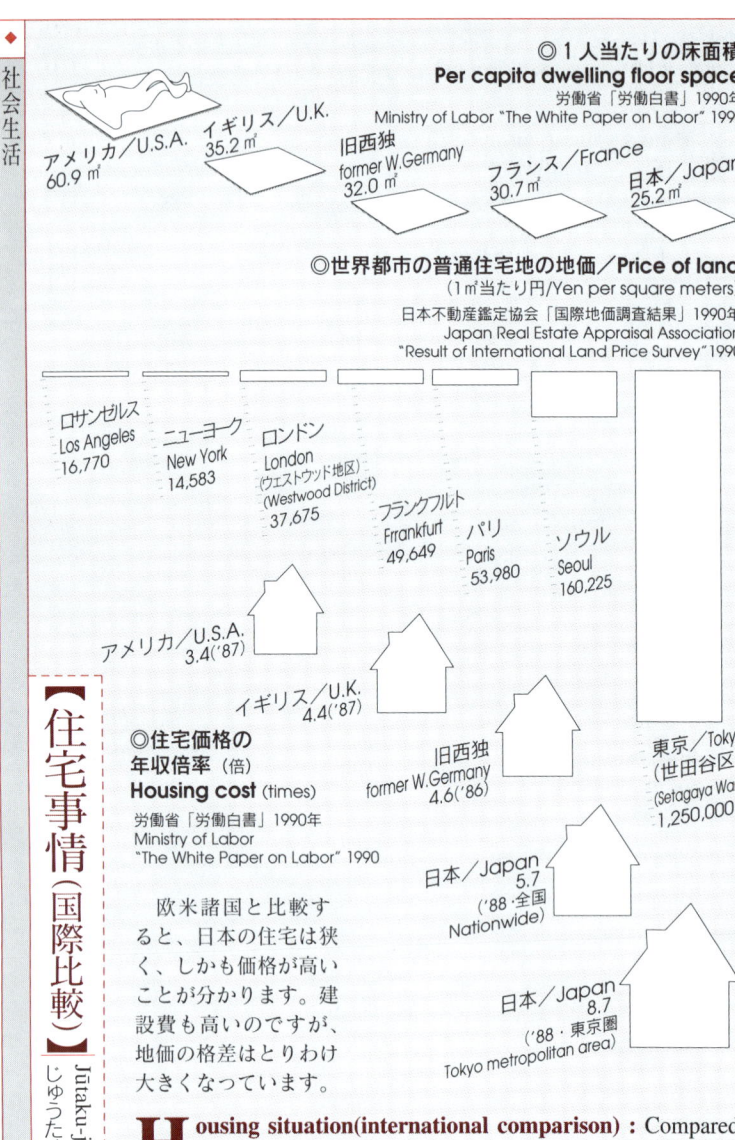

◎１人当たりの床面積
Per capita dwelling floor space
労働省「労働白書」1990年
Ministry of Labor "The White Paper on Labor" 1990

アメリカ／U.S.A.
60.9 ㎡

イギリス／U.K.
35.2 ㎡

旧西独
former W.Germany
32.0 ㎡

フランス／France
30.7 ㎡

日本／Japan
25.2 ㎡

◎世界都市の普通住宅地の地価／**Price of land**
(1㎡当たり円/Yen per square meters)
日本不動産鑑定協会「国際地価調査結果」1990年
Japan Real Estate Appraisal Association
"Result of International Land Price Survey"1990

ロサンゼルス
Los Angeles
16,770

ニューヨーク
New York
14,583

ロンドン
London
（ウェストウッド地区）
(Westwood District)
37,675

フランクフルト
Frrankfurt
49,649

パリ
Paris
53,980

ソウル
Seoul
160,225

アメリカ／U.S.A.
3.4('87)

イギリス／U.K.
4.4('87)

◎住宅価格の
年収倍率 (倍)
Housing cost (times)
労働省「労働白書」1990年
Ministry of Labor
"The White Paper on Labor" 1990

旧西独
former W.Germany
4.6('86)

東京／Tokyo
（世田谷区）
(Setagaya Ward)
1,250,000

日本／Japan
5.7
('88・全国
Nationwide)

日本／Japan
8.7
('88・東京圏)
Tokyo metropolitan area)

欧米諸国と比較す
ると、日本の住宅は狭
く、しかも価格が高い
ことが分かります。建
設費も高いのですが、
地価の格差はとりわけ
大きくなっています。

【住宅事情（国際比較）】
Jūtaku-jijō
じゅうたくじじょう

Housing situation(international comparison) : Compared
to Western countries, Japanese housing is small and costly.
Construction expense is high, too, but the difference is
particularly big in land prices.

【団地】
Danchi
だんち

　団地は中層から高層の集合住宅が計画的に建設されたものです。人口が集中した都市部における深刻な住宅不足への対策として、建設されるようになりました。住民に必要な公共施設も取り込んで、総合的な住環境の創造を目指したものですが、居住面積の狭さ、高層部に住むことにより及ぼされるいくつかの影響、周辺の既成住宅地の住民との摩擦など、さまざまな問題が指摘されてきました。

　都市部の住宅問題は依然として解決されていないため、入居希望者は非常に多く、入居者は抽選で決められます。しかし最近は、都心部から遠く狭い団地は敬遠されるようになってきています。

Apartment-house complex : *Danchi* is systematically built groups of mid-sized to high-rise apartment. It has been built to counter the vast lack of housing in cities, where the population is concentrated. It is built with an overall living environment in mind, taking into account the necessary public facilities for the residents, but a number of problems surfaced, such as the small living space, the various consequences of living in a high-rise, and friction with people living in existing residential areas nearby.

　Because the urban residential problem remains unresolved, the exceedingly large numbers of people hope to get into *danchi*, so the tenants are determined by lottery. Recently, however, small *danchi* that are far from the heart of the city are being shunned.

【町内会】

Chōnaikai
ちょうないかい

　町内会は地域住民の自治組織です。第2次大戦中は、軍国主義政権の末端組織として機能していたため、戦後廃止されましたが、配給などの処理のために自主的に再組織され、現在に至っています。法的に定められた組織ではなく、会員から集めた会費で運営されています。

　現在の町内会の仕事は、防災、防犯、衛生に関するものが主で、地方行政の下部組織としての役割を果しています。情報は**回覧板**と呼ばれる書類ばさみにまとめられ、各家庭で回覧されたり、路上の掲示板で伝達されたりします。

　また、ゴミ置き場の清掃などの共益的な活動も、多くの場合、町内会の管理で行われています。

Block associations : *Chōnaikai* are self-governing organizations of local residents. In the Second World War, they functioned as militaristic organizations in direct contact with the people and hence were abolished after the war; but they were independently reorganized to manage distribution and other systems and continue to exist. They are not legally constituted organizations and are run by fees collected from the membership.

The current work of *chōnaikai* principally concerns disaster and crime prevention and sanitation, and they fulfill a role in the substructure of regional administrations. Information is collected in folders called **circular notices** and passed around each household, and is also notified on bulletin boards on streets.

Moreover, the *chōnaikai* manages most of the activities for the common benefit, such as cleaning garbage collection sites.

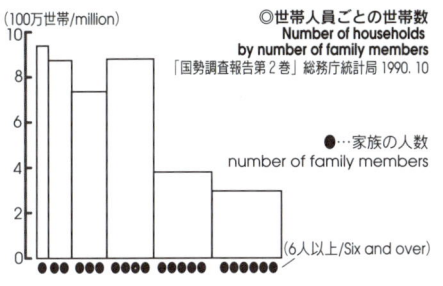

(100万世帯/million)

◎世帯人員ごとの世帯数
Number of households
by number of family members
「国勢調査報告第2巻」総務庁統計局 1990. 10

●…家族の人数
number of family members

(6人以上/Six and over)

【核家族】
Kaku-kazoku
かくかぞく

　「核家族」とは文化人類学の用語で、夫婦と子供だけの家族を意味しますが、日本では社会問題を考える際のキーワードとして、広く使われています。1960年代を中心とする**高度成長期**に、都市部では地方から単身で出てきた若者が家庭を作ることが多かったため、必然的に夫婦と子供だけの核家族が増えました。また都市部の住宅事情のもとでは大家族が一緒に住むことは困難だったため、核家族とならざるを得ませんでした。この核家族は、一方ではニューファミリーと称され、消費社会の担い手となって文化風俗をリードしてきましたが、他方では、取り残された老人が孤独とならざるを得ない状況を生んできたのです。

Nuclear family : *Kaku-kazoku*, a term used in cultural anthropology, means the immediate family of husband, wife and children only, and it is widely used as a key word when considering social issues in Japan. In the **period of high economic growth**　centered in the 1960s, because there were numerous young people who came alone from outlying regions and made their families in urban areas, *kaku-kazoku* inevitably increased. In addition, with the shortage of residence in which large families could live together, people could not help becoming *kaku-kazoku*. On one hand, *kaku-kazoku* was called the new family, and took the lead in culture and manners as driving force of the consumer society, it has, on the other hand, created the conditions that isolate the old people left behind.

【銭湯】
Sentō
せんとう

　料金を払って入る公衆浴場のことですが、歴史は古く、**江戸時代**（1603〜1867）にさかのぼります。江戸（今の東京）は18世紀前半には人口100万人を超え、大都会としての機能を備えていました。銭湯も都会に必要な共同施設として、また地域住民の社交場として栄えたのです。**江戸時代**の滑稽本や**浮世絵**などに、よく銭湯の場面が描写されています。近代以降も銭湯の必要性は高く、利用者もたくさんいましたが、戦後の**高度成長期**以後は、ほとんどの家に**風呂**が付き、アパートも**風呂**付きが増えて銭湯は急激に減少してしまいました。現在、銭湯は生き残りをかけてサウナや健康器具を設備し、変貌を遂げつつあります。

Public bath : This refers to public bathhouses that one uses for a fee. They go far back in history to the **Edo Period**(1603-1867). Edo(present-day Tokyo) in the first half of the eighteenth century had a population that exceeded 1,000,000 and featured the functions of a large city. *Sentō* flourished as public facilities necessary for a city and as places of social exchange for local residents. *Sentō* scenes are often portrayed in the comic books and *ukiyoe* of the **Edo Period**. Even after modernization, *sentō* were very necessary and a lot of people used them, but after the **period of high economic growth** most homes came with **baths** and apartments with **baths** increased; thus, *sentō* suddenly decreased in number. Today, *sentō*, their survival at risk, are undergoing transformation with the installment of saunas and health equipment.

【学歴社会】 がくれきしゃかい／Gakureki-shakai

日本の社会は長く学歴が重視されてきました。就職の際に**大学**名が重要視されたり、組織内の人事に学閥の力関係が影響を与えることも少なくありません。実際の能力そのものより学歴が重視されるため弊害が多く、最近は学歴にこだわらず広く人材を求めるようになりつつあります。高級官僚には東大卒が多いため、最近は他大学卒業者を多く採用するよう、総理大臣自ら指導したほどです。

Credential society : For a long time, Japanese society has seen academic background as important. When job hunting, importance is attached to the name of one's **university**, and the power relationships of university factions are frequently influential on personnel in the organization. Because academic background is regarded as more important than actual ability, there are many abuses; recently, people of talent are being widely sought after without emphasizing academic background. This is happening to the extent that the Prime Minister himself, because there are so many Tokyo University graduates at high levels in the bureaucracy, has directed that more graduates of other universities be accepted.

【就職活動】 しゅうしょくかつどう／Shūshoku-katsudō

大学・短大生の就職活動は、最終学年になる少し前から始まります。まず会社案内を読んで各企業の情報を得た後、会社説明会に出席したり会社訪問をしたりして志望先を絞り込みます。そして筆記試験や面接で合格すれば、非公式の採用通知である内定をもらうという手順で行われます。学生の多くは、夏休みが終わるころまでには就職先が決まります。

Job hunting : *Shūshoku-katsudō* for **university** and junior college students begins a little before the beginning of the final year of school. After first reading company guides and obtaining information on the businesses, they select their desired places by attending company information meetings and making company visits. If they are successful at a written examination and interviews, they will then receive an informal decision that is an unofficial notice of employment. Most students obtain their place of employment by the end of summer vacation.

【情報社会】
Jōhō-shakai
じょうほうしゃかい

　日本の情報社会化は1970年代以降急速に進み、コンピュータによる情報処理の高速化と多様な通信メディアの発達によって、高度な情報社会が実現されつつあります。日本の情報化における特徴の１つは、日本語が１バイトのアルファベットと違い、２バイトを必要とすることです。これはコンピュータ内で情報を処理する際にメモリーを多く必要とするため、ソフトウェアの開発では多くの労力を必要とします。一方日本ではトロンという基本ソフトが開発され、すべての情報処理システムをこのトロンで統一する計画もあります。トロンは国際的にも注目され、国際規格の通信言語の１つとして採用されています。

Information-oriented society : Japan's transformation to *jōhō-shakai* advanced rapidly after 1970. The highly information-oriented society continues to be realized through the quickening of information management by computer and the development of diverse communication media. One of the main features of Japan's information orientation is that Japanese has made necessary a two-byte alphabet that is different from the one-byte alphabet. That requires a lot of effort to develop software, because of the necessity to have a lot of memory for managing information by computer. In Japan basic software known as TRON has been developed and there is even a plan to unify all information management systems with TRON. TRON has also caught international attention and is being adopted as a standard international communication language.

【通勤電車】 つうきんでんしゃ／Tsūkin-densha

日本の大都市における通勤電車は、混雑がひどいことでは世界的に有名です。混雑解消のために路線を複々線化したり、車両を改造してドアを増やしたりしていますが、根本的な改善にはなりません。特に東京は、人口が集中し過ぎるのが地価高騰と通勤ラッシュの原因であるとされ、遷都論も具体的に検討されています。東京で電車に乗るコツは、ラッシュ時間を避けることでしょう。

Commuter trains : *Tsūkin-densha* in large Japanese cities are notorious around the world for being terribly crowded. To solve the congestion, four-track lines have been layed, and each train car has been remodeled with more doors, but this has not resulted in fundamental improvement. Particularly in Tokyo, which is overpopulated, high land prices and the commuter rush hour have produced concrete discussions on moving the capital. The knack of riding the trains in Tokyo is surely to avoid rush hour.

【自動車】 Jidōsha じどうしゃ

日本は鉄道が極めて発達しているため、アメリカと比較すると乗用車の所有台数は5分の1です。通勤も鉄道を利用する人が圧倒的に多く、また便利です。従って、車を持っている人はレジャーに利用することが多く、**正月**や夏休みあるいはゴールデンウィークなどには各地の高速道路が渋滞します。自然回帰の風潮からか、最近はスポーツカーよりは4WDなどのRV車に人気があります。

Automobiles : Because Japan's railroads are highly developed, passenger car ownership is about one-fifth that of America. An overwhelming majority of people use the railroad for commuting and it is convenient. Accordingly, most people who have cars use them for leisure; during **New Year**, summer vacation and Golden Week,which is a series of consecutive holidays from the end of April to the beginning of May, highways everywhere are crowded. Perhaps because of the return-to-nature movement, recently recreational vehicles like the 4WD are more popular than sportscars.

【高齢化社会】Kōreika-shakai.
こうれいかしゃかい

　日本は現在世界一の長寿国です。他方で出生率は年々低下し、高齢化社会になりつつあります。全人口に占める65歳以上の比率は、1970年には7.1％（9.9％）でしたが1990年には12％（12.7％）にまで上昇しています（カッコ内はアメリカ）。先進国では同様の傾向があるとはいえ、アメリカと比較すると高齢化のスピードは早まっています。さらに第2次大戦後の「団塊の世代」があと15年足らずで60歳を迎えると、心配されるのが「年金」の問題です。そのときは若い人々が多額の年金資金を支払わなければ、高齢者への年金支給ができなくなるのです。そのため年金の加入を拒否する人が出るなど、今から論議が盛んです。

Aging society : Japan is the country with the longest life expectancy in today's world. On the other hand, with the birth rate dropping year by year, Japan has continued to become a *kōreika-shakai*. The percentage of those above 65 in the population was 7.1%(9.9% in U.S.) in 1970 but rose to 12%(12.7% in U.S.) in 1990. Advanced countries have this same tendency, but, when compared to the United States, the speed of Japan's aging is faster. Moreover, when the populous postwar generation turns 60 in fewer than 15 years, it will be concerned about the issue of "pensions." At that time, if young people do not pay large sums into their retirement funds, there will be no pension allowances for the aged. Consequently, a lively debate about this is beginning, with people coming out against participation in pensions.

【高齢化の現状】
Kōreika no genjō
こうれいかのげんじょう

◎日本の年齢別人口構成図
Population formation chart by age

…1950年は出生率、死亡率がともに高いのでピラミッド型だが、1990年にはすでに釣り鐘型になっている。2つの山は、戦後のベビーブームの世代と、その子供の世代である。

…The chart forms a pyramid shape in 1950, for the high rates of birth and death, it forms a hunging bell shape in 1990. The two curves are baby boomer genaration of postwar Japan and its children's generation.

国勢調査　各10月1日現在/National Census, as of October 1 each year.

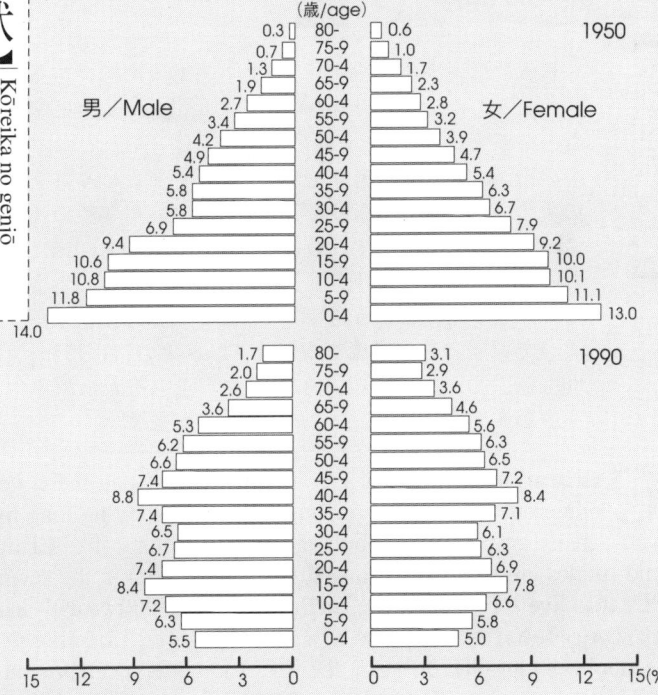

高齢化は、死亡率・出生率の低下によって起きます。日本の平均寿命は世界のトップレベルにあり、また出生率は減少し続けているため（p.181参照）、日本の高齢化は世界に例を見ない速さで進んでいます。

Present condition of the aging society : The aging society is caused by low rates of death and birth. The average life span of the Japanese is at the top level of the world, and the birth rate continues to decrease(see p.181). Thus, the aging society of Japan is growing in a speed that cannot be found in other parts of the world.

　日本には古来長寿を願い、また祝う数々の風習がありました。そのため、おめでたいものの象徴には長寿に関係したものが多いのです。「**鶴**は千年、**亀**は万年」といって長寿の象徴であり、**海老**は尾が曲がっているためやはり長寿の象徴です。長寿を喜び合うために、一定の年齢に達するごとにお祝いをします。最初に長寿を祝うのは60歳になったときで、この歳を「**還暦**」といいます。自分の生まれた**干支**に還った、という意味です。この日には子供や孫が集まって家族全員で**還暦**を祝います。60歳の次には70、77、80、88、90、99、108歳と続きます。それぞれに故事や歳を表わす文字に関係した意味を持っています。

Celebration of long life : Traditionally, in Japan there were numerous practices of praying for and celebrating long life. Thus, many auspicious symbols are related to long life. **Cranes** and **turtles** are symbols of long life as can be seen in the saying, "**Cranes** live for 1,000 years, **turtles** live for 10,000 years," and a **shrimp**, **lobster**, or **prawn** with its curved tail likewise symbolizes long life. To share the joy of longlife, a celebration is held at certain ages. Long life is first celebrated at age 60. This age is referred to as "*kanreki*," which means a return to one's original birth combination of the **sexagenary cycle**. On this date, children and grandchildren gather together and the whole family celebrates one's **60th birthday**. Celebrations continue after age 60 at ages 70, 77, 80, 88, 90, 99, and 108. Each age respectively carries meaning related to the characters used to express the age or to historical facts.

◎年齢別離婚率の推移／Change in the rate of divorce by age

…既婚女性1,000人対
…Rate per 1,000 of married women

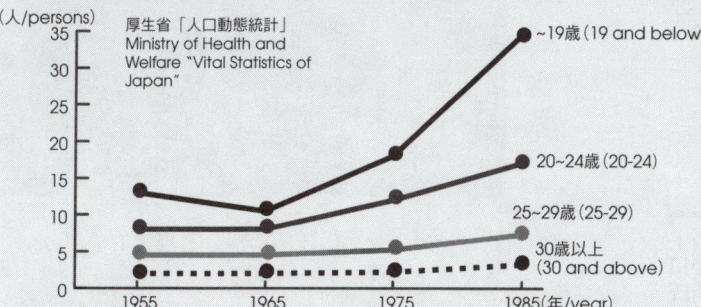

厚生省「人口動態統計」
Ministry of Health and Welfare "Vital Statistics of Japan"

~19歳 (19 and below)
20~24歳 (20-24)
25~29歳 (25-29)
30歳以上 (30 and above)

◎離婚件数／Number of divorces

厚生省「人口動態統計」
Ministry of Health and Welfare "Vital Statistics of Japan"

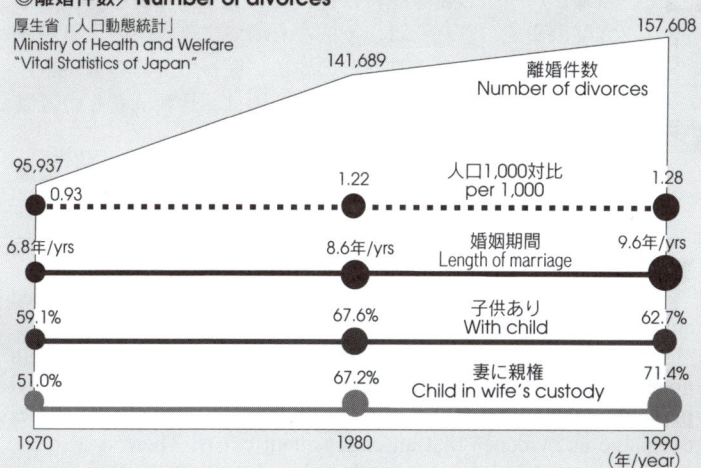

	1970	1980	1990
離婚件数 Number of divorces	95,937	141,689	157,608
人口1,000対比 per 1,000	0.93	1.22	1.28
婚姻期間 Length of marriage	6.8年/yrs	8.6年/yrs	9.6年/yrs
子供あり With child	59.1%	67.6%	62.7%
妻に親権 Child in wife's custody	51.0%	67.2%	71.4%

(年/year)

経済的に自立する女性が増えると結婚年齢は上昇します。一方、経済的に自立していれば離婚しても生活には困らないため、離婚率もまた上昇します。

Divorce : As the number of financially independent women increases, the marriage age rises. Meanwhile, financial independence guarantees livelihood after divorce, so that divorce rate also rises.

【離婚】
Rikon
りこん

【結婚式】
けっこんしき
Kekkonshiki

　現代の日本の結婚式は、伝統的な部分と現代的な部分が混在して、さまざまな形式で行われています。

　仲介者である仲人が男女を引き合わせる**見合い**。婚約成立の証として両家が金品を贈り合う**結納**。婚礼の際に新郎新婦が三つ組の盃を順番に使って、交互に神酒を飲む**三三九度**の儀式。これらは伝統的なものです。専門の式場で**神道**、**仏教**、**キリスト教**などの作法に従って夫婦の誓いをしたり、新婚旅行に出かけたりするのは、比較的新しい習慣です。

　結婚式には儀式と**披露宴**という2つの要素があり、**披露宴**は大勢の知人を招いて、ホテルなどで盛大に行われます。

Wedding ceremonies : Contemporary Japanese weddings are a mix of traditional and contemporary aspects and are carried out in a variety of ways.

There are the **formal meeting with a view to marriage** by which a go-between introduces the man and woman, and the **betrothal presents**, which are gifts of money and goods that the two families exchange as evidence that an engagement exists. There is also the **exchanges of nuptial cups** ritual during the marriage ceremony in which the bride and groom, using a set of three sake cups by turns, alternately drink sacred sake. These are traditional aspects. Holding the ceremony at a specialized wedding hall in accordance with **Shinto**, **Buddhist** or **Christian** rites and going on honeymoons are comparatively recent practices.

In *kekkonshiki* there are two essential elements; the ritual ceremony and the **wedding reception**. Large numbers of friends are invited to the **wedding reception**, which takes place in grand style at hotels.

◎日本人の平均初婚年齢の変遷
Change in the average age for the first marriage

経済企画庁「国民生活白書」1992年
Economic Planning Agency
"The White Paper of national's living condition" 1992

【結婚事情】

けっこんじじょう／Kekkon-jijō

女性の高学歴化や社会進出に伴い、日本人の平均初婚年齢は高くなっています。こうした傾向は、出生率の低下の原因の1つになっています。

Marriage situation : As women proceed for higher education and society, the average age for the first marriage is becoming older. This kind of tendency is one of the reasons for the decrease in the birth rate.

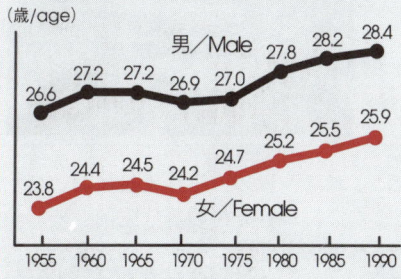

（歳/age）

男／Male
26.6　27.2　27.2　26.9　27.0　27.8　28.2　28.4

23.8　24.4　24.5　24.2　24.7　25.2　25.5　25.9
女／Female

1955　1960　1965　1970　1975　1980　1985　1990

◎女性の年代別結婚に関する意識
Women's opinion regarding marriage according to age groups

総理府「女性に関する世論調査」1990年
Prime Minister's Office "Public opinion poll regarding women" 1990

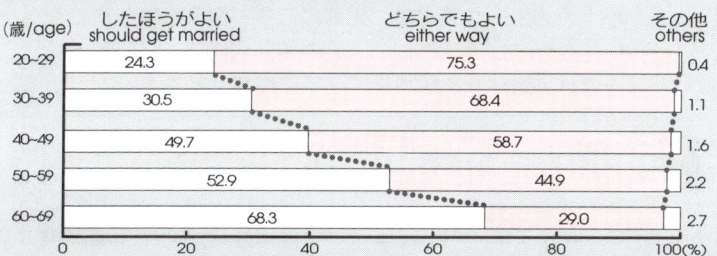

（歳/age）	したほうがよい should get married	どちらでもよい either way	その他 others
20~29	24.3	75.3	0.4
30~39	30.5	68.4	1.1
40~49	49.7	58.7	1.6
50~59	52.9	44.9	2.2
60~69	68.3	29.0	2.7

0　20　40　60　80　100(%)

◎見合い結婚と恋愛結婚の割合の変化
Change of ratio of arranged and love marriage

経済企画庁「国民生活白書」1992年／Economic Planning Agency "The White Paper of national's living condition" 1992

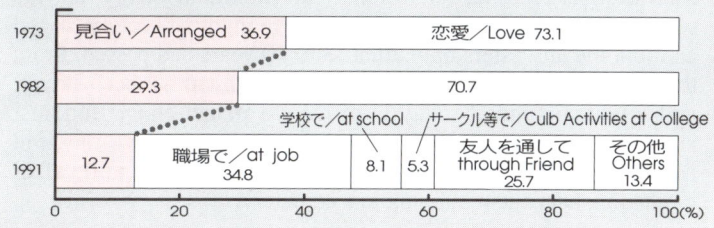

| 1973 | 見合い／Arranged 36.9 | 恋愛／Love 73.1 | | | |
| 1982 | 29.3 | 70.7 | | | |

| 1991 | 12.7 | 職場で／at job 34.8 | 学校で／at school 8.1 | サークル等／Culb Activities at College 5.3 | 友人を通して through Friend 25.7 | その他 Others 13.4 |

0　20　40　60　80　100(%)

【葬式】
Sōshiki
そうしき

　日本人古来の死生観によれば、人の一生は死後においても一定期間連続しています。しかも死後の霊は生前と変わらぬ人格を持ち、子孫から供応を受け、やがて神になって子孫を守護すると考えられていました。近親者が死ぬと遺族は死後49日間は喪中といって心身を清浄に保ちます。その後１年、７年と一定期間ごとに死者の**供養**をし、33年か50年が過ぎて初めて死者は神になって先祖の仲間入りすると考えられていました。中世以降は**仏教**の影響が強くなり、現代の典型的な葬式は、死者に対して**僧**に読経をしてもらい、翌日には**通夜**を行い、その後**告別式**をして死者に別れを告げ、遺体は火葬の後、墓地に埋葬されます。

Funerals : Accirding to the Japanese view of death from ancietnt times, one's time continues on even after death for a certain period. Moreover, spirits after death were considered to have the same personality as before death, received warm hospitality from their descendants, and later became gods and protect their descendants. When a close relative dies, people go into mourning and keep both mind and body clean for 49 days following the death. Subsequently, **memorial services** are held at each designated time, for instance, the first anniversary and the seventh anniversary, and the dead was thought to become a god and join the anscesters only after 33 to 50 years had passed. From the midieval times on, the influence of **Buddhism** has been strong, and a typical funeral today is to have a **priest** chant Buddhist sutras for a deceased, hold a **wake** on the following day, bid farewell to the deceaced in a **farewell service**, and, after cremation, bury the remaining in a cemetery.

開発途上国の人口増加は、今や地球規模の問題となっており、一方、先進国では出生率と死亡率の低下による高齢化が進んでいます（p.175参照）。出生率の低下は今後も進む見込みですが、高齢者の割合が高くなることにより、死亡率は漸増することが予想されます。

Birth and death rate : Growing population in developing countries has now become the problem on the earth wide scale, meanwhile the tendency for an aged society is getting bigger in advanced countries, due to a decrease in both the birth and the death rate (see p.175). The birth rate is expected to decrease even more in future, however, for the increasing rate of the aged, the death rate is expected to make a gradual increase.

…1990年の国際連合による人口動向アセスメントに基づく中位の推計値。出生率と死亡率は、人口1,000人に対する出生数と死亡数で、それぞれ5年間の平均。…The estimated average value based on population trend assessment in 1990 by the United Nations. The birth and the death rate are each the number of births and deaths to a population of one thousand, and are taken from the average of five years.

しゅっしょうりつとしぼうりつ／Shusshōritsu to shiboritsu

【出生率と死亡率】

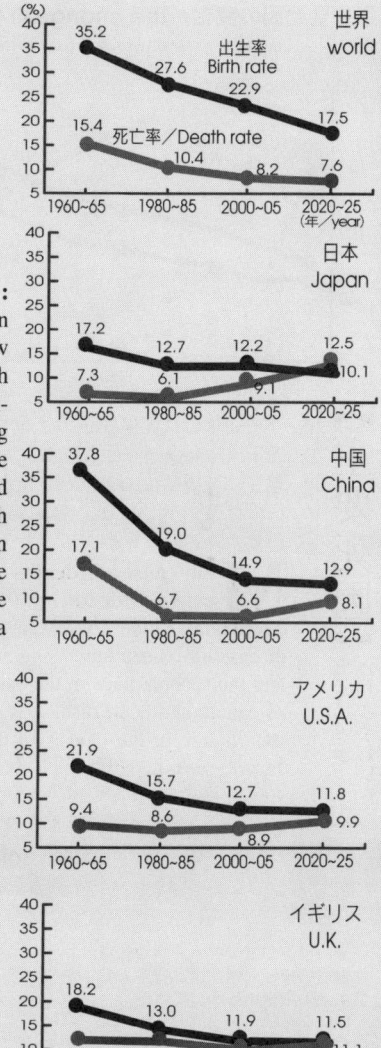

世界 world
出生率 Birth rate
35.2　27.6　22.9　17.5
死亡率／Death rate
15.4　10.4　8.2　7.6
1960~65　1980~85　2000~05　2020~25 (年／year)

日本 Japan
17.2　12.7　12.2　12.5
7.3　6.1　9.1　10.1
1960~65　1980~85　2000~05　2020~25

中国 China
37.8　19.0　14.9　12.9
17.1　6.7　6.6　8.1
1960~65　1980~85　2000~05　2020~25

アメリカ U.S.A.
21.9　15.7　12.7　11.8
9.4　8.6　8.9　9.9
1960~65　1980~85　2000~05　2020~25

イギリス U.K.
18.2　13.0　11.9　11.5
11.8　11.7　10.9　11.1
1960~65　1980~85　2000~05　2020~25

◎出生率・死亡率の推移と予測
Change and estimate of birth and death rate
国際連合「世界の将来人口」1990年／The United Nations "The future population of the world" 1990

◎主要死因の変化／**The change in main causes of deaths**

厚生省「人口動態統計」／Ministry of Health and Welfare "Vital Statistics of Japan"

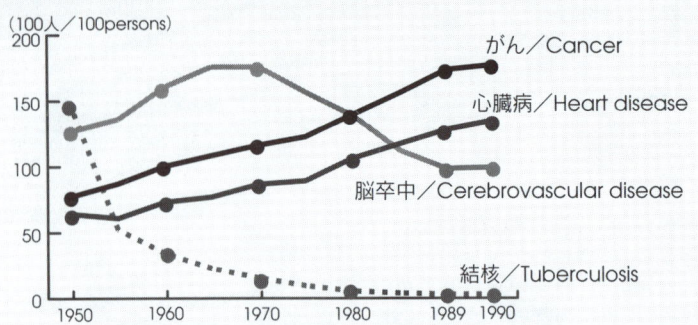

（100人／100persons）

がん／Cancer
心臓病／Heart disease
脳卒中／Cerebrovascular disease
結核／Tuberculosis

1950　1960　1970　1980　1989　1990

【主要死因】Shuyō-shiin　しゅようしいん

　1950年には死因順位の2位であった脳卒中（1位は結核）は、70年以降減少傾向にあります。一方、がんと心臓病は年々増加し、現在の死因順位の1位と2位を占めています。心臓病とがんが多いのは欧米型であり、死因のこのような変化の背景には、日本人の食生活の欧米化があると考えられます。

Main causes of deaths : Apoplexy, which was the second cause of death in 1950(the first was tuberculosis,) is decreasing since 1970. On the other hand, cancer and heart disease have been increasing every year, and they occupy the first and the second place in the causes of deaths. To have many cases of cancer and heart disease is categorized to a Western type, and the change in the causes of deaths indicates Westernization of Japanese eating habits as its background.

◎1人1日あたり主要食品別栄養摂取量
Daily Intake per person of main foods

'60の摂取量を100とした場合
measured by taking the intake of '60 as 100

油脂／Oils
動物性食品／Fats
野菜／Vegetables
砂糖／Suger
米／Rice

1960　1970　1980　1990

…米の摂取の減少と、油脂や動物性食品の摂取の増加は、日本人の食生活の欧米化を示している。
…Decline in the intake of rice and increase in intake of oils, fats, and animal proteins indicate the Westrnized Japanese eating habits.

厚生省「国民栄養調査」
Ministry of Health and Welfare "Nationals' Nutrition Survey"

娯楽

【宝くじ】
たからくじ
Takarakuji

　宝くじは当籤金つき抽選券で、海外でのロッタリーやナンバー・ゲームと似ています。地方自治体で発行されており、収益は地方自治体の財源となります。

　江戸時代（1603〜1867）に寺社の再建や修理にあてるため発売された**富くじ**を起源とするもので、第1回宝くじは、1945年、政府によって1枚10円で発売されました。1等賞金は10万円、ほかに生地・タバコなども当たるとあって、物資の乏しかった当時は爆発的な人気を呼びました。

　現在では、最高賞金は1億円に達するものもあります。しかも賞金には所得税がかからないとあって、あまりの人気に予約制がしかれるほどです。

***T**akarakuji* is a public lottery with money as its prize. It resembles the lottery or numbers games in other countries. *Takarakuji* tickets are issued by local self-governing bodies which take the proceeds as a source of revenue.

The practice began in the **Edo Period** (1603-1867) as a **lottery** sold to provide for reconstruction and repair of Buddhist temples and Shinto shrines. The first *takarakuji* ticket was sold for ¥10 in 1945 by the government. The first prize money was ¥100,000 and other prizes were items like cloth and cigarettes. In those poverty-stricken times, it ignited an explosive popularity.

Nowadays, the top prize reaches as much as ¥100,000,000. Adding to that, the prize money is exempt from income tax, so that its popularity is as high as that tickets are sold on a reservation basis.

【カラオケ】 Karaoke

　カラオケの「カラ」は「空っぽ」、「オケ」は「オーケストラ」を指します。つまり、ボーカル部分がないオーケストラ音楽という意味です。カラオケの装置が1970年代中期に発売されると、飲み屋やバーなどに置かれてカラオケ・ブームとなり、庶民の娯楽として浸透しました。好きな曲をカラオケ伴奏に合わせて歌えばストレス解消になり、場を盛り上げることもできるとあって、つきあいの場にも欠かせないものとなっているのです。

　最近は、中国をはじめとするアジアやアメリカ、ヨーロッパにも輸出されており、高い人気を得ています。

Singing with prerecorded accompaniment : The *kara* of *karaoke* means "empty" and *oke* means "orchestra." That is, it means an orchestra without vocals. When *karaoke* equipment was first sold in the mid–1970s, it was set up in taverns and bars; a *karaoke* boom ensued, spreading as popular entertainment for everybody. Singing favorite songs along with the taped *karaoke* accompaniment releases stress and enlivens the atmosphere; it has become a necessity for both social and personal associations. In recent years, *karaoke* has been exported to China and other Asian countries and even to the United States and Europe. It enjoys high popularity everywhere.

【テレビゲーム】 Terebi-gēmu

　現在の子どもの遊びは戸外より室内中心になっていますが、テレビゲームはその最たるものです。海外、特にアメリカでもテレビゲームの人気は高く、メーカーの「ニンテンドー（**任天堂**）」といえばテレビゲームをさすほどです。エレクトロニクス技術を応用したコンピュータゲームの一種で、1978年から79年にかけて「インベーダーゲーム」が大流行し、その先駆けとなりました。今では内容もスポーツや冒険ものなど多様化してきました。最も人気がある「ドラゴンクエスト」シリーズの発売前には長蛇の列ができ、社会的なブームになりました。しかし過度の使用は視力低下やてんかんの発作の原因となるとの指摘もあります。

Video games : Current children's games occur indoors more than outdoors, and the representative of them are *terebi-gēmu*. Overseas, especially in the United States, *terebi-gēmu* are so popular that the name of one maker, **Nintendō**, is synonymous with video games. It is a kind of computer games applying electronic technology; its forerunner was "Space Invaders," a computer game, whose popularity has swept Japan from 1978 to 1979. The contents of games have now become diversified, using sports and various kinds of adventures for their set-ups. Long lines have formed prior to the sale of the most popular "Doragon Quest" series of games, which have become a social boom. However, there are indications that excessive use causes reduced eyesight and epilepsy.

【ゲームセンター】 *Gēmu-sentā*

　アメリカのカジノやピンボール・マシンなどの文化に影響され、1969年ごろから登場した遊興場です。スロットマシンなどもありますが、コンピュータで開発された映像によるゲームが主流です。インベーダー・ゲームが爆発的にヒットし、現在は「バーチャル・リアリティー」（仮想現実）を体験できる高度な機械に人気があります。10〜20代の若者の遊び場として繁華街に多く見られます。

Game centers : These are places of amusement which appeared around 1969 with influence from the culture of American casinos and pinball machines. There are slot machines too, but most of the games are based on computer-generated images. The "Space Invaders" game has made an explosive hit, and now sophisticated machines with which one can experience "virtual reality" are popular. As places to hang around for young people in their teens and twenties, *gēmu-sentā* are mostly found in amusement districts.

【ディスコ】 *Disuko*

　東京や大阪などの大都市に多く見られますが、18歳未満は入場が規制されています。音楽、ダンス、ファッションにおいて流行の発信源となることが多く、とりわけ東京のディスコは流行最先端の場所といえます。華やかなファッションに身を包んだ若者たちが、音楽に合わせて自由に踊りを楽しみます。最近は人気のディスコの入場券が付いたCDも発売され、話題になりました。

Disco : These are much in evidence in big cities like Tokyo and Osaka, but entrance is prohibited for those under eighteen. They have become the sources of transmitting new waves of music, dance, and fashion, especially the *disuko* in Tokyo are said to be on the cutting edge of the new waves. Young people, dressed up in showy fashions, enjoy dancing to the music in their own ways. Recently, CDs sold with tickets to popular *disuko* attached have caught people's attention.

【パチンコ】Pachinko

1920年ごろにアメリカから伝わったコリント・ゲームを改良したものといわれています。多くの人の娯楽となっていますが、18歳未満の人は行うことができません。鋼鉄製の玉をばねではじいて、盤面にあるいくつかの穴に入れると、10個以上の玉が出てくるしくみです。昔は手動で玉をはじいていましたが、今は電動式になりました。獲得した玉は、タバコやお菓子など、さまざまな賞品と交換できます。

Pachinko is said to be an improvement on the "Corinth Game" which was brought from the United States around 1920. It has become a diversion for many people, but is prohibited to play for those under eighteen. The game involves launching steel balls with a spring flipper and, if they go into the several holes on the game board, 10 or more balls come out. In the past, the balls were flipped manually using the flipper, but now that is substituted by manipulating a handle which works electronically to flip the balls. Accumulated balls can be exchanged for various prizes such as cigarettes or sweets.

【麻雀】Mājan まーじゃん

麻雀は**明治時代**（1868〜1912）末期、中国からアメリカを経由して日本に伝わったゲームで、「**牌**」と呼ばれる136個の四角い駒を用いて4人で得点を争います。当初は貴族や金持ちの遊びでしたが、第2次大戦後庶民に普及しました。大学生やサラリーマンのつき合いによく利用されていましたが、次第にすたれつつあります。

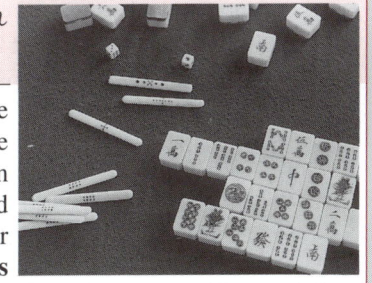

Mah-jong is a game brought to Japan in the **Meiji Period** (1968-1912) from China by way of the United States. Four players compete for points, using 136 **square pieces of tile**(*pai*). It was originally a game for the nobility and the wealthy, but after the Second World War it spread to the common people. It has often played in friendly gatherings of university students or businessmen, but it is gradually going out of fashion.

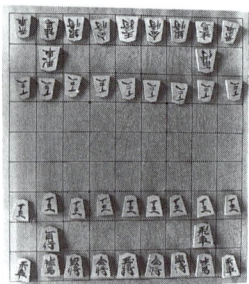

【将棋】

Shōgi
しょうぎ

日本の伝統的なゲームで、8世紀ごろ**碁**とともに中国から日本に伝わり、その後独自の改良が加えられて、一般に広まりました。チェスによく似ていますが、相手から取った**駒**を自分の持ち駒として再び使用できる点が異なります。縦長の五角形をした木製の**駒**には、王や将軍などの地位や役割を示す文字が書かれており、その種類は全部で8つです。

2人の対戦者は、81個の正方形のます目が描かれた**将棋盤**の上で**駒**を動かします。それぞれが20枚の**駒**を持ち、初めに**将棋盤**の所定の位置に並べます。交互に駒を動かして、相手の**王将**を早く追いつめた方が勝ちとなるもので、毎年、全国名人戦も行われています。

Japanese chess : This is a traditional Japanese game which came to Japan from China together with the game of *go* in the eighth century, and became popular after distinctive improvement. It is quite similar to chess, but with the difference that a player can re-use as his own the **pieces** taken from the opponent. Characters indicating rank and role, such as king or shogun, are written on the pieces, which are made of wood carved in an irregular pentagonal shape. In all, there are eight different ranks.

Two opponents move their **pieces** on the *shōgi* **board** which has 81 squares. Each player has 20 **pieces** , lined up at the beginning in fixed positions. They move their **pieces** by turns and the first one to corner the opponent's **king** wins. A national championship for master players is held every year.

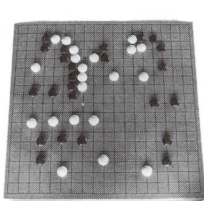

【囲碁・碁】

Igo, Go
いご・ご

　囲碁は日本の代表的な室内娯楽の1つで、8世紀に中国から伝わりました。当初は貴族の遊びでしたが、13世紀ごろから大衆に普及し、現在に至っています。このゲームは2人で行うもので、361個の目（交点）のある正方形の**碁盤**を使い、目の上に1人が黒い**碁石**、もう1人が白い**碁石**を交互に並べていきます。自分の石で相手の石を囲めばそれを取ることができ、多く取った方が勝ちです。

　上手な人が白い石を使い、黒い石を持った人から先に打ちます。互いの実力の差に応じて、あらかじめ黒石をいくつか**碁盤**の目に置いておくというルールがあるので、実力に差がある人同士でも互角に勝負することができます。

Igo, a representative Japanese indoor game, was introduced from China in the eighth century. At first it was a game for the nobility, but from about the thirteenth century on it spread to the masses. This game is played by two persons using a square *go board* with a grid, which has 361 intersecting points called *me*(eyes). The players alternately play their *go stones*–one using black, the other white–on the *me*. One can take the opponent's stones by surrounding them with his own; the one who takes the most stones wins.

A skilled player uses the white stones, and the player with black stones is given priority to start the game. There is a rule establishing that some black stones must be placed on the *go board* in advance, to accommodate the relative differences in the players' ability. Thus, even players of different ability can have even matches.

【漫画】
Manga
まんが

日本では漫画は大衆文化の１つとなっています。子供向けから少年・少女向け、サラリーマンやOL向けなど、それぞれの年齢層に合わせた漫画雑誌が数多く発行されており、スーツ姿のサラリーマンが電車内で漫画雑誌を読む光景も珍しくありません。しかし、中には単なる娯楽を超えた作品もあり、最近では経済、歴史などを漫画で分かりやすく解説した本も出版され、好調な売れ行きを見せています。

Comics : In Japan *manga* have become a part of mass culture. Large numbers of *manga* magazines are being published, aimed at various age brackets; boys, girls, white collar businessmen, young female office workers (known as OL–"office ladies"), and others. It is not unusual to see white collar businessmen in suits reading *manga* magazines in trains. However, there are also works that go beyond simple entertainment. Recently, books with easy-to-understand *manga* explanations of economics, history, and so on have been published and show a favorable demand.

【レンタルビデオ】
Rentaru bideo

映画館の３分の１以下の料金で、自宅で気軽に映画が見られることから需要が多くなり、ここ10年足らずの間にレンタルビデオ・ショップの数は急激に増加しました。ビデオ・ソフトの売上高も、映画の興行収入の倍以上となり、今や映画は映画館で見るものではなく、ビデオ化されたものを借りて見るものとなりつつあります。そのため、閉館を余儀なくされた映画館も少なくありません。

Video rental : There is a lot of demand for this, since the movies can be watched leisurely at home at the cost less than one-third of movie theaters'; in the span of barely ten years the number of video rental stores has increased rapidly. Gross sales of video software, too, have more than doubled the exhibition income for movies. Movies now are no longer to be seen only in theaters but increasingly are seen after being put on video. Consequently, quite a few movie theaters have been forced to close down.

【競馬・競輪】

けいば・けいりん／Keiba, Keirin

日本では賭博は禁止されていますが、競馬、競輪、競艇などは公営ギャンブルとして公認されています。特に競馬は人気が高く、近年は女性ファンも多くなりました。日本中央競馬会による中央競馬と、地方自治体による地方競馬とがあり、大きなレースはテレビ中継もされています。

競輪もまた、当初は地方財政の復興を目的に始められたものですが、国民の娯楽としても定着しています。

Horse racing, bicycle racing : Gambling is prohibited in Japan, but horse racing, bicycle racing and boat racing are authorized for gambling under public management. Horse racing is especially popular and recently female fans have increased. Major races are run by the Japan Racing Association and local races are run by autonomous local bodies; big races are televised.

Keirin, bicycle racing, was initially begun with the goal of reviving local finance, and it is also taking root for the people.

【海外旅行】

かいがいりょこう／Kaigai-ryokō

1990年には日本からの出国者数は1千万人を超え、今や新婚旅行は海外が当り前、大学生の卒業旅行も海外が多くなりました。ハワイを含むアメリカには人気があり、アメリカの観光入国者数では2位英国に1.4倍の差をつけて日本が断然トップです。* オーストラリアや東南アジア、ヨーロッパなども人気があります。**正月**やゴールデンウィーク、夏休みは成田空港が最も混雑するシーズンです。

Trips abroad : In 1990 the number of people who traveled outside Japan exceeded 10 million; honeymoons overseas are now quite common and most graduation trips for college students also are overseas. It is popular to go to the united states, including Hawaii, and, among tourists entering the united states, Japan is decisively at the top with a difference of 1.4 times more than the U.K. in the second place.* Australia, Southeast Asia, and Europe are also popular places to travel. **New Year**, "Golden Week" (a series of holidays from the end of April to the beginning of May), and summer vacation are the most congested seasons at New Tokyo International Airport (Narita).

*注：1989年度の統計による／statistics from 1989

【温泉】
Onsen
おんせん

　日本には温泉が多く、日本人ほど温泉好きな国民は世界でも珍しいといわれています。さまざまな泉質の温泉があり、昔からけがや病気を治すためにも温泉は利用されてきました。

　著名な温泉場には旅館やホテルが立ち並び、大きなリゾート地を形成しています。しかし最近は大自然と静寂を求めて山奥の一軒家の温泉に人気が集まり、開放的な**露天風呂**で自然とのふれあいを楽しむ人も増えました。温泉が体をいやし、自然が心をいやすのです。旅行雑誌で温泉の特集が組まれることも多く、温泉ツアーも盛んに行われています。

Hot spring : It would be unusual for a nation anywhere in the world to have as many *onsen* or to love them as much as Japan. There are various hot springs with different qualities of water, from ancient times heal wounds and sickness.

　Japanese inns and hotels are lined up at famous hot-spring spots forming large resort areas. However, recently, with the demand for the great outdoors and silence, isolated *onsen* deep in the mountains have become popular, and there are more and more people who enjoy the contact with nature in **open-air baths**. *Onsen* heal the body and nature heals mind and heart. Travel magazines frequently feature *onsen* in special issues, and *onsen* tours are very popular thing to do.

【余暇活動】

Yoka-katsudō
よかかつどう

諸外国と比較して、ゴルフ、テニス、ボウリング、遊園地、国内観光旅行などへの参加率が高い日本の余暇活動は、「高費用・行楽中心型」であるといえそうです。

Leisure activities : In comparison to other countries, leisure activities in Japan are focused on playing golf, tennis, and bowling, going to amusement parks, and domestic sightseeing can be referred to as "expensive and excursion-oriented."

◎余暇活動参加率の5カ国比較 (%)／Comparison of the rate of participation in leisure activities among 5 countries (%)

…**A**-日本/Japan、**B**-アメリカ/U.S.A.、**C**-イギリス/U.K.、
D-フランス/France、**E**-旧西ドイツ/former W. Germany

「レジャー白書'92」財団法人余暇開発センター
＊印は「7カ国比較国際レジャー調査」（余暇開発センター）による
"1992 Leisure Survey" the Leisure Development Center
＊marked part is from "International Leisure Survey among Seven Countries" (the Leisure Development Center)

	A	B	C	D	E
＊「好きでよくするスポーツや趣味があるか」という質問に「ある」と回答した人の比率 / Ratio of respondents who answered "yes" to a question, "Do you have favorite sports or hobbies that you often do?"	47.0	76.9	80.0	73.5	70.6
スポーツ部門 / Sports					
ジョギング／Jogging	16.3	25.8	16.6	25.6	20.3
サイクリング[1]／Cycling	7.4	24.2	20.0	35.3	44.6
サッカー／Soccer	2.1	3.8	10.1	7.4	11.9
水泳／Swimming	21.0	40.0	46.0	31.8	51.4
ゴルフ／Golf	16.1	11.2	10.7	1.5	2.0
テニス／Tennis	11.0	8.9	10.1	12.3	8.3
スキー／Skiing	9.8	8.8	4.3	12.0	10.2
釣り／Fishing	14.7	32.5	9.9	15.2	3.4
ボウリング／Bowling	22.3	25.4	11.0	15.3	19.8
趣味・創作部門 / Culture					
映画鑑賞[2]／movies	25.5	50.9	39.7	40.8	36.5
音楽会・コンサート／Recitals and concerts	16.2	35.1	27.5	14.3	26.4
クラシック音楽鑑賞[3]／Listening to classical music	13.1	31.1	25.8	35.6	24.7
社交ダンス／Social dance	4.2	9.3	5.9	20.7	33.2
読書／reading	48.7	65.8	70.2	72.5	59.1
写真撮影[4]／Taking photographs	19.2	29.0	30.8	27.7	25.0
娯楽部門 / Amusement					
宝くじ／Lottery	25.4	24.7	5.2	15.8	29.7
競馬／Horse racing	6.0	6.9	6.6	4.7	2.1
外食[5]／Dining-out	41.7	60.8	57.4	54.1	54.6
ホームパーティー／House Party	8.3	30.4	20.9	41.2	34.8
観光・行楽部門 / Travel and outdoors					
遊園地／Amusement parks	26.0	30.8	25.9	21.5	19.2
ドライブ／Driving	46.4	62.7	47.7	60.2	58.6
キャンプ／Camping	7.0	23.5	13.6	18.7	9.8
国内観光旅行[6]／Domestic travel	40.2	30.0	31.3	33.8	40.4
外国旅行／Travel abroad	6.8	11.3	34.1	22.6	32.4
ハイキング／Hiking	11.5	18.0	11.3	27.3	36.7

1…サイクルスポーツ全般/Cycle sports、2…映画館での/at theater、3…レコード、テープ等による/recorded、4…映画、ビデオ含む/ including movies and video、5…日常的なものを除く/excluding daily ones、6…宿泊つき/with a lodge

ことば

ろんご
ro 呂

そんぞ流

【日本語】
Nihongo
にほんご

　日本語は言語学的にどの語族に属するかについては定説がありません。英語やフランス語が属する印欧語族とは全くその構造を異にするため、西洋から見れば習得は難しい言語と言われています。

　日本語は長期間、比較的安定した共同体の中で形成されてきました。そのため成員同士が既知の事柄についてはあえて発話しなくても理解できるので、発話のある部分を省略する形式が発達しました。また相手に自分の言いたいことを察してもらうことも期待できるため、断言する形式は忌避されます。これが時に西洋人からは、日本人は自分の意見をはっきり言わない、という誤解につながるようです。

Japanese : There is no established theory as to which language family *Nihongo* linguistically belongs to. Its structure is completely different from that of the Indo-European languages, to which English and French belong, so as seen from the West it is a language difficult to acquire.

　Nihongo was formed within a comparatively stable community for a long time. Thus, the Japanese, as members of the community, could have understood each other without utterance, on matters already well-known to them; so the form of abbreviating certain part of utterance was developed. In addition, because it is expected that the other person will realize what one wants to say, strong assertions are avoided. On this point, Western people sometimes are tied into the misunderstanding that Japanese do not clearly express their opinions.

【文字】 Moji もじ

現在の日本語は、3種類の文字から成り立っています。すなわち、表意文字としての**漢字**及び表音文字の**平仮名**と**片仮名**です。もともと**日本語**には文字がなかったのですが、5世紀ころに**漢字**を使って記録するようになりました。その**漢字**を日本人は日本語風に読むことを考えだし、さらに**漢字**を基に表音文字を作り出したのです。このような文字の基礎が確立したのは**平安時代**（794〜1185）で、この文字のおかげで世界最古の長編小説『**源氏物語**』も紫式部によって完成されました。現在、**片仮名**は主に外来語を表すのに使い、**漢字**と**平仮名**で文章をつづります。また、ローマ字を含めた表音文字のみで表記することも可能です。

Characters : Modern Japanese consists of three kinds of *moji*: the ideographic **Chinese characters** known as *kanji* and the phonetic characters known as *hiragana* and *katakana*. Originally, **Japanese** had no *moji*, but in the fifth century documents came to be recorded using **Chinese characters**. The Japanese devised the way of reading those **Chinese characters** in a Japanese way and, based on **Chinese characters**, created the phonetic characters. The basis for phonetic *moji* was established in the **Heian Period**(794-1185), and it is with such *moji* that MURASAKI Shikibu completed the world's oldest novel, "**Genji Monogatari**"(The Tale of Genji). Today, *katakana* is mainly used for foreign words, and **Chinese characters** and *hiragana* for composing sentences. In addition, it is possible to write only in phonetic characters, including Roman letters.

【音】 Oto, On
おと・おん

日本語の音は以下の「50音図」（網伏せ部分）のとおりで、これですべての日本語を表記することも可能です。

Sounds, syllable : The sounds in **Japanese language** exactly follow the "Japanese syllabary; chart of the fifty sounds" below(the shaded area). It is possible to express all the Japanese words with these fifty sounds.

	a	i	u	e	o			
あ行	あ	い	う	え	お			
か行	ka か	ki き	ku く	ke け	ko こ	kya きゃ	kyu きゅ	kyo きょ
さ行	sa さ	shi し	su す	se せ	so そ	sha しゃ	shu しゅ	sho しょ
た行	ta た	chi ち	tsu つ	te て	to と	cha ちゃ	chu ちゅ	cho ちょ
な行	na な	ni に	nu ぬ	ne ね	no の	nya にゃ	nyu にゅ	nyo にょ
は行	ha は	hi ひ	fu ふ	he へ	ho ほ	hya ひゃ	hyu ひゅ	hyo ひょ
ま行	ma ま	mi み	mu む	me め	mo も	mya みゃ	myu みゅ	myo みょ
や行	ya や	i い	yu ゆ	e え	yo よ			
ら行	ra ら	ri り	ru る	re れ	ro ろ	rya りゃ	ryu りゅ	ryo りょ
わ行	wa わ	(wi) ゐ	u う	(we) ゑ	o を			
	n ん							
が行	ga が	gi ぎ	gu ぐ	ge げ	go ご	gya ぎゃ	gyu ぎゅ	gyo ぎょ
ざ行	za ざ	ji じ	zu ず	ze ぜ	zo ぞ	ja じゃ	ju じゅ	jo じょ
だ行	da だ	di ぢ	du づ	de で	do ど			
ば行	ba ば	bi び	bu ぶ	be べ	bo ぼ	bya びゃ	byu びゅ	byo びょ
ぱ行	pa ぱ	pi ぴ	pu ぷ	pe ぺ	po ぽ	pya ぴゃ	pyu ぴゅ	pyo ぴょ

【日本語教育】
Nihongo-kyōiku
にほんごきょういく

現在世界各国、特に環太平洋地域では**日本語**の教育が盛んです。その理由は日本人と接触し、会話する必要が増えたからにほかなりません。

1980年代の後半から急激に**日本語**学習者が増えたため、教師や教材の数が不足しています。そのため、日本側も**日本語**の教科書を寄贈したり教師を派遣したり、各国に対してさまざまな支援を実施しています。来日する外国人も増え、国内の**日本語**教育施設もまた増えつつあります。日本語能力試験が、1984年に初めて実施されました。日本国内及び世界各国で受験することができます。1992年には受験者数が68,496名となっています。

Japanese-language education : At present in many countries around the world, especially in circum-Pacific regions, **Japanese-language** education is flourishing. The reason is nothing but the increased necessity to contact and converse with the Japanese.

Because in the late 1980s students of **Japanese language** increased abruptly, the number of instructors and the amount of instructional material are insufficient. Thus, Japan, for its part, has put into effect various kinds of support in a number of countries , such as donating **Japanese-language** textbooks and dispatching instructors. Foreigners coming to Japan have also increased, and domestic institutions for **Japanese-language** education also keep on increasing. In 1984, a Japanese-ability examination was held for the first time. It can be taken in Japan as well as many other countries around the world. The number of people who took the exam in 1992 was 68,496.

山田は
外出して
おります。

社外

（山田）社長は
外出され
ています。

社内

【敬語】
Keigo
けいご

　日本語では敬語が著しく発達し、これを**日本語**の特色の
ひとつに数える見方もあります。しかし敬語は**日本語**だけ
でなくアジアの多くの言語、中国語、韓国語、ヴェトナム
語、タイ語、ビルマ語、ジャワ語などにも発達しています。
これらに共通するのは、相手には**尊敬語**を使い、自分につ
いては**謙譲語**を使うことです。この敬語は社会的な場面で
誤って使うと相手に失礼になり、また教養がないとみなさ
れるので、注意を要します。**日本語**の敬語でさらに注意を
要するのは、話す相手によって尊敬か謙譲かが変わること
です。例えば自社の社長について社内で話せば**尊敬語**を使
いますが、社外の人間には**謙譲語**を使うのです。

Honorific language : In **Japanese**, *keigo* is remarkably
developed and is counted as a key characteristic of the
language. However, *keigo* has developed not only in **Japanese** but
also in most Asian languages, such as Chinese, Korean,
Vietnamese, Thai, Burmese and Javanese. Common among these
is using **exalted terms** for others and **humble terms** for oneself.
This requires attention, because if *keigo* is used wrongly in social
settings it is rude to the other person and, in addition, one is
regarded as lacking education. The reason why **Japanese** *keigo*
requires attention is that respect or humility change depending on
the person to whom one speaks. For example, in speaking about
the president of one's own company inside the company, **exalted
terms** are used, but to people outside the company **humble terms**
are used.

【方言】
Hōgen
ほうげん

　日本は各地方が山岳地帯にさえぎられているため、各共同体が簡単に往来することができず、それぞれ独自の方言が発達しました。例えばラテン系の言語の中でフランス語とスペイン語は非常によく似ていて、それぞれラテン語の方言ということも可能ですが、**日本語**の方言もそれに近い違いを持っている場合があります。かつては東北地方と九州地方では互いにことばを通じさせるのが非常に困難だった時代もありました。そのため近代になってから、主に東京のことばを基準に徐々に共通語が形成されました。しかし、方言はその地域の文化を担っているので、むしろ最近はそれを大切にする運動が起こっています。

Dialects : Various regions in Japan are separated by mountains, so communities, unable to come and go easily, developed their own respective *hōgen*. Among Latin-based languages, for example, French and Spanish are quite similar and it is possible to call them *hōgen* of Latin; similarly **Japanese** dialects in some cases also have close differences. There was even a time when it was extremely difficult for people Tōhoku and people Kyūshū to communicate with each other. Therefore, in the modern era a common language was gradually formed, principally taking the language of Tokyo as standard. However, because dialects are part of a region's culture, recently a movement to emphasize their importance has arisen.

教育

【義務教育】
Gimukyōiku
ぎむきょういく

　日本の義務教育期間は小学校6年、中学校3年の計9年で、新学期は4月に始まります。3学期制が敷かれ、各学期はそれぞれ夏休み、冬休み、春休みによって区切られています。

　クラスごとに決まった教室があり、実技や実験などを行う授業を除いては、そこで授業を受けます。公立の小中学校では、昼食には給食という一律のメニューが出され、やはり同じ教室で食べます。ほとんどの中学校には制服があり、生徒はそれを着用して登校します。

　文部省は学習内容や教科書を細かく管理しており、全国でほぼ同一内容の授業が行われています。そのため、画一的ながらも均質で高水準の教育が可能となっているのです。

Compulsory education : The *gimukyōiku* time period in Japan is nine years, six in elementary school and three in junior high, and the new school year begins in April. The three-term system is adopted, each term marked respectively by the summer, winter and spring vacations.

Every class has its own fixed classroom where its students take all the courses, except for ones in which practical training and laboratory works are carried out. At public elementary and junior high schools, lunch is provided on a standardized menu, and it is eaten in the same classroom. Nearly all junior high schools require their students to attend wearing school uniforms.

The Ministry of Education closely supervises curriculum and textbooks, and classes with much the same content are taught throughout the country. As a result, through uniformity and homogeneity, a high standard of education becomes possible.

　日本の学校制度は、第２次大戦後、アメリカの制度を参考にして改革されました。小学校６年、中学校３年の義務教育を基本としています。

The Japanese school system was reformed after the Second World War with reference to the American system. It is based on compulsory education of six years in elementary school and three in junior high.

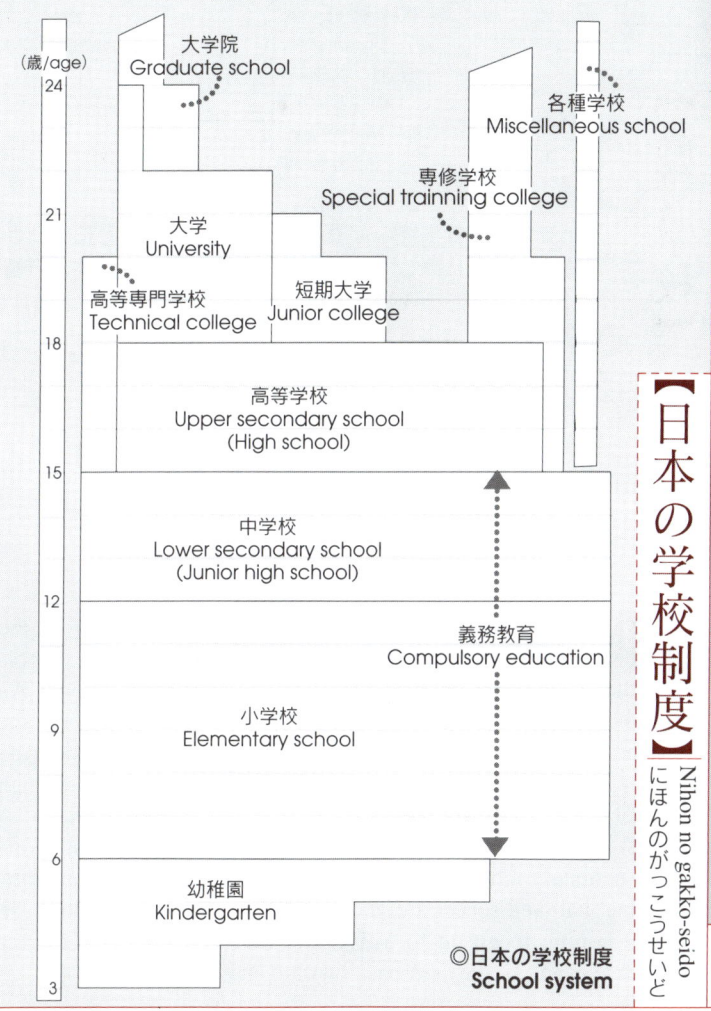

(歳/age)

24	大学院 Graduate school
	各種学校 Miscellaneous school
21	大学 University
	専修学校 Special trainning college
	短期大学 Junior college
18	高等専門学校 Technical college
	高等学校 Upper secondary school (High school)
15	中学校 Lower secondary school (Junior high school)
12	
	義務教育 Compulsory education
9	小学校 Elementary school
6	
	幼稚園 Kindergarten
3	

◎日本の学校制度
School system

【日本の学校制度】
Nihon no gakko-seido
にほんのがっこうせいど

◎高校生のスポーツ、部活動加盟状況（人）
High school student's participation in sports activities(persons)
…男女総合ベスト10
…top10

バスケット／basketball	203,783
バレーボール／volleyball	176,052
サッカー／soccer	155,786
硬式野球／baseball	146,036
陸上競技／track&field	138,392
ソフトテニス／softball tennis	133,687
バドミントン／badminton	98,808
卓球／table tennis	83,571
剣道／Japanese fencing	79,841
柔道／judo	65,721

【高等学校】Kōtōgakkō
こうとうがっこう

　通常は「高校」という略称で呼ばれ、進学を希望する生徒のための普通科と、職業科とに大別されます。入学に際しては入学試験が実施され、試験の点数のほか、中学での成績も考慮した上で合格者が決定します。現在の高校進学率は約95パーセントで、中途退学者は増加傾向にあるものの、約2パーセント程度です。

　多くの高校では制服が決められています。クラブ活動は盛んで、スポーツはほとんど全国大会があり、野球やサッカーなどの人気スポーツの全国大会はほとんどテレビで中継されます。3年になると**大学**進学希望者は受験勉強のために忙しくなり、クラブ活動も控え目になります。

High school : High schools are usually referred to by the shortened form of *kōkō*, and are divided into regular schools for students aiming at higher education and vocational schools. An entrance exam is required to enter a school and, in addition to the exam score, successful students are determined by considering junior high grades. Today, the rate of students advancing to high school is 95%, with an increasing dropout rate of about 2%.

Most *kōkō* require uniforms. Club activities abound, most sports have national tournaments, and the tournaments for popular sports like baseball and soccer are generally televised. In the senior year, those hoping to go on to **university** are busy studying for the entrance exam, so they cut back on club activities.

【大学】 Daigaku だいがく

　日本の大学はふつう４年制ですが、医・歯学部では６年制、**短期大学**では２年制がとられています。大学生の７割は男子学生ですが、**短期大学**はそのほとんどが女子短大です。第２次大戦以後現在のような制度になり、カリキュラムも最初の２年間は一般教養が中心で、専門科目は後半の２年間に集中しています。しかし、４年生になると**就職活動**のため学問に集中できなくなるなど、戦後半世紀近くを経て現実と合わない面が出てきているため、大学の制度的・カリキュラム的な改革の必要性が指摘されています。

　国際的には初・中等教育に対する評価が高い反面、大学教育については高い評価を得ているとはいえません。

University : Japanese *daigaku* are usually four years, but medical and dental schools are six years and **junior college** two. 70% of university students are male, but most **junior colleges** are women's colleges. After the Second World War, the present system was adopted, with the first two years focused on liberal studies and the major subjects concentrated in the last two years. However, because of **job hunting** in the senior year, students are unable to concentrate on their studies; and because in the nearly half century that has passed since the war aspects of the system have emerged that do not fit with reality, the necessity of reform in the university system and curriculum is being suggested.

In contrast to the high international regard for Japanese elementary and secondary education, Japanese university education has not obtained high marks.

【大学進学事情】

Daigaku-shingaku-jijō
だいがくしんがくじじょう

大学への進学率は、1989年に女子が男子を追い抜き、現在に至っています。

帰国子女の増加は、日本人の海外進出が増加していることを、大検志願者の増加は、高校を中退して大学を目指す人の増加を、それぞれ推測させます。

◎大学への進学率
The ratio of students who go on to colleges

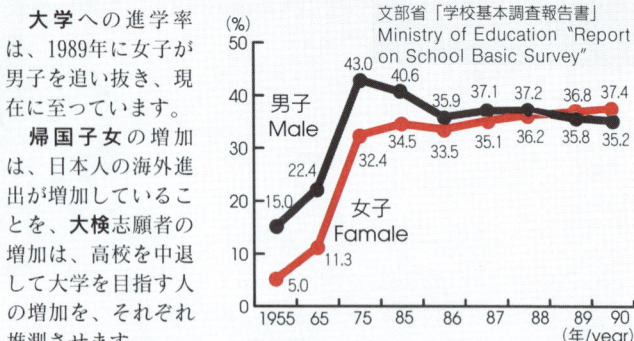

文部省「学校基本調査報告書」
Ministry of Education "Report on School Basic Survey"

男子 Male

女子 Famale

| | 1955 | 65 | 75 | 85 | 86 | 87 | 88 | | 90 (年/year) |
男子: 15.0, 22.4, 43.0, 40.6, 35.9, 37.1, 37.2, 36.8, 37.4
女子: 5.0, 11.3, 32.4, 34.5, 33.5, 35.1, 36.2, 35.8, 35.2

The situation of going on to the university : In 1989, the percentage of female students who went on to **universities** have exceeded that of male students', and have continued to be so until today.

The increase in the number of **returnee children** indicates the increase of the Japanese going overseas, and the growing number of people who take **The University Entrance Qualification Examination** indicate the increase of people who quit of high school and aim at going to university by themselves.

◎帰国子女数／The number of returnee children
…小学生、中学生、高校生の合計
…Total of elementary, secondary, and high school students
出典同上／The same source as above

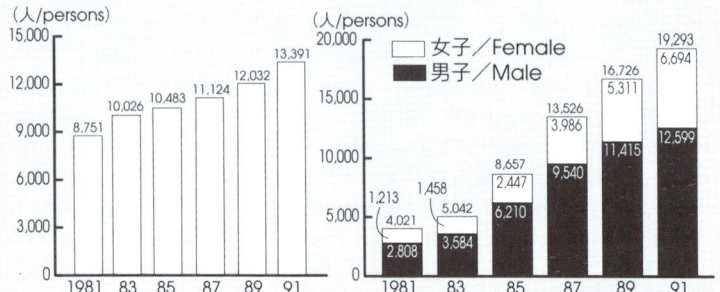

（人／persons）

	1981	83	85	87	89	91
	8,751	10,026	10,483	11,124	12,032	13,391

（人／persons）

女子／Female
男子／Male

	1981	83	85	87	89	91
女子	1,213	1,458	2,447	3,986	5,311	6,694
	4,021	5,042	8,657	13,526	16,726	19,293
男子	2,808	3,584	6,210	9,540	11,415	12,599

◎大検志願者数の変化
Shift in the number of applicants for The University Entrance Qualification
文部省生涯学習局課／Ministry of Education, Life-long Learning Bureau

【大学院】Daigakuin だいがくいん

国際的に見ると、日本の大学生の大学院への進学率は低く、大学院教育の水準も高いとはいえません。特に、科学の基礎研究における設備の拡充と人材の養成が課題とされています。なお、進学率が低い理由には、博士号の取得が非常に困難なこと、一般企業に就職するには年齢が高くなるので不利になること、日本の**大学**の教員は終身在職なので、新人が教員の職を得にくいことなどが挙げられます。

Graduate school : From an international point of view, the rate of Japanese university students advancing to *daigakuin* is low and the educational standards of Japanese graduate schools are not that high. In particular, the expansion of facilities and cultivation of talented students in the field of basic scientific research are their task. Several reasons are offered for this low rate: it is extremely difficult to obtain a doctorate, it is a disadvantage to look for a job in the average company at an older age, and it is difficult for a newcomer to find a faculty position because faculty members at Japanese **universities** are tenured for life.

【生涯教育】しょうがいきょういく／Shōgai-kyōiku

生涯教育という言葉は、1970年代以降、日本でも使われるようになりました。しかし、生涯教育を保障するために学校制度を改革するという方向ではなく、主婦や高齢者が、個人の内面生活の充実のために教養を身につける場を提供するという方向で制度化されてきました。**高齢化社会**の到来や、労働時間の短縮による余暇の増加によって、この制度が改めて関心を集めています。

Lifelong education : The term *shōgai-kyōiku* came into use in Japan after 1970s. Its objective was not to reform the school system to guarantee *shōgai-kyōiku*; it became institutionalized with the objective of offering places where housewives and the elderly could acquire education to fulfill their individual inner lives. With the advent of the **aging society** and the increase in free time from the reduction in working hours, this institution has taken on renewed interest.

【帰国子女】きこくしじょ／Kikokushijo

日本企業の海外進出に伴い、海外で生まれたり育ったりした子供も増えています。しかし帰国後の子供たちは、学力や言語面でクラスで疎外されることも多いため、学校側も特別な受け入れ態勢を少しずつ整備してきました。帰国子女を対象にした入試制度を取り入れた学校も増えています。最近では語学力や国際性などが評価され、かえって帰国子女に対する評価が高まってきています。

Returnee children : Accompanying the advance of Japanese companies abroad, children born or raised abroad have increased. However, these children after returning have often been alienated in classes because of their academic and linguistic abilities, so school authorities have adjusted gradually to a special attitude of acceptance. Schools also have increased that have adopted an entrance exam policy for *kikokushijo*. Recently, with linguistic ability and an international outlook in high demand, appreciation toward *kikokushijo* is growing.

【留学】Ryūgaku／りゅうがく

第2次大戦後はアメリカの基金などで日本の優秀な人材が留学して、帰国後日本の復興に寄与しました。最近は円高の状況もあって日本人学生の留学は年々増加傾向にあります。数週間から1カ月程度の語学留学をする高校・大学生も増えました。留学先はアメリカやオーストラリアなど英語圏が大半を占めています。また、欧米の方が博士号を取りやすいこともあって、**大学院**への留学も増えています。

Studying abroad : After the Second World War, Japan's best and brightest people did *ryūgaku* with funds from American foundations, and on returning to Japan they contributed to Japan's restructuring. Recently, with the rise in the value of the yen, Japanese students doing *ryūgaku* have been increasing every year. High school and university students doing language study abroad for a few weeks to a month have also increased. English-speaking countries like America and Australia make up the majority of *ryūgaku* destinations. In addition, since it is easier to take a doctorate in Europe and America, *ryūgaku* for **graduate school** has also increased.

【専門学校】

Senmongakkō
せんもんがっこう

　専門学校は普通課程の学校と違い、特定の職業で必要な知識や能力を育成する学校です。中学校または高校卒業者を対象とする専門学校としては、高等専門学校と専修学校とがあります。そのほかに各種学校と呼ばれる学校があり、語学、服飾、看護、料理などをはじめとしてさまざまな分野の専門教育が行われています。**予備校**もこの中に分類されます。

　日本は学歴が将来の出世に重要な意味を持つ社会ですが、最近は**大学**ではなくこうした専門学校を選択する学生も増えています。**学歴社会**が徐々に崩れつつあり、選択肢が多様化しているためです。

Specialized schools : *Senmongakkō*, as distinct from schools with regular curricula, are schools that cultivate the necessary knowledge and skills for special vocations. There are two kinds of special schools for graduates of junior high schools and high schools, technical colleges and special training colleges(see p.201). There are others called miscellaneous schools for professional education in all sorts of fields, such as language, fashion, nursing and cooking. **Cram schools** too are included among these schools.

 Japan is a society in which one's academic background carries great meaning for future success in life, but in recent years students choosing such *senmongakkō* over **universities** have increased. It is a consequence of that the **credential society** is gradually collapsing and the range of choices has diversified.

【受験戦争】じゅけんせんそう／Jukensensō

　かつては「4当5落」(睡眠時間を4時間にして勉強すれば受かるが、5時間では受からない) などといわれ、その激烈な様を戦争に例えたものでした。しかし日本の**終身雇用制**が崩れ始めるとともに、学歴の重要性も昔ほどではなくなり、入社試験の面接で出身学校を問わない会社も出てきました。今も受験は厳しい競争の中で行われていますが、将来への選択肢が増えていることも事実です。

Examination wars : At one time, it was said, "if you study on four hours of sleep, you pass the university entrance exam, on five hours, you fail", and that intensely pressured situation has been compared to war. However, as Japan's **lifetime employment system** is beginning to collapse, one's academic background is no longer as important as in the past, and companies have emerged that are not asking about one's university in the interview for the company's entrance exam. *Juken* are still carried out in an atmosphere of fierce competition, but the fact is that the range of choices for the future is broadening.

【塾・予備校】じゅく・よびこう／Juku,Yobikō

　学校の勉強を補う民間の教育機関です。日本の学校は一律の内容を一定の速度で教えるため、授業についていけない生徒や、逆に高レベルの学校を目指す生徒は塾や予備校での勉強が必要となります。全国的なチェーン展開をしている大規模校も多く、通信衛星を使った授業を行うなど一大産業分野を形成しています。塾や予備校は、今や公教育を補うものとして不可欠な存在です。

Cram schools / Preparatory schools : These are private educational institutions that supplement regular school study. Because Japanese schools teach uniform contents at a fixed rate, students who are unable to follow the lessons and, conversely, students aiming for high-level schools find it necessary to study at *juku* and *yobikō*. There are numerous large-scale schools that have developed nationwide chains and they are building up a large business sector that features lessons using communications satellites. *Juku* and *yobikō* have now become indispensable as supplements to public education.

【夜間学校】
やかんがっこう／Yakan-gakkō

中・高・**大学**で働きながら学習を続けたい人のための定時制の学校ですが、さまざまな境遇の人に対する教育機関としても機能しています。例えば夜間中学を例にとると、第2次大戦のため十分な教育が受けられなかった人々に再教育の機会を提供してきましたし、最近は、日本に帰国した中国残留孤児や在日韓国人が夜間中学で日本語を勉強することも多くなっています。

Night schools : These are part-time schools at junior highs, high schools and **universities** for people who want to continue their learning while working, and they function as educational institutions for people in all sorts of situations. Take, for example, junior high night school. It offers retraining for people who were not able to receive sufficient education because of the Second World War. In addition, recently many repatriated orphans who had been left behind in China and Koreans living in Japan have studied Japanese in junior high night schools.

【大検】
Daiken／だいけん

大検は「大学入学資格検定試験」の略で、文部省が毎年実施している検定試験です。大学や短大入学のためには高校卒業が資格として必要ですが、高校を卒業できなかった人でも、この試験に合格すれば高校卒業と同等の資格が認定されます。近年は、高校の教育環境に不適応、不満足な生徒が高校を中途退学し、大検を受けて大学進学の道を開こうとする例も増えてきています。

Daiken is an abbreviation of "The University Entrance Qualification Examination" and is carried out every year by the Ministry of Education. High school graduation is necessary as a requirement to enter university or junior college, but even those who did not graduate from high school can, by passing this exam, be recognized as having an equal qualification as high school graduation. In recent years, students who are unable to adjust to and are unsatisfied with the high school educational environment drop out, and instances of trying to open up the road to higher learning by taking *daiken* are increasing.

【英語教育】 Eigokyōiku えいごきょういく

　日本では、中学1年から英語教育が始まり、**大学**を卒業するまでに最低8年間は英語を学ぶことになりますが、一向に英語を話せるようにはなりません。その原因のひとつは読解力中心の教育にあります。さらに日本語と英語は系統の違う言語であり、構造にも語いにも共通性がないために習得が困難なのです。しかし近年は国際共通語としての英語でコミュニケートする必要性が高まり、聞き話す英語力が求められています。従って、英会話を学ぶ学生や社会人が急速に増え、民間の「英会話学校」が台頭してきました。中学や高校、大学でもコミュニケーションを主眼とした英語教育に力を入れるようになってきました。

English-language education : In Japan, *eigo kyōiku* begins in the first year of junior high and, until one graduates **university**, English is studied for at least 8 years—but not at all so that it can be spoken. One reason for this is that instruction focuses on the skill of reading. In addition, because Japanese and English belong to different families of languages with no commonalities neither in structure nor words. However, in recent years the necessity has increased to communicate in English as the international language and the ability to listen to and speak English is in demand. Accordingly, students and adults who study English conversation have increased rapidly, and private "English conversation schools" have become prominent. Junior highs, high schools and universities are also now putting strength into English-language education which is making communication its chief aim.

政治

【憲法】
Kenpō
けんぽう

　日本では、**明治時代**（1868〜1912）に憲法の制定や国会の開設を求める自由民権運動が起こり、1889年に大日本帝国憲法が制定されました。しかしこの憲法では主権は**天皇**にあり、人権を尊重する近代憲法とはいえないものでした。現行の**日本国憲法**は、敗戦直後の1946年、アメリカの要請のもとに制定されました。主権は国民にあり、**天皇**は日本国の象徴であるとする**象徴天皇制**と、軍隊の保持や国の交戦権を認めない**恒久平和主義**が大きな特徴です。しかし、憲法は政治状況によって都合のいいように解釈され、現実には自衛隊という軍隊が存在するなどの矛盾を抱えており、憲法自体を見直そうとする動きも出始めています。

The constitution : In Japan during the **Meiji Period**(1868-1912), the Freedom and People's Right Movement arose calling for the enactment of a constitution and the establishment of the Diet, and in 1889 the Constitution of the Empire of Japan was enacted. However, sovereignty in this constitution rested with the **Emperor**, so it was not a modern constitution respecting human rights. The present **Constitution of Japan** was enacted at the request of the United States in 1946 immediately after Japan lost the war. Sovereignty rested with the people, its chief characteristics being the **Emperor as a symbol**, by which the **Emperor** stands as a symbol of the nation of Japan, and **permanent pacifism**, which does not approve maintaining an army or the right of the nation to wage war. However, the constitution is conveniently interpreted depending on political conditions, and in fact it contains the contradiction of having military forces called the Self-Defense Forces; there is an emerging movement to take another look at the constitution itself.

【三権分立】

さんけんぶんりつ
Sanken-bunritsu

国家権力を行政・立法・司法に分けて、互いに牽制させることで権力の濫用を防止しようとする三権分立の制度は、日本でも採用されています。現行の**日本国憲法**でそうであるだけではなく、**明治時代**（1868〜1912）の大日本帝国憲法下でも三権は分立していました。しかし、行政部が一部の司法権を有していたり、**天皇**の統治権が三権の上位に設定されていたりしていたため、不完全なものでした。

三権分立の形態は、非常に厳密なアメリカ型と、比較的ゆるやかなイギリス型がありますが、日本はイギリスに似た**議院内閣制**をとっているため、アメリカほど厳格な三権分立制度にはなっていません。

◎日本の統治機構
Japanese Government Organization

立法 国　会	衆議院	
	参議院	
	裁判官弾劾裁判所	
	裁判官訴追委員会	
	国立国会図書館	

総理府	総務庁
法務省	北海道開発庁
外務省	防衛庁
大蔵省	経済企画庁
文部省	科学技術庁
厚生省	環境庁
農林水産省	沖縄開発庁
通商産業省	国土庁
運輸省	国家公安委員会
郵政省	公正取引委員会
労働省	宮内庁
建設省	
自治省	

行政 内　閣	内閣官房	
	内閣法制局	
	人事院	
会計検査院	安全保障会議	

司法 最高裁判所	高等裁判所	地方裁判所	簡易裁判所
		家庭裁判所	

Separation of the three powers [of administration, legislation, and judicature] : The system of *sanken-bunritsu,* which is calculated to prevent the abuse of power by dividing the power of the State into legislative, judicial and administrative functions and allowing mutual checks, has also been adopted in Japan. This is not only true in the existing **Constitution of Japan**; the three powers were also divided in the Constitution of the Imperial Japan of the **Meiji Period**(1868-1912). However, it was imperfect, because the administrative branch had some judicial power and the sovereignty of the **Emperor** was established above the three powers.

The form of *sanken-bunritsu* has very strict U.S. forms and comparatively loose U.K. forms, but because Japan has taken the **parliamentary system of government**, similar to the system in U.K., its *sanken-bunritsu* system is not as strict as in U.S..

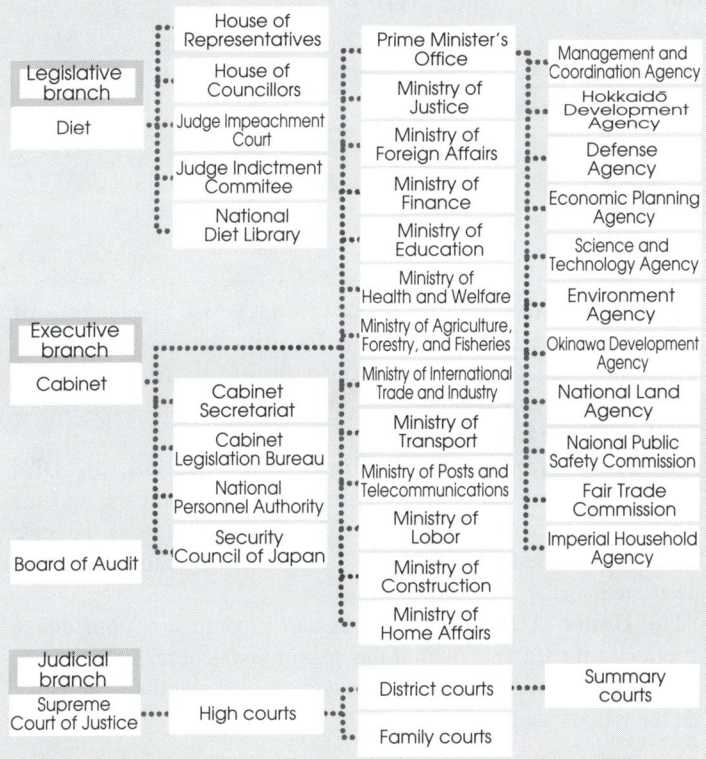

Legislative branch

Diet
- House of Representatives
- House of Councillors
- Judge Impeachment Court
- Judge Indictment Commitee
- National Diet Library

Executive branch

Cabinet
- Cabinet Secretariat
- Cabinet Legislation Bureau
- National Personnel Authority
- Security Council of Japan

Board of Audit

- Prime Minister's Office
- Ministry of Justice
- Ministry of Foreign Affairs
- Ministry of Finance
- Ministry of Education
- Ministry of Health and Welfare
- Ministry of Agriculture, Forestry, and Fisheries
- Ministry of International Trade and Industry
- Ministry of Transport
- Ministry of Posts and Telecommunications
- Ministry of Lobor
- Ministry of Construction
- Ministry of Home Affairs

- Management and Coordination Agency
- Hokkaidō Development Agency
- Defense Agency
- Economic Planning Agency
- Science and Technology Agency
- Environment Agency
- Okinawa Development Agency
- National Land Agency
- Naional Public Safety Commission
- Fair Trade Commission
- Imperial Household Agency

Judicial branch

Supreme Court of Justice — High courts — District courts — Summary courts

Family courts

【内閣】
Naikaku
ないかく

　内閣は国の行政全般を担当します。国内行政、外交、条約の締結、法律案や予算の作成、最高裁判所の長官の任命などが主な仕事となります。

　日本では**議院内閣制**がとられているため、**国会**が国会議員の中から総理大臣を指名し、総理大臣が他の国務大臣を任命します。国務大臣は20名以内で、その過半数が国会議員でなければなりません。

　衆議院は内閣不信任案を提出することができ、これが可決された場合は、内閣は総辞職するか、あるいは**衆議院**を解散して、国民の意思を問うことになります。

The Cabinet : *Naikaku* is in charge of all aspects of administering the country. Its principal work involves domestic affairs, diplomacy, concluding treaties, drafting legislative proposals and budgets, and appointing the chief justice of the Supreme Court.

In Japan, adopting the **parliamentary system**, the **Diet** designates the prime minister from within its members, and the prime minister appoints the other State ministers. Among the State ministers, limited to 20 or less in number, the majority must be Diet members.

The **House of Representatives** can present non-confidence motion in the Cabinet, and, if this passes, *naikaku* resigns enmasse or the **House of Representatives** is dissolved and the issue is put to the will of the people.

◎内閣
Cabinet

総理大臣	Prime Minister
副総理*	Deputy Prime Minister*
外務大臣	Minister of Foreign Affairs
法務大臣	Minister of Justice
大蔵大臣	Minister of Finance
文部大臣	Minister of Education
厚生大臣	Minister of Health and Welfare
農林水産大臣	Minister of Agriculture, Forestry and Fisheries
通商産業大臣	Minister of International Trade and Industry
運輸大臣	Minister of Transport
郵政大臣	Minister of Posts and Telecommunications
労働大臣	Minister of Labor
建設大臣	Minister of Construction
自治大臣	Minister of Home Affairs
官房長官	Chief Cabinet Secretary
総務庁長官	Director General of the Management and Coordination Agency
北海道・沖縄開発庁長官	Director General of the Hokkaido/Okinawa Development Agency
防衛庁長官	Director General of the Defence Agency
経済企画庁長官	Director General of the Economic Planning Agency
科学技術庁長官	Director General of the Science and Technology Agency
環境庁長官	Director General of the Environment Agency
国土庁長官	Director General of the National Land Agency

＊注：必要に応じて設置　Note : Set up at need

◎歴代内閣
List of Cabinets(since 1945)
自治省/Ministry of Home Affairs

東久邇	Higashikuni	8/17/1945〜	福田	Fukuda	12/24/1976〜
幣原	Shidehara	10/9/1945〜	大平	Ōhira	2/7/1978〜
吉田	Yoshida	5/22/1946〜	鈴木	Suzuki	7/17/1980〜
片山	Katayama	5/24/1947〜	中曽根	Nakasone	1/27/1982〜
芦田	Ashida	3/10/1948〜	竹下	Takeshita	11/6/1987〜
吉田	Yoshida	10/15/1948〜	宇野	Uno	6/3/1989〜
鳩山	Hatoyama	12/10/1954〜	海部	Kaifu	8/10/1989〜
石橋	Ishibashi	12/23/1956〜	宮沢	Miyazawa	11/5/1991〜
岸	Kishi	2/25/1957〜	細川	Hosokawa	8/9/1993〜
池田	Ikeda	7/19/1960〜			
佐藤	Sato	11/9/1964〜			
田中	Tanaka	7/7/1972〜			
三木	Miki	12/9/1974〜			

【国会】
こっかい
Kokkai

　国会は**衆議院**と**参議院**の2院からなる国家の最高機関であり、唯一の立法機関です。日本は**議院内閣制**であるため、総理大臣を指名するのも国会です。また、**内閣**が作成した国家予算の審議と議決も行います。

　どちらの議院の議員も国民の直接選挙によって選出され、任期は衆議院議員が4年、参議院議員は6年です。**参議院**では3年ごとに議員の半数が改選されます。

　衆議院は任期も短く、解散もあるので、国民の意思をより強く反映するものとして、**参議院**より強い権限が与えられています。

The Diet : *Kokkai* consists of two chambers, the **House of Representatives** and **House of Councillors**, and is the highest organ of state and the only legislative one. Because Japan adopts the **parliamentary system of government**, *kokkai* designates the prime minister. Also, it deliberate and decide the national budget prepared by the **Cabinet**.

　The members of both houses are elected by direct vote of the people. Their terms of service are four years for representatives and six for councillors. In the **House of Councillors**, half the members are elected every three years.

　The **House of Representatives** has a shorter term of service and can be dissolved; hence, regarded as more strongly reflecting the will of the people, it has more authority than the **House of Councillors**.

【選挙】
Senkyo
せんきょ

　明治時代（1868～1912）には、選挙権は一定額以上の税金を納めている25歳以上の成人男子のみに与えられていました。1925年には成人男子すべてに選挙権を与える男子普通選挙法が成立しましたが、女性に選挙権が認められたのは、第2次世界大戦後のことです。現在では**憲法**によって、20歳以上の成年者による普通選挙が保障されており、被選挙権は公職選挙法によって、衆議院議員と都道府県知事が30歳以上、それ以外は25歳以上になると与えられます。

　近年では、たび重なる汚職などにより国民の政治不信が高まったため、政権交代がしやすいように、中選挙区制から小選挙区制へと選挙制度が改められました。

Elections : In the **Meiji Period**(1868-1912), the right to vote was granted only to adult men above the age of 25 who paid more than the fixed amount of tax. In 1925, the Universal Manhood Suffrage Law was enacted granting the right to vote to all adult males, but the right to vote for women was legalized only after the Second World War. At present, universal suffrage is guaranteed by the **constitution** for all adults from the age of 20; eligibility to stand for election, according to the Public Office Election Law, is granted to those over 30 to be members of the House of Representatives and to be a prefectural governor, and to those over 25 for all other offices.

In recent years, instances of corruption have piled up and the people's distrust of politics has heightened; consequently, the election system has been reformed from medium-size constituency system to small one to make for easier transitions of political power.

政府 政治改革法案を国会提出

【政治改革】
Seiji-kaikaku
せいじかいかく

　1955年以降1993年まで、日本の政治は自由民主党がほぼ政権を独占してきました。その間、**高度経済成長政策**により、日本は戦後の荒廃から立ち直り奇跡的な復興を遂げました。一方、1党が政権を独占してきたために政界・官界・財界が癒着し、汚職がはびこるようになったのです。

　1993年、これに対する国民の批判が強まると、自民党から分裂した新党と他の野党とが連合を組み、**選挙**で勝利して連立内閣を組織しました。この**内閣**の下で選挙制度改革、政治献金の規制を内容とする政治改革が実行されました。このような動きは、冷戦が終結し、世界が新しい秩序を模索して激しく動いている状況に対応しています。

Political reform : From 1955 to 1993, Japanese politics were dominated by the Liberal Democratic Party. During that time, with the **policy of high economic growth**, Japan stood up from the postwar devastation and achieved a miraculous recovery. Meanwhile, one party had been monopolizing political power, creating a giver-receiver relationship between the political, bureaucratic and financial worlds, and corruption became rampant. In 1993, when the people's criticism against this strengthened, the Japan New Party, which had split from the Liberal Democratic Party, and other opposition parties formed an alliance, won an **election**, and organized a coalition cabinet. Under this **Cabinet**, political reform, consisting of reform of electoral system and regulation of political contributions, was put into effect. Such actions are corresponding to the vigorously changing situation of the cold war ending and the world grouping for a new order.

経済・経営

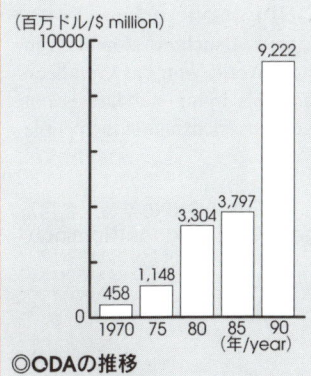

(百万ドル/$ million)

1970	75	80	85	90
458	1,148	3,304	3,797	9,222

(年/year)

◎ODAの推移
Change in ODA

DAC（開発援助委員会）
DAC=(Development Assistance Committee)

日本の政府開発援助（ODA）額は世界第1位です。しかしODA以外にも、日本の経済力に見合った対外援助が世界中から求められています。

Official Development Assistance : Official Development Assistance (ODA) of Japan is the highest in the world. However, foreign aids besides ODA that match Japan's economic power is being required from all over the world.

【政府開発援助】

Seifu-kaihatsu-enjo
せいふかいはつえんじょ

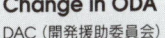

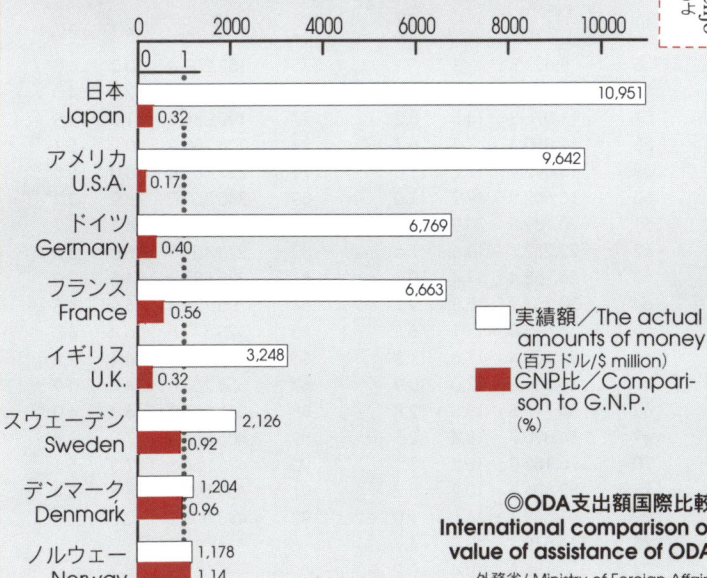

	実績額	GNP比
日本 Japan	10,951	0.32
アメリカ U.S.A.	9,642	0.17
ドイツ Germany	6,769	0.40
フランス France	6,663	0.56
イギリス U.K.	3,248	0.32
スウェーデン Sweden	2,126	0.92
デンマーク Denmark	1,204	0.96
ノルウェー Norway	1,178	1.14

□ 実績額／The actual amounts of money (百万ドル/$ million)

■ GNP比／Comparison to G.N.P. (%)

◎ODA支出額国際比較
International comparison of value of assistance of ODA

外務省/ Ministry of Foreign Affairs

【国民総生産】
Kokumin sō-seisan
こくみんそうせいさん

日本のGNPは、世界の最高水準にあります。第2次大戦で壊滅的な打撃を受けながら、ここまで発展してきたスピードは奇跡とさえいわれました。しかし、国民の生活レベルは必ずしもこれに比例していません。生活者重視の改革が、これからの政府の課題となっています。

Gross National Product (GNP) : GNP of Japan is the highest in the world. The speed of such development, in spite of crushing defeat in the Second World War, has even been called a miracle. However, the people's living standard is not necessarily in proportion to this. Reforms focusing on the people are task of the government from now on.

◎日本のGNPの推移（名目）
Change in GNP of Japan(Nominal)
経済企画庁「国民経済計算」
Economic Planning Agency
"Report on National Accounts"

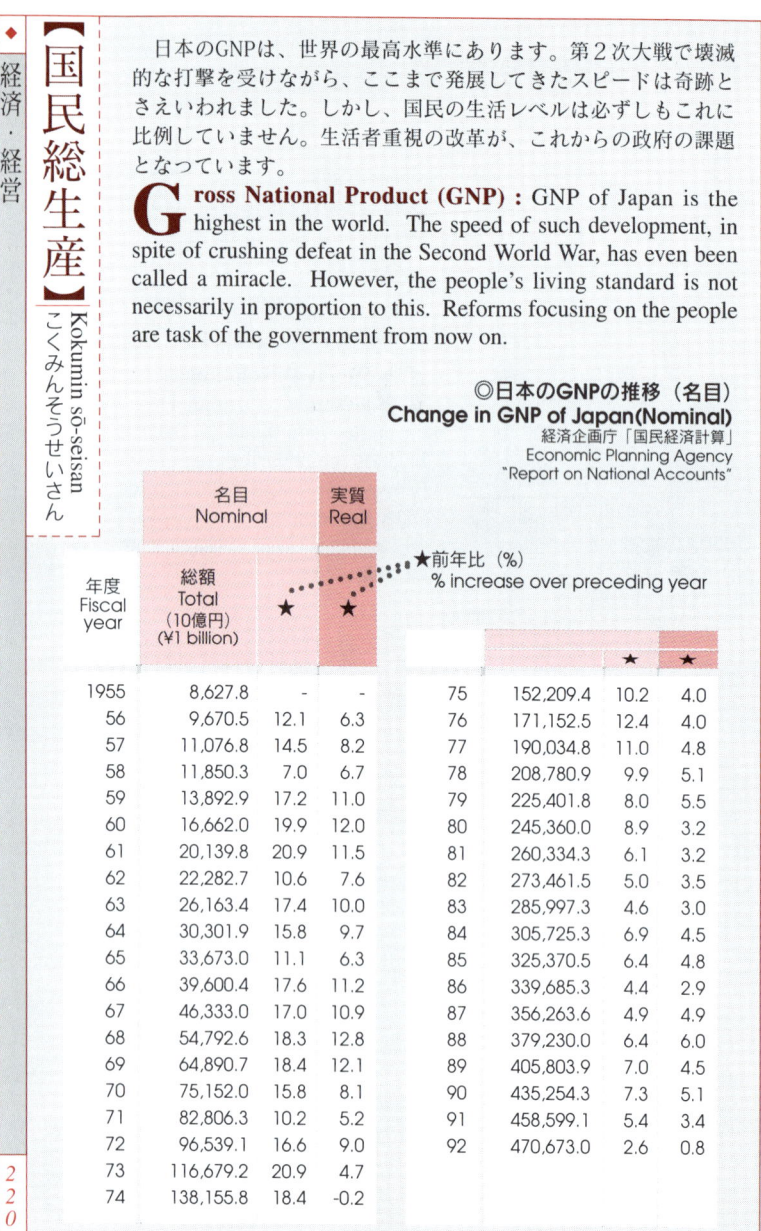

★前年比（％）
% increase over preceding year

年度 Fiscal year	総額 Total (10億円) (¥1 billion) 名目 Nominal	★	★ 実質 Real		年度	総額	★	★
1955	8,627.8	-	-		75	152,209.4	10.2	4.0
56	9,670.5	12.1	6.3		76	171,152.5	12.4	4.0
57	11,076.8	14.5	8.2		77	190,034.8	11.0	4.8
58	11,850.3	7.0	6.7		78	208,780.9	9.9	5.1
59	13,892.9	17.2	11.0		79	225,401.8	8.0	5.5
60	16,662.0	19.9	12.0		80	245,360.0	8.9	3.2
61	20,139.4	20.9	11.5		81	260,334.3	6.1	3.2
62	22,282.7	10.6	7.6		82	273,461.5	5.0	3.5
63	26,163.4	17.4	10.0		83	285,997.3	4.6	3.0
64	30,301.9	15.8	9.7		84	305,725.3	6.9	4.5
65	33,673.0	11.1	6.3		85	325,370.5	6.4	4.8
66	39,600.4	17.6	11.2		86	339,685.3	4.4	2.9
67	46,333.0	17.0	10.9		87	356,263.6	4.9	4.9
68	54,792.6	18.3	12.8		88	379,230.0	6.4	6.0
69	64,890.7	18.4	12.1		89	405,803.9	7.0	4.5
70	75,152.0	15.8	8.1		90	435,254.3	7.3	5.1
71	82,806.3	10.2	5.2		91	458,599.1	5.4	3.4
72	96,539.1	16.6	9.0		92	470,673.0	2.6	0.8
73	116,679.2	20.9	4.7					
74	138,155.8	18.4	-0.2					

【貿易】
Bōeki
ぼうえき

　日本は地下資源がほとんどないので、原材料を輸入して製品を輸出する貿易立国です。しかし日本が輸出に努力すればするほど貿易の黒字が増えてしまうこととなり、日本の輸出に世界各国が規制を加えるようになりました。同時に日本の非関税障壁を撤廃する要求も高まったのです。

Trade : Japan, with few underground resources, is a country built on the business of importing raw materials and exporting manufactured products. However, the more Japan puts effort into export, the more the trade surplus increases, resulting in countries around the world putting restrictions on Japan's exports. At the same time, there is a growing demand to remove Japan's non-tariff barriers.

◎輸出額、輸入額/Value of exports, value of imports

経済企画庁「経済白書」1992年
Economic Planning Agency "Economic Survey of Japan" 1992

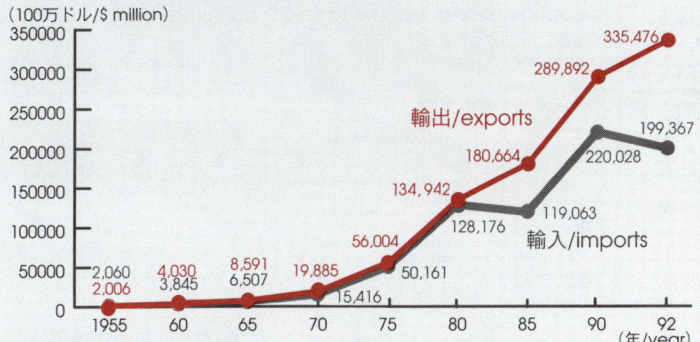

(100万ドル/$ million)

輸出/exports

輸入/imports

◎貿易収支/Trade balance

日本銀行「国際収支統計月報」
Bank of Japan "Balance of Payments Monthly"
(100万ドル/$ million)

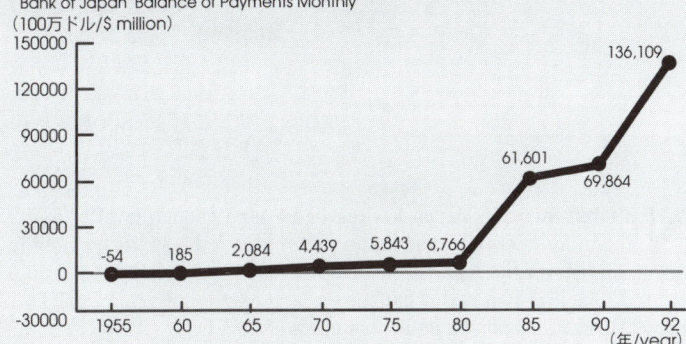

◎1人当たり国民所得の推移
Per capita national income

経済企画庁「国民経済計算年報」
Economic Planning Agency
"Annual Report of National Accounts"

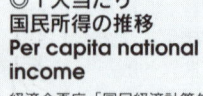

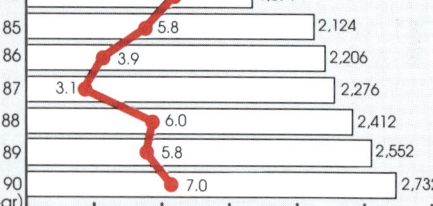

●—● 前年比
% increase over preceding year

□ 円表示/In yen

年/year	円表示(¥1,000)	前年比(%)
1965	266	10.4
70	571	16.8
75	1,085	9.6
80	1,671	7.1
85	2,124	5.8
86	2,206	3.9
87	2,276	3.1
88	2,412	6.0
89	2,552	5.8
90	2,732	7.0

◎OECD諸国の1人当たり国民所得（1990年）
Per capita national income of OECD countries(1990)

経済企画庁「国民経済計算年報」
Economic Planning Agency"Annual Report on National Accounts"

1人当たり国民所得（ドル）
Per capita national income (dollars)

スイス／Switzerland	29,305
ルクセンブルク／Luxembourg	25,403
スウェーデン／Sweden	19,426
フィンランド／Finland	19,103
日本／Japan	19,035
デンマーク／Denmark	18,417
ノルウェー／Norway	17,845
ドイツ／Germany	17,461
アメリカ／U.S.A.	17,379
カナダ／Canada	15,770
フランス／France	15,721
ベルギー／Belgium	15,490
オーストリア／Austria	14,997
オランダ／Netherlands	14,822
イタリア／Italy	14,810

【国民所得】
Kokumin-shotoku
こくみんしょとく

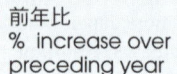
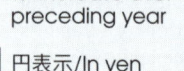
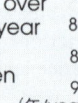

日本は、今や経済大国といわれるほど経済的な実力は世界でトップクラスですが、1人当たりの国民所得も順調に伸びてきました。1990年で10年前の2.5倍にも増加しています。これをOECD加盟各国と比較してみると、第5位となります。

National income : Japan has reached a high enough level of world economic strength that it can now be called a major economic power, and per capita national income has also been steadily increasing. As of 1990, it is two and a half times larger than ten years ago. This places Japan fifth among member countries of OECD.

【高度成長期】

Kōdo-seichōki
こうどせいちょうき

　高度成長期とは、1950年代から1970年代の十数年間の、経済成長率が年平均10パーセントを越えた時期をさします。この時期の日本では、技術革新により新産業が生まれ、生産技術が飛躍的に向上する一方、労働力にも恵まれ、生産された製品は国外へ大量に輸出されています。そして高度成長期を境に、日本の国民生活は大衆的規模で上昇しました。政府の所得倍増計画が実現し、家庭には電化製品がつぎつぎに導入されるなど、生活も大きく変化したのです。しかし年月が経つにつれ、都市への人口集中と農村の過疎化、環境破壊や公害が大きな問題となり始め、1973年のオイル・ショックとともに、高度成長期は終焉を迎えました。

Period of high economic growth : *Kōdo-seichōki* refers to the period of some 20 years from the 1950s to the 1970s when the rate of Japan's economic growth exceeded an average of ten percent per year. During this period of time, whole new industries were born through technical innovation, and manufacturing techniques improved by leaps and bounds while there was also a strong labor force, and manufactured goods were exported in large numbers to foreign countries. In *kōdo-seichōki* the lives of the Japanese people improved on a mass scale. The income-doubling program by government was realized and, with the introduction of electrical products one after another into people's homes, their lives changed significantly. However, as time passed, the concentration of population in the cities, the depopulation of farming villages, and environmental destruction and pollution started to become large problems, and, together with the Oil Crisis of 1973, *kōdo-seichōki* met its final moments.

【バブル経済の崩壊】
──けいざいのほうかい／Baburu-keizai no hokai

　国土の狭い日本では、土地が最も確実な資産と見なされています。バブル経済とはこうした「土地中心主義」を基礎にした、「実態の価値以上に膨らんだ（泡）経済」を指します。1980年代後半の日本は、まさにバブル経済全盛期でした。銀行の過剰融資により地価が急騰、さらに企業がその土地を担保に借金して株に投資したため、株価も急騰したのです。しかし90年代に入ると、金融引き締めや土地融資の規制強化などで地価上昇に歯止めがかけられ、バブル経済も崩壊しました。首都圏の地価は下落へと転じ、株価も低迷するなど、かつて日本を支配した「地価も株価も下がることはない」という神話を覆したのです。

The collapse of the "Bubble Economy": In land-scarce Japan, real property is regarded as the most certain asset. The "Bubble Economy" indicates "an economy swollen beyond its actual value," which is based on "land centrism." The second half of the 1980s was truly the golden age of the "Bubble Economy." Land prices rose sharply through excessive bank financing, and furthermore businesses secured loans against that land and invested in stocks; hence stock prices too rose sharply. However, in the 1990s the brakes were applied to the rise in land prices by such measures as tightening credit and strengthening control over financing, and the "Bubble Economy" collapsed. Land prices around Tokyo made a downward shift and stock prices also hovered low, and the myth that "neither land nor stocks will fall," which once controlled Japan, was disproved.

【日本的経営】
Nihonteki-keiei
にほんてきけいえい

　その特質を3つ挙げると、**終身雇用制**、**年功序列**、**企業別組合**となるでしょう。欧米では労働力や経営力などの機能を雇用するのに対し、日本では人間の能力のすべてを雇用すると考えるため、従業員は1つの企業に**定年**まで勤務することが前提となり、勤続年数に応じて賃金や地位も上がっていきます。また、企業内部に組織された組合も、労使間の共存共栄にうまく働き、これらが一体となって従業員の企業に対する**忠誠心**が培われ、組織も円滑に運営されてきたのです。日本の経済的繁栄にはこれらの特質が大きく貢献したとされています。

Japanese-style management : The three principal elements of Japanese management are probably **lifetime employment system**, the **seniority system** and **company-based unions**. In contrast to Europe and the United States, where people are employed for their labor and management functions, in Japan people are employed for their total capabilities. A premise for employees, therefore, is to work until the **mandatory retirement age** at one company, with salary and rank going up in accordance with the number of years one works there. The labor unions, too, which are organized within the company, work well in the co-existence and co-prosperity between labor and management —working as one body—and this fosters employee's **loyalty** to the company and makes for smooth management of the organization. These kinds of special features have contributed to Japan's economic prosperity.

【食費】 Shokuhi しょくひ

日本の家計の総支出に対する食費の割合は、ヨーロッパとはほぼ同水準ですが、アメリカよりは高くなっています。

日本人の食事の内容は、女性の社会進出や独身者の増加によって、外食や調理食品の割合が高くなってきています。

Food expenses: The ratio of the food expense to the whole family budget is almost at the same level as that of Europeans' but higher than that of Americans'.

Regarding the substance of what Japanese eat, due to participation of woman to society and the increasing number of single persons, the percentage of eating out and eating prepared foods is getting high.

◎食品物価の国際比較
International comparison of food expense

…東京での小売価格を100とした場合
…measured by taking retail prices in Tokyo as 100.

経済企画庁「物価レポート」／Economic Planning Agency "Price Report"

注：1 ドル＝129円で計算（1990年）
Note : measured in the exchange rate of US$1=¥ 129(1990)

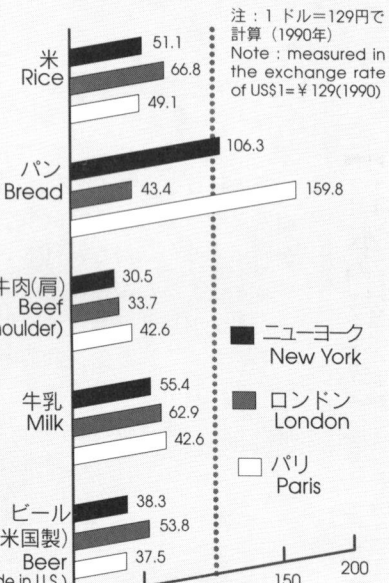

米 Rice — 51.1 / 66.8 / 49.1

パン Bread — 106.3 / 43.4 / 159.8

牛肉(肩) Beef (shoulder) — 30.5 / 33.7 / 42.6

牛乳 Milk — 55.4 / 62.9 / 42.6

ビール（米国製）Beer (made in U.S.) — 38.3 / 53.8 / 37.5

■ ニューヨーク New York
■ ロンドン London
□ パリ Paris

0　50　100　150　200

◎**食費における外食・調理食品の割合の変化**
Change in the percentage of eating out and eating prepared foods in the whole food expense

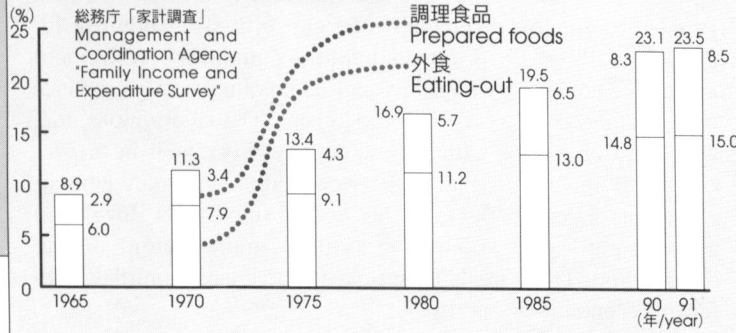

(%)

総務庁「家計調査」
Management and Coordination Agency "Family Income and Expenditure Survey"

調理食品 Prepared foods
外食 Eating-out

	1965	1970	1975	1980	1985	90	91
合計	8.9	11.3	13.4	16.9	19.5	23.1	23.5
調理食品	2.9	3.4	4.3	5.7	6.5	8.3	8.5
外食	6.0	7.9	9.1	11.2	13.0	14.8	15.0

(年/year)

東京の物価は食品以外の分野でも、家賃、エネルギー・水道、被服などの分野で割高になっています。東京の方が安いものもありますが、海外旅行が一般的になってきたことなどから、格差を強く実感する人が増えてきています。

International comparison of commodity prices : Commodity prices in **Tokyo** are expensive in fields of house rent, energy, water supply, and clothes, in addition to foods. Some commodities are cheaper in **Tokyo**; however, as **trips abroad** becomes popular, there are increasing numbers of people who strongly realize the difference.

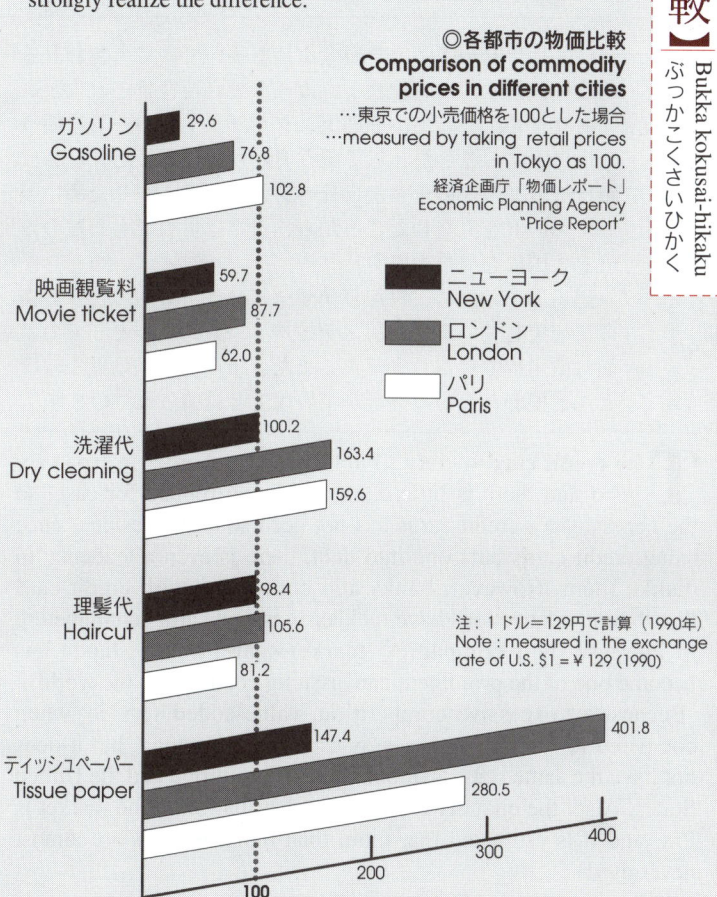

◎各都市の物価比較
Comparison of commodity prices in different cities
…東京での小売価格を100とした場合
…measured by taking retail prices in Tokyo as 100.
経済企画庁「物価レポート」
Economic Planning Agency "Price Report"

■ ニューヨーク New York
■ ロンドン London
□ パリ Paris

注：1ドルは129円で計算（1990年）
Note : measured in the exchange rate of U.S. $1 = ¥ 129 (1990)

ガソリン Gasoline
29.6
76.8
102.8

映画観覧料 Movie ticket
59.7
87.7
62.0

洗濯代 Dry cleaning
100.2
163.4
159.6

理髪代 Haircut
98.4
105.6
81.2

ティッシュペーパー Tissue paper
147.4
401.8
280.5

0　100　200　300　400

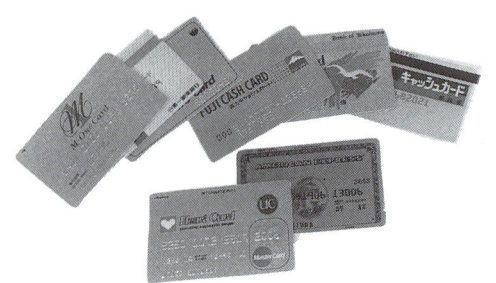

【カード社会】——しゃかい Kādo-shakai.

日本は治安がよいので現金を持ち歩いていても奪われる危険性が低く、クレジット・カードの必要性はそれほど高くありませんでした。その上、クレジット・カードを使うのは借金することだとして厭う風潮もありました。しかし、銀行や流通関係の企業が自社のシェアを拡大するために競ってカードを乱発したことから、日本は世界でも有数のカード大国になったのです。

過当競争のため、付加価値サービスは諸外国に比べて格段に充実していますが、ステイタス・シンボルとしての価値は欧米程ではありません。また、市場流通量は低く、ほとんど使われないカードが半数以上と見積られています。

The credit card society : Public peace and order in Japan are good and there is little danger of being robbed for cash, so the necessity for credit cards has not been so high. Besides, since using credit cards puts one into debt, there is even a tendency to dislike them. However, banks and companies with credit card distribution connections have recklessly issued cards in competing to increase their companies' market share; hence, Japan has become one of the prominent card-issuing countries in the world.

Because of excessive competition, value-added service, when compared to foreign countries, is especially thorough, but it does not have the same status symbol value as in Europe and the United States. Also, the quantity of cards for distribution in the market is low, and it is estimated that more than half the cards are almost never used.

【カード発行枚数】

Kado hakkō-maisū
——はっこうまいすう

　クレジット・カードは、金融・流通関連各社が競って利用者の拡大に励んだため、急速に普及しました。特に若い世代の使用者の教育が不十分なことなどから、多重債務を抱え込んで自己破産に陥る人も急増しています。

The number of credit cards issued : With financial institutions and distribution companies competitively making efforts to increase users, credit cards have rapidly spread. However, particularly due to ignorance, some of the young generation of users, have made multiple obligations and end up in bankruptcy.

◎クレジットカードの発行枚数と自己破産件数
The number of credit cards issued and self bankruptcy cases

…85年あたりの自己破産件数の多くは、サラ金*利用で債務返済不能になったもの。

…Most bankruptcy cases around 1985 are caused by insolvency of obligations due to repeated use of *sarakin*.

サラ金：サラリーマン金融。無担保で金を借りられるが高利なため、負債を返済できずに破産する利用者が1984年ごろを中心に続出した。
Sarakin : A consumer credit business catering to wage workers. Centering around 1984, bankruptcy of users "who could not fulfill obligations" occurred one after another.

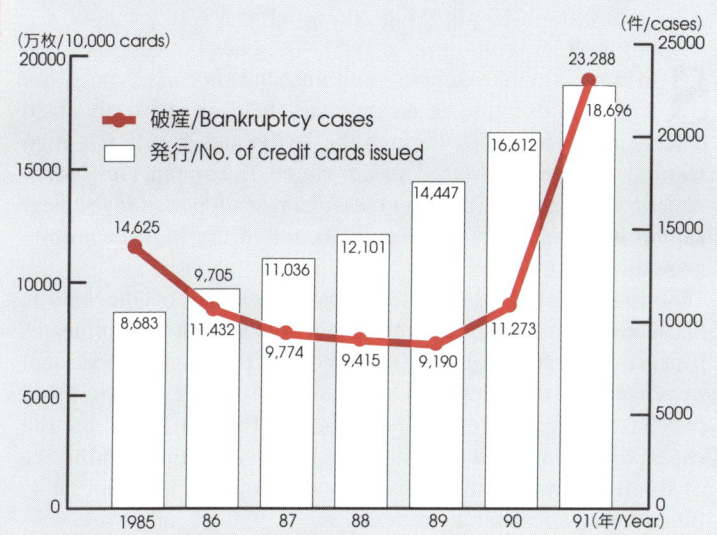

（万枚/10,000 cards） （件/cases）

- 破産/Bankruptcy cases
- 発行/No. of credit cards issued

年/Year	発行	破産
1985	8,683	14,625
86	11,432	9,705
87	9,774	11,036
88	9,415	12,101
89	9,190	14,447
90	11,273	16,612
91	18,696	23,288

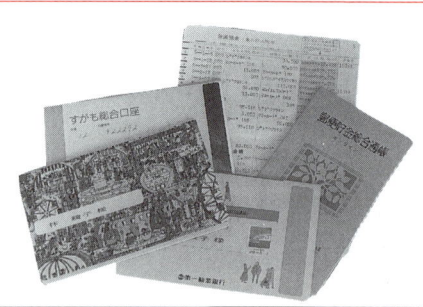

【貯蓄】
Chochiku
ちょちく

　日本の家計の貯蓄率は近年漸減傾向にあるものの、1960年代から70年代を通じては約20パーセントを維持し、現在も欧米先進国と比較して高い水準にあります。この貯蓄率の高さが投資資金の支えとなり、**高度成長**を助ける要因にもなりました。

　日本人の貯蓄率が高いのは、病気や災害時、あるいは老後の生活において、社会保障に対する不安が強いことと、子供の教育費や住宅の建設・購入費が非常に高額になるという事情があるからだと考えられています。また、韓国や台湾の貯蓄率も非常に高いことから、質素倹約を重んじる儒教的価値観の影響も少なくないと考えられます。

Savings : The rate of household financial *chochiku*, which has tended to decrease in recent years, held steady at about 20 percent from the 1960s through the 1970s and is still at a high standard when compared to advanced European and North American countries. This high *chochiku* rate supported investment capital and even became a causal factor of the **high economic growth.**

　The reason for the Japanese people's high rate of *chochiku* is because there is strong concern about social security in times of illness, accident or old age and because there are educational expenses for children and extremely high construction and purchase expenditures for one's home. In addition, since the *chochiku* rate in Korea and Taiwan is also quite high, the influence of Confucian values that respect simple frugality must not be so little on the *chochiku* rate in Japan.

【財テク】
Zaiteku
ざいてく

　財テクとは「財務テクノロジー」の略称です。これは「資金を証券投資や不動産などで運用して利益を上げること」を意味し、1986年ごろから一般化しました。**円高不況**の進展によって設備投資に消極的になった日本企業は、余剰資金を有価証券や土地に積極的に投資し、配当金や売却金で利益を上げようと考えたのです。

　この「財テクブーム」は企業のみならず個人にも波及し、高利の抵当証券やマンション、首都圏の土地への個人投資が活発に行われました。この過剰な財テクブームが地価高騰の一因になったともいえるでしょう。しかし**バブル経済の崩壊**とともに、財テクブームも一段落したようです。

Financial management : *Zaiteku* is an abbreviation of *zaimu tekunorojii,* which means "Raising profit by utilizing capital for securities investments, real estate and the like" and has been widely used since 1986. Japanese companies conservative about capital investment because of the **recession by yen appreciation** have eagerly invested surplus capital in securities or in real estate and tried to raise profits with money from dividends or sales.

　This *zaiteku* boom has spread not only to companies but to individuals who have vigorously invested in high-yield securities or in apartment houses or land in Tokyo. This excessive *zaiteku* boom can be said to be one cause of the steep increase in land prices. However, the *zaiteku* boom has apparently come to an end with the **collapse of the** "**Bubble Economy**."

【在日外国人】

Zainichi-gaikokujin
ざいにちがいこくじん

1992年には総人口に占める外国人登録者の割合は1.03％となり、5年間で1.3倍になりました。80％近くがアジア出身者、特に韓国・北朝鮮出身者ですが、その割合は低下し南米出身者が増えて14.6％になっています。これはブラジルやペルーの日系人やその家族が帰国、定住したためです。アメリカやオーストラリアなどの移民で作られた国とは違って、日本は外国人の入国管理が厳しく、特に労働目的での入国には厳しい条件を設けています。

Foreigners in Japan : The percentage of foreign residents to the total population was 1.03% as of 1992, which has grown 130% in five years. Nearly 80% of them is people from Asia, especially from South and North Korea, but its ratio was lowered, and people from South America have increased to 14.6%. It is the result of that the second or later generation of Japanese immigrants to Brazil and Peru returned to Japan with their families and settled down. Different from countries built by immigrants, such as the United States or Australia, Japan has a strict entry administration, and has set up strict conditions for entries on working purpose.

◎外国人登録者の推移
Change in foreign residents

法務省/Ministry of Justice

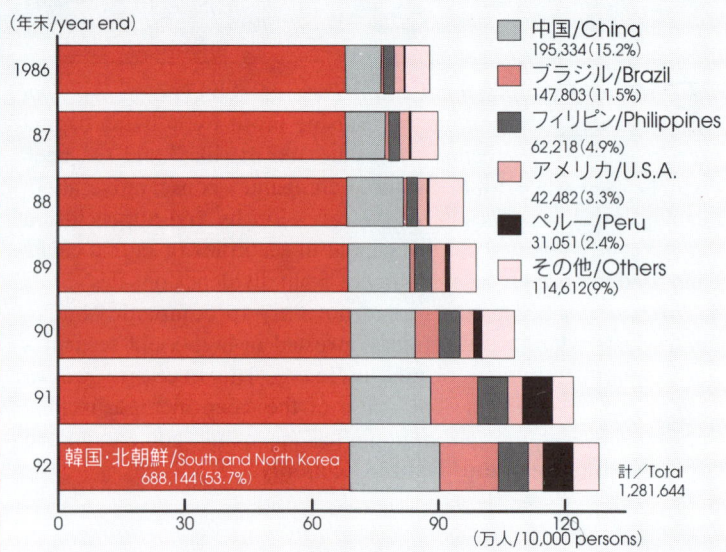

中国/China
195,334 (15.2%)

ブラジル/Brazil
147,803 (11.5%)

フィリピン/Philippines
62,218 (4.9%)

アメリカ/U.S.A.
42,482 (3.3%)

ペルー/Peru
31,051 (2.4%)

その他/Others
114,612 (9%)

韓国・北朝鮮/South and North Korea
688,144 (53.7%)

計/Total
1,281,644

(万人/10,000 persons)

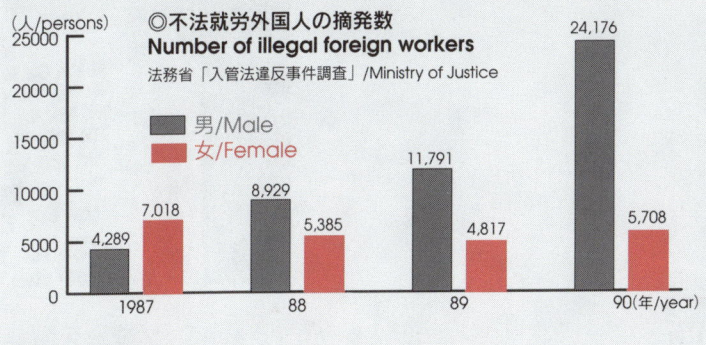

(人/persons)
◎不法就労外国人の摘発数
Number of illegal foreign workers
法務省「入管法違反事件調査」/Ministry of Justice

男/Male
女/Female

	1987	88	89	90(年/year)
男/Male	4,289	8,929	11,791	24,176
女/Female	7,018	5,385	4,817	5,708

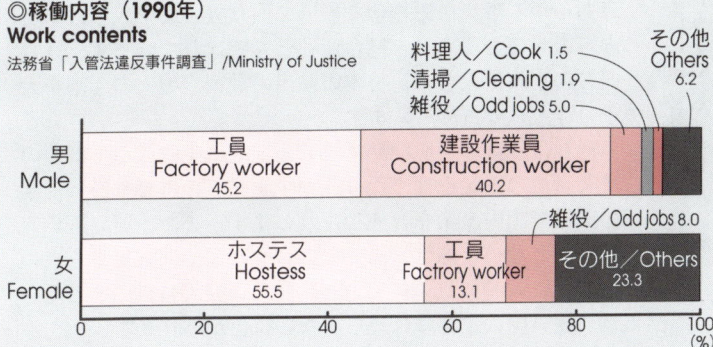

◎稼働内容（1990年）
Work contents
法務省「入管法違反事件調査」/Ministry of Justice

料理人／Cook 1.5
清掃／Cleaning 1.9
雑役／Odd jobs 5.0
その他 Others 6.2

男 Male
工員 Factory worker 45.2
建設作業員 Construction worker 40.2

雑役／Odd jobs 8.0

女 Female
ホステス Hostess 55.5
工員 Factrory worker 13.1
その他／Others 23.3

0　　20　　40　　60　　80　　100(%)

　円が国際的に強い通貨となり、日本で働けば大金が稼げると考える人々が増えています。しかし入国審査が厳しいため、**バブル経済**時代は、観光ビザなどで入国して働き、ビザの期限が切れてもそのまま滞在し続ける不法就労者が急増しました。しかしバブルが崩壊すると失業者が増え、不法就労者も漸減する傾向にあります。

Foreign Workers : Yen has become an internationally strong currency, and there are increasingly more people who think that working in Japan will make it possible to earn a large sum of money. However, because of strict inspections for entry, illegal workers, who entered the country on tourist or other visa for work and stayed after the visa had expired, have rapidly increased during the period of "**Bubble Economy.**" As "Bubble Economy" collapsed and the number of the unemployed grew, illegal workers are gradually decreasing.

【外国人労働者】
がいこくじんろうどうしゃ／Gaikokujin-rōdosha

【商社】
Shōsha
しょうしゃ

　日本の商社は、地球上のあらゆる場所で、あらゆる商品とあらゆる事業をあらゆる形態で取り扱います。その事業内容の多様さゆえに、総合商社とも呼ばれています。総合商社の規模は大きく、日本の輸出の5割、輸入の4割を大手9社だけで占めています。

　商社は外国の資源開発に協力し、それを輸入して国内の産業資源の不足を補ったり、中小企業への融資や海外市場の開拓で国内産業を育成したりします。また、貿易不均衡が問題となった際は、海外との合弁事業や輸入促進を進めるなど、政府の政策に協力し、経済の発展に貢献するという、諸外国の企業には見られない特色があります。

Commercial firms : Japanese *shōsha* do business in all sorts of places around the world with all sorts of goods and enterprises, in all sorts of forms. Because of their diversity within those enterprises, they are called general trading companies(*sōgō shōsha*). The size of general trading companies is such that only nine large companies control 50% of Japan's exports and 40% of the imports.

　Shōsha cooperate in the development of resources in foreign countries, they then import those resources to supplement deficiencies in industrial resources and nurture domestic industries with financing for smaller companies and by cultivating foreign markets. In addition, they also cooperate with government policies and contribute to the development of the nation's economy, a characteristic not evident in other countries' companies; for example, they promote imports and joint ventures with foreign countries when the trade imbalance becomes a problem.

【転勤】 Tenkin てんきん

　日本では、企業が**終身雇用制**をとっていることもあって、社員は企業への帰属意識が強く、家庭の事情より会社の都合を優先させるのが当然だと見なされる傾向にあります。従って、転勤を命じられたらそれを断ることは困難でした。しかし、転勤すると受験を控えた子供には教育上不利になるし、持ち家があれば、不在時の管理もしなければなりません。そのような場合は、父親は妻と子供を残し、単身で勤務地に赴任することになります。家族が別れて生活することには経済的にも精神的にも問題が多いため、**単身赴任**は社会問題にもなっていますが、最近では企業も社員の希望を優先させるなど、対応策をとり始めています。

Change of job location : Business in Japan has the **lifetime employment system** and employees have a strong sense of belonging to the company. The fact that employees prioritize the company over the family tended to be regarded as natural. Accordingly, if one is ordered to do *tenkin*, it is difficult to refuse. However, *tenkin* puts children at a disadvantage with exams approaching, and, if one owns a house, it must be managed in one's absence. In such cases, the father leaves his wife and children behind and sets out to his place of work alone. Because there are a lot of problems, both economic and emotional, in living apart from the family, **taking up one's post apart from one's family** has become a social issue; but recently businesses are making employees' wishes a priority and have begun to deal with the issue.

◎おもな週休制の形態別企業数割合（1991年）
Rate of corporations by basic form of a weekly holiday(1991).
注：調査対象は従業員30人以上の5,200社。
労働省「平成3年賃金労働時間制度等総合調査」による。
Note: Survey on 5,200 corporations
with 30 or more employees.

週休一日半制
a five-and-a-half-day week 1.2%
その他／Others 0.2%

週休1日制
a six-day week
20.4%

全企業数
The total of
corporations.
100%

月一回以上の週休2日制
One or more five-day week per month.
78.2%

【労働時間】
Rōdō-jikan
ろうどうじかん

　日本人は第2次大戦後、壊滅的打撃を受けた経済を復興し、生活を豊かにするために懸命に働きました。そのため、1960年代を中心とする**高度成長期**を経て日本は経済大国に成長しましたが、一方で輸出超過や相変わらずの長時間労働に対しては、他の先進国から仕事中毒だと批判されてきました。そこで政府は完全週休2日制の普及や有給休暇の取得率の向上などで、年間実労働時間を減らす方針を打ち出したのです。**バブル経済の崩壊**後の不景気は、図らずも**時短**を促進する効果がありました。日本の企業戦士たちは突然手にした自由時間に戸惑いながらも、教養講座やボランティア活動に参加するなど、新しい生き方を模索しています。

Working hours : After the Second World War, the Japanese people reconstructed their economy, which had suffered a deadly blow, and desperately worked to enrich their lives. Japan thus passed through the **period of high economic growth** centered in the 1960s and grew into a major economic power. Yet, with respect to the excess in exports and the same long working hours, Japan had been criticized by other advanced countries as being workaholic. Thus, by spreading five-day week and improving the frequency of paid vacations, the government began to hammer out a policy of reducing the actual annual worktime. The recession following the **collapse of the "Bubble Economy"** unintentionally and effectively promoted the **reduction in working hours**. Although bewildered by the freetime that suddenly came into their hands, business warriors in Japan are groping for a new way of living by, for example, taking cultural courses and participating in volunteer activities.

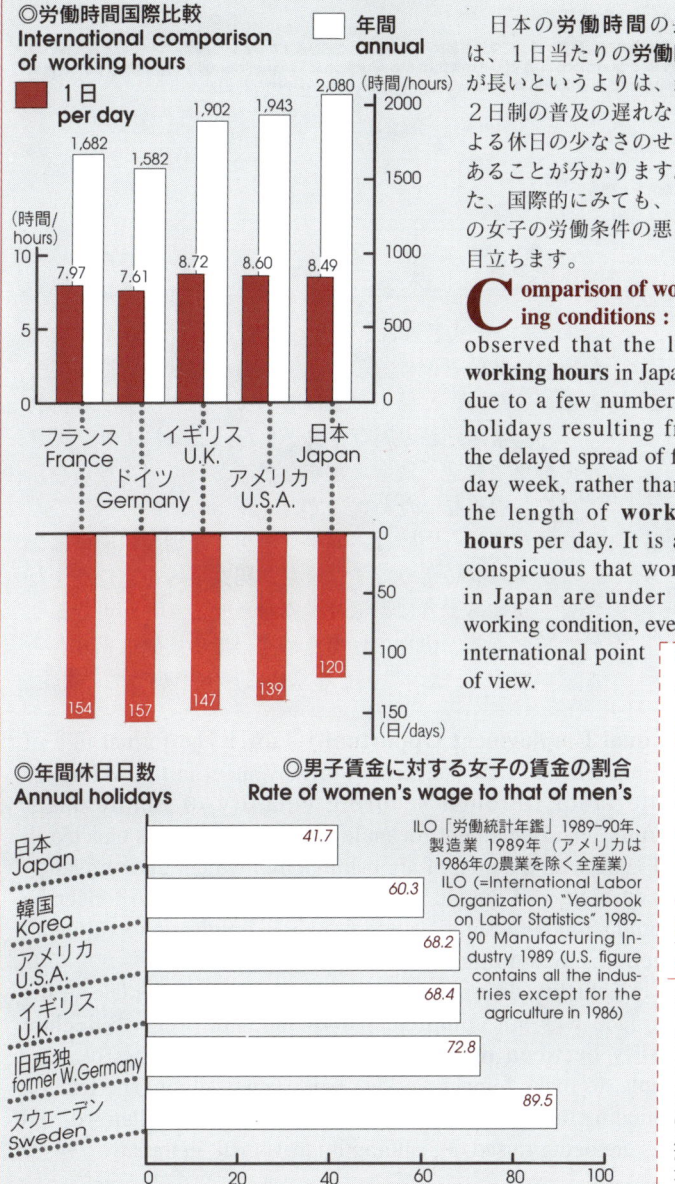

◎労働時間国際比較
International comparison of working hours

☐ 年間 annual
■ 1日 per day

	フランス France	ドイツ Germany	イギリス U.K.	アメリカ U.S.A.	日本 Japan
per day	7.97	7.61	8.72	8.60	8.49
annual	1,682	1,582	1,902	1,943	2,080
days	154	157	147	139	120

◎年間休日日数
Annual holidays

◎男子賃金に対する女子の賃金の割合
Rate of women's wage to that of men's

	%
日本 Japan	41.7
韓国 Korea	60.3
アメリカ U.S.A.	68.2
イギリス U.K.	68.4
旧西独 former W.Germany	72.8
スウェーデン Sweden	89.5

ILO「労働統計年鑑」1989～90年、製造業 1989年（アメリカは1986年の農業を除く全産業）
ILO (=International Labor Organization) "Yearbook on Labor Statistics" 1989-90 Manufacturing Industry 1989 (U.S. figure contains all the industries except for the agriculture in 1986)

　日本の**労働時間**の長さは、1日当たりの**労働時間**が長いというよりは、週休2日制の普及の遅れなどによる休日の少なさのせいであることが分かります。また、国際的にみても、日本の女子の労働条件の悪さが目立ちます。

Comparison of working conditions : It is observed that the long **working hours** in Japan is due to a few numbers of holidays resulting from the delayed spread of five-day week, rather than to the length of **working hours** per day. It is also conspicuous that women in Japan are under bad working condition, even in international point of view.

【労働条件比較】
Rōdō-jōken hikaku
ろうどうじょうけんひかく

◎「あなたの職場では配置・昇進について男女平等は進んだと思いますか」という質問についての回答（1991年）
Answers to a question, "Do you think that the situation for sexual equality regarding personnel positioning and promotion at your work has been improved?"(1991)

東京都「男女雇用平等モニター」調査

女性／Female	思う／Yes 33.2%	思わない／No 66.8%	

男性／Male	思う／Yes 43.1%	思わない／No 53.8%	無回答／Not answer 3.1%

【男女雇用機会均等法】 だんじょこようきかいきんとうほう／Danjo koyō kikai kintōhō

　この法の正式名称は『雇用の分野における男女の均等な機会及び待遇の確保等女子労働者の福祉の増進に関する法律』といい、雇用における男女差別を解消する目的で、1986年4月から施行されました。これにより、従業員の募集・昇進・賃金・**定年**などにおいて男女差別をしてはならなくなったわけです。

　しかしながら実際は、職場での男女差別の撤廃にはなかなか至らないようです。また、**男女平等**をうたうがために、女性労働者にも深夜勤務をさせることが可能になったことなど、男女の仕事をめぐっての軋轢（あつれき）は相変わらず続いており、法の見直しを求める声も上がっています。

Equal Employment Opportunity Law : The formal title of this law is: "Law concerning improvement in the welfare of female labor, through securing equality of employment opportunity and treatment for male and female." It was enacted in April 1986 with the goal of abolishing employment discrimination between male and female. This meant there would no longer be discrimination between male and female in employee recruitment, promotion, pay or **mandatory retirement age**.

　But in actuality discrimination between male and female in the workplace was not completely abolished. In order to declare **equality between male and female**, it became possible, for example, to make female workers work late at night. The friction surrounding men and women at work continued unchallenged, and voices are being raised demanding improvement in the law.

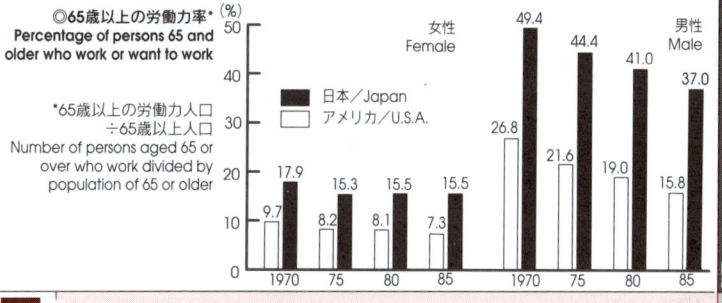

◎65歳以上の労働力率*
Percentage of persons 65 and older who work or want to work

*65歳以上の労働力人口 ÷65歳以上人口
Number of persons aged 65 or over who work divided by population of 65 or older

女性 Female
男性 Male

日本／Japan
アメリカ／U.S.A.

女性 Female: 9.7, 17.9 (1970), 8.2, 15.3 (75), 8.1, 15.5 (80), 7.3, 15.5 (85)
男性 Male: 26.8, 49.4 (1970), 21.6, 44.4 (75), 19.0, 41.0 (80), 15.8, 37.0 (85)

【定年】 Teinen ていねん

　日本のほとんどの企業では、定年制が採用されています。定年制とは、ある定められた年齢に達すれば、本人の意思にかかわらず退職しなければならないという制度です。定年となる年齢は、55歳から60歳というのが一般的で、近年は多少引き上げられる傾向にあります。退職の際は退職金というまとまったお金が支給され、その額は、大企業に何十年も勤めてからの退職であれば2,000万から3,000万ほどになります。

　定年制は、老齢による退職というよりは、**終身雇用制**に対する**雇用調整**の役割を果たすものですが、ふつう取締役以上の重役には定年はありません。

Mandatory retirement age : Most Japanese companies have introduced a *teinen* system, which means that on reaching a certain age a person must retire from work, whether he wants to or not. The age limit is usually from 55 to 60; the average age has tended to rise a little in recent years. On retiring, a lump sum of money, called a retirement allowance, is given, and, if it is a retirement after working for many years at a large company, the amount is as much as ￥20 to ￥30 million.

The role of the *teinen* system is, rather than requiring retirement from work for old age, an **employment adjustment** in connection with the **lifetime employment system**, but executives above the director level generally have no *teinen*.

【自動販売機】
Jidō-hanbaiki
じどうはんばいき

　自動販売機は日本中至るところに普及しています。扱っている商品も、酒類やたばこから花束、下着まで多岐にわたっています。日本はたぶん、世界で最も自動販売機が普及している国でしょう。店が閉まっていても、自動販売機があれば商品を購入できるので、消費者にとっては便利ですし、販売者にとっても人件費や店舗経費がほとんどかかりません。しかし、自動販売機が日本で普及している最大の理由は「安全」にあります。治安が悪ければ、自動販売機は普及する前に破壊されるか盗まれていることでしょう。従って自動販売機の普及は、日本人の現代生活の型と日本経済の発展の秘密の一端を物語っているともいえます。

Vending machines : *Jidō-hanbaiki* are everywhere throughout Japan. Products in them range widely, from alcoholic drinks and cigarettes to flowers and underwear. *Jidō-hanbaiki* are probably more widespread in Japan than anywhere else in the world. Even when stores are closed, items can be purchased from *jidō-hanbaiki*, so they are convenient for consumers; even for sellers there are almost no personnel or store expenses. However, the biggest reason why *jidō-hanbaiki* have proliferated in Japan is "safety." Without public peace and order, *jidō-hanbaiki* would probably have been broken or stolen before becoming so widespread. Thus, the proliferation of *jidō-hanbaiki* tells partly about how the Japanese people presently live their lives and partly about the secret of the development of the Japanese economy.

日本の象徴

【天皇】 Tennō てんのう

　天皇は、**日本国憲法**で「日本および日本国民統合の象徴である」と規定されています。現在の明仁天皇は、紀元前660年に即位したとされる初代の神武天皇から数えて125代目の天皇に当たります。この間、天皇の役割は実権者であったり名目上の最高地位者であったりしました。1889年（明治22年）に公布された明治憲法（大日本帝国憲法）で、政治権力と軍事権力を持つ元首とされていた天皇は、第2次大戦の敗戦後に施行された**日本国憲法**により、その権力を失いました。以来、現在に至るまで、天皇は、国家的な儀礼としての国事行為のみを行い、国政に関する機能は持たないというシンボルとしての存在となっています。

The Emperor : In the **Constitution of Japan**, it is stipulated that "the Emperor shall be the symbol of the State and of the unity of the people." The current *tennō*, Akihito, is the 125th *tennō*, counting from Jinmu *Tennō*, who was the first to be enthroned in 660 B.C.. In this span, the role of *tennō* was at times one of real power, at times only the nominal sovereign. In the Meiji Constitution (the Constitution of the Empire of Japan) which was proclaimed in 1889 (Meiji 22), *tennō* was made the chief of state with political and militaly power; but he lost that power with the **Constitution of Japan** which went into effect following the defeat in the Second World War. From then until now, *tennō* exists as a symbol without function in the administration of government and only carries out affairs of state as national ceremonies.

【皇室】
Kōshitsu
こうしつ

　天皇を中心とした一族のことを皇室、または皇族といいます。皇室には名字がなく、天皇から与えられた「宮」という称号を用います。例えば現皇太子は浩宮徳仁といい、海外ではプリンス・ヒロの愛称で親しまれています。日本国憲法の施行後は、戸籍法を適用されないこと、選挙権・被選挙権を持たないこと、養子をとることができないことなどを除いては、一般国民と同様の国法が適用されます。

　皇室に関する公の事務は、国務の一部として総理府の外局である宮内庁が司っています。また、皇室に関する重要事項を審議するための皇室会議は、総理大臣ほかの政府関係者と皇族の要人で構成されています。

Imperial Household : The family headed by the **Emperor** is called *kōshitsu* or *kōzoku*. *Kōshitsu* has no surname but uses the appellation *miya*(meaning "prince," or "princess") granted by the **Emperor**. For example, the current Crown Prince is called Hiro-no-miya Naruhito, and he is commonly known overseas by the friendly name Prince Hiro. After the **Constitution of Japan** went into effect, the laws of the country applied to the Imperial Household in the same way as to ordinary citizens, with the exceptions of the Family Registration Act, the right to vote or stand for election, and the right to adopt children.

The Imperial Household Agency, an extra-ministerial bureau of the Prime Minister's Office, administers public matters involving *kōshitsu* as a part of the affairs of state. In addition, meetings to deliberate important *kōshitsu* matters are made up of the Prime Minister, other government-connected officials and key figures of the Imperial family.

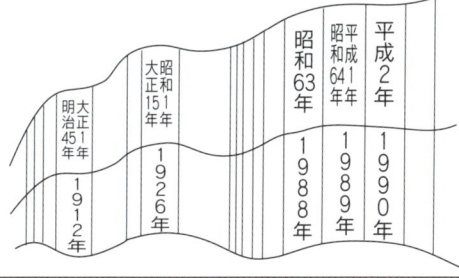

昭和63年
昭和64\平成元年
平成2年

1912年
1926年
1988年
1989年
1990年

【元号】
Gengō
げんごう

　日本では西暦で年を表す習慣も定着してきましたが、多くの場面ではまだ日本独自の年号を使用しています。この独自の年号とは、中国で皇帝が時をも支配するという思想から始まり、日本では645年に「大化」と号したのが最初です。**天皇**が制定権を持っていた時代は、**天皇**の即位や天変地異などによってしばしば元号が改められましたが、明治以降は一世一元になり、皇位が継承されるときにのみ改められることになっています。1989年に明仁天皇が皇位を継承したことによって、元号は「昭和」から「平成」へと変わりました。なお、過去の**天皇**を表すときにはこの元号を付けて「昭和天皇」などと呼ぶ習わしがあります。

Era names : In Japan the custom of expressing the years by the Christian calendar has begun to take root, but in most scenes the original Japanese era designation is still being used. This original era designation began in China from the notion of the **Emperor** as dominant even over the time period, and it happened first in Japan with the Taika designation in the year 645. *Gengō*, which **emperors** had the authority to establish for their reigns, were frequently changed with an **emperor**'s enthronement or with natural calamities, but from the Meiji Period on *gengō* marked a single **emperor**'s reign and were changed only upon succeeding to the throne. For Emperor Akihito's succession to the throne in 1989, the *gengō* changed from "Shōwa" to "Heisei." Moreover, when referring to past **emperors**, it is customary to use *gengō*, saying, for example, the "Shōwa Emperor."

♩=69

ki mi ga - yo - wa chi yo ni - - ya chi yo ni

sa za re i shi no i wa o to na ri te

ko ke no mu - su - ma - - de

作者不詳
Words : Anonymous
作曲：林広守
Music : HAYASHI Hiromori

【国歌】
こっか
Kokka

　日本の国歌は「君が代」です。「君」とは**天皇**のことを指し、歌詞の内容は「**天皇**の治世がいつまでも続きますように」という願いが込められています。

　この歌は、もともと**天皇**が世の中を統治していた時代である10世紀初頭に編纂された『**古今和歌集**』にある**和歌**からとられています。そのため、天皇制が廃止された現代において、この歌を国民が国歌として歌うことに関してはさまざまな異論があります。しかし目下のところ、この歌は国歌として国家的祭典、国際的行事、学校や祝祭日などにおいて歌われています。国技である**相撲**でも、千秋楽の優勝者表彰のときには観客全員が起立して歌います。

The national anthem : The Japanese *kokka* is "*Kimi-ga-yo*." "*Kimi*" refers to the **Emperor**, and the words contain the prayer: "May the **Emperor**'s reign last forever."

　This song was originally taken from one of *waka*, **classical Japanese poems**, in the "**Kokinwakashū**", compiled in the early tenth century, an era when the **Emperor** reigned over the people. Consequently, today when the original emperor system has been abolished, various objections have been raised about the people singing this song as *kokka*. However, at present it is sung as *kokka* at national festivals, international events, schools, and on national holidays. With *sumō*, the national sport, it is also sung on the last day of a tournament when the champion receives his awards, by the whole spectators standing up.

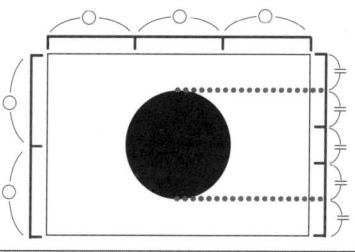

【国旗】
Kokki
こっき

　法で定められてはいませんが、白地に赤い丸を描いた旗が、日本の国旗として使われています。「日本」とはもともと「太陽が昇る国」という意味であり、したがって赤い丸は日の出の太陽を象徴しています。英国旗を「ユニオン・ジャック」、米国旗を「星条旗」というように、日本の国旗は「**日の丸**」といいます。

　この「**日の丸**」は旗以外に赤い丸単独でも用いられ、さまざまなシンボルとしても使われます。第2次大戦中には、**日の丸**は「**特攻隊**」やその他の悲劇のシンボルとしても使われたため、戦争中の不幸な記憶と結び付き、国旗としてふさわしくないと考える人もいます。

The national flag : The Japanese *kokki* has a red circle on a white background. "*Nippon*"(Japan) basically means "land of the rising sun," so the red circle is a symbol of the rising sun. Just as the British flag is called "the Union Jack" and the American flag "the Stars and Stripes," the Japanese flag is called "*hinomaru*."

This red circle of *hinomaru* is used independently for all kinds of symbols. There are people who do not think that *hinomaru* is appropriate as *kokki*, for it was used as a symbol for the "suicide units" and other tragedies in the Second World War, thus it is connected with tragic memories of the war.

【国花】
こっか
Kokka

　日本人に最も愛好され、日本を象徴する花といえば**桜**です。日本人は、１週間ほどで散ってしまう**桜**から、美しさとともに無常感や物悲しさ、あるいは潔さを読みとります。

　この花と日本人の叙情は昔から深く結び付いていて、**平安時代**（794～1185）以来、**和歌**にもよく詠まれています。**昭和時代**（1926～1989）初期から第２次大戦までの間は、この**桜**の散りぎわの潔さが軍国主義に利用されて、特攻隊の死が美化されたりしたのです。今ではその美しさが平和のシンボルとして、日本から海外に贈られ、アメリカのワシントンD.C.のポトマック河畔やベルリンの壁跡に、その薄桃色の花を春ごとに咲かせています。

The national flower : The flower that is most beloved by the Japanese people and that symbolizes Japan is the **cherry blossom**. From the **cherry blossom** which falls only within a week or so, the Japanese sense beauty, as well as transience, melancholy, and perhaps honor of graceful resignation.

The lyricism of the Japanese people has been closely connected with this flower from ancient times; since the **Heian Period**(794-1185), it has been often included in classical Japanese poems. From the early years of the **Showa Period**(1926-1989) until the Second World War, the way that the **cherry blossom** quickly and gracefully falls was appropriated into militarism to beautify the deaths of the suicide units. Today, Japan has sent cherry trees with their beauty overseas as the symbol of peace, and their light pink flowers bloom every spring, for example, beside the Potomac River in Washington, D.C., and on the remains of the Berlin Wall.

【菊】
Kiku
きく

　菊は中国が原産ですが、8世紀ごろ日本に伝来した後、日本人の好みに合わせてさまざまな改良が加えられ、今や春の**桜**と同様に日本を代表する秋の花となっています。そのため品種は非常に多く、花の色は白、黄、桃、紅など、また大きさも大菊・中菊・小菊などがあります。17世紀にはオランダ経由でヨーロッパに渡り、高い評価を受けました。香りがよく、気品の漂う菊は**皇室**の紋章ともなっており、また、死者や先祖を慰める**墓参り**にも菊は欠かせません。菊は日本人の持つ繊細な美的意識の象徴と見なされ、ルース・ベネディクトの日本研究の書『**菊と刀**』のタイトルともなっています。

Chrysanthemums : *Kiku* were originally produced in China and were brought to Japan in the eighth century. They underwent various improvements that appeal to Japanese tastes, and now have become the typical fall flower of Japan just as the springtime **cherry blossom**. Thus, there is an extremely wide range of varieties, in white, yellow, pink, and red colors and large, middle and small sizes. In the seventeenth century, they were brought to Europe by way of Holland and received high appreciation. The *kiku*, with its fragrance and aura of elegance, is the crest of the **Imperial Household**, and the flowers are indispensable for **visiting graves** to honor the dead and ancestors. The *kiku* is regarded as a symbol of the subtle sense of beauty held by the Japanese people; it was even used in the title of Ruth Benedict's book on Japan, "**The Chrysanthemum and the Sword**."

【国鳥】
Kokuchō
こくちょう

　日本を代表する鳥は**キジ**です。**キジ**は日本固有の鳥で、古くから人々に親しまれており、1947年に国鳥に指定されました。人里離れた雑木林や草原に住み、雄は顔が赤く体全体が暗い緑色で尾が長く、雌は淡い褐色で黒い斑点があり、雄より小さく尾も短いという特徴があります。

　秋から冬にかけて狩猟の対象とされ、古くから食肉用として珍重されてきました。婚礼の祝い物として用いられることも多くありました。

　鳥の中でも最上とされ、雄と雌が互いを求めて鳴く声に哀愁があり、そのため、歌や**俳句**では妻子を恋うる心情の象徴とされています。

The national bird : The bird that represents Japan is the **pheasant**. Native to Japan, the **pheasant** has been a familiar bird to the people since ancient times and was designated *kokuchō* in 1947. It lives in wooded areas and grassy fields away from human habitation. Its main features including, for males, red faces, dark green bodies and long tails, and for females, light brown color with black spots; females are smaller and have shorter tails than males.

In fall and winter they were objects of hunting and from ancient times were highly valued for eating. They also were often used as celebratory material for weddings.

Among birds, they are considered the finest; because of the sorrow in the cries of males and females for each other, they are taken as symbols in classical Japanese poems and **poems in seventeen syllables** of the feelings of love for one's family.

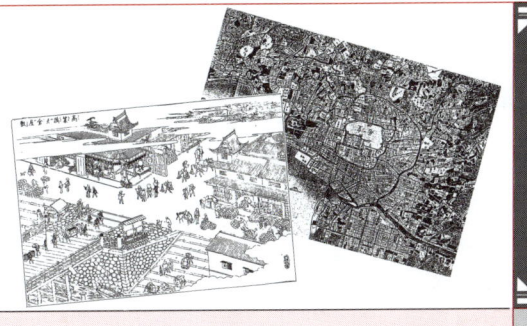

【東京】Tokyo とうきょう

日本の首都は東京です。昔は江戸といい、**江戸時代**の名前の由来ともなっています。1457年に武将・太田道灌が江戸に城を築き、その後1603年には**徳川家康**が江戸に幕府を開き、**江戸時代**が始まりました。それまでは一地方都市だった江戸はこの300年間に独自の文化を築き、幕府が崩壊する1867年までに人口100万の世界一の都市となっていました。現在では人口1,200万人、伝統とハイテクの混在する国際都市であり、ニューヨーク、ロンドンと並ぶ世界金融の中心でもあります。中心部には緑に囲まれた広大な敷地に**天皇**の住む**皇居**があり、その周囲に国会議事堂を初めとする政治関連施設、それにビジネス街が連なります。

Tokyo : The capital of Japan is Tokyo. It used to be called Edo which is the source for the name of the **Edo Period.** A warrior ŌTA Dōkan built a castle in Edo in 1457, and in 1603, the **Edo Period** started when **TOKUGAWA Ieyasu** founded a feudal government at Edo. A regional city until then, Edo established a unique culture over a three hundred year period and became the world's largest city with a population of one million until the overthrow of the government in 1867. Today, it is an international city of twelve million population where tradition and high technology coexist, and is a center of world finance ranked with New York and London. The center of the city is the **Imperial Palace**, where the **Emperor** resides, settled in an extensive ground surrounded by green. Political institutions including the Diet Building and a business district stretch around this center.

【富士山】
Fuji-san
ふじさん

　富士山は、その美しさゆえに広く世界に知られている日本一高い山です。標高は3,776メートル、日本のほぼ中心部に位置し、史上たびたび噴火してきました。1707年以降は火山活動を休止していますが、地質学上は活火山です。

　富士山は日本三霊山の１つで、古来信仰の対象として崇められてきました。特に**江戸時代**（1603〜1867）には、信仰のための登山が盛んに行われています。

　その偉大さと美しさはまた、日本の多くの芸術家を魅了し、優れた作品が残されています。浮世絵画家・**葛飾北斎**には「富嶽三十六景」という優れた作品があり、「赤富士」など世界に知られる名作もあります。

Mount *Fuji* : *Fuji-san* is Japan's highest mountain, known throughout the world for its beauty. It is 3,776 meters high, located almost in the middle of Japan, and in the past erupted frequently. Since 1707 volcanic activity has ceased, but geologically it is a dormant volcano.

Fuji-san is one of Japan's three sacred mountains and has been an object of worship since ancient times. In the **Edo Period**(1603-1867) in particular, it was frequently climbed as an expression of faith.

Its grandeur and beauty have fascinated many Japanese artists, who have left behind outstanding works of art. There is, for example, the outstanding work called the "*Fugaku Sanjūrokkei*" by the *ukiyoe* artist KATSUSHIKA **Hokusai**, which contains worldly known masterpieces like the "*Akafuji.*"

【芸者】
Geisha
げいしゃ

　「フジヤマ、ゲイシャ」といえば、最近までは日本をよく知らない人々が神秘的な東洋の島国を表すときに使われるステレオタイプの表現でした。有名になった原因は、芸者のやさしい心遣いが西洋の男性を感激させたからでしょうか。しかし今では日本への無知を告白する表現と見なすべきです。芸者とは、祝宴の席に興を添えることを職業とする女性のことです。**日本髪**を結い、**着物**を着て旅館や**料亭**に出かけ、唄を歌い、**三味線**を弾き、**日本舞踊**を踊ります。娼婦を兼ねた時代もあったため性的なイメージが強いのですが、現在ではむしろ伝統的な芸を受け継ぐ、貴重な職業と見なされる傾向にあります。

*G*eisha : The term "*Fujiyama, geisha*" was until recently a stereotypical expression used by people who are not familiar with Japan to express the mysterious Oriental island country. The reason the term became famous is perhaps because the gentle and thoughtful manners of the *geisha* deeply impressed Western men. However, now it should be regarded as an expression of ignorance about Japan. *Geisha* are women who make a profession of providing entertainment for banquets. They do up their hair in the **Japanese coiffure**, go out to traditional inns and **traditional Japanese-style restaurants** wearing **kimonos**, sing traditional songs, play the ***shamisen*** and perform **classical Japanese dance**. There was a time when they were also prostitutes, so the sexual image is strong, but now the tendency is rather to regard them as working for a valuable profession that inherits traditional arts.

年中行事／祝祭日

しめ飾り

【正月】
Shōgatsu
しょうがつ

　正月とは1月のことですが、祝う期間はふつう最初の3日間または1週間で、日本人には最も大事な期間です。学校も会社も1～2週間休みとなり、家族と離れて暮らしている人の多くも、帰省して家族と一緒に過ごします。正月を迎えるにあたっては大掃除をし、**門松やしめ飾り**、**鏡餅**の準備をします。**大晦日**の夜には**寺**で**除夜の鐘**が鳴らされ、**年越しそば**を食べて新年を迎えるのです。**和服**を着ることも多く、元旦には寺社へ**初詣**に行って新年の健康と幸福を祈ります。届いた**年賀状**に目を通すことや、子どもにとっては**お年玉**をもらうことも、正月の楽しみの1つです。

New Year : Although *Shōgatsu* means January, we generaly celebrate it for the first 3 days or the first week of January. *Shōgatsu* is the most important days for the Japanese. Schools and businesses close for one to two weeks, and many people who live away from their families return home to spend this time with their families. To prepare for *shōgatsu*, a general house cleaning is done, and **New Year's pine and bamboo decorations**, **sacred straw festoon**, and **round mirror-shaped rice cakes** are set out. On **New Year's Eve**, **bells speeding the old year** are rung at **temples** and the New Year is welcomed by eating **year-crossing noodles**. On New Year's Day, many wear **Japanese-style garments** and people go for the **first temple or shrine visit of the New Year** and pray for health and happiness in the new year. *Shōgatsu* is also enjoyed by reading **New Year's cards** and by children receiving **New Year's gift**.

【おせち料理】

Osechi-ryōri
おせちりょうり

おせち料理は、正月三が日に食べる特別な料理です。漆塗りの**重箱**には、口取り、焼き物、煮物、酢の物などが色とりどりに盛りつけられます。見た目が豪華である上、長持ちするのが特徴で、三が日くらいは主婦の家事が軽減されるようにという配慮もあって、現在のおせち料理ができあがったようです。地方によって多少の違いはありますが、おせちの中身はだいたい決まっています。そして鯛は「めでたい」、数の子は「子孫繁栄」昆布巻は「よろこぶ」といったように、おせちの中身にはそれぞれ願いが込められているのです。

The New Year dishes : *Osechi-ryōri* are special side dishes eaten on the first three days of the new year. **Tiered lacquer boxes** are abundantly loaded with multi-hued side dishes, grilled or boiled dishes and vinegared dishes. It appears that present-day *osechi-ryōri* was developed with the particular practice of keeping it as is for a while, because it is splendid to look at, and also out of consideration for reducing housewives' work for three days. There are some regional differences but *osechi* contents are essentially fixed. Those contents are respectively charged with wishes: for example, **sea bream**(*tai*) is "auspicious"(*mede**tai***), herring roe(*kazu no ko*) indicates "the prosperity for one's descendants", and sea tangle roll(*kobu maki*) means "happiness"(*yoro**kobu***).

【しめ飾り】 しめかざり／Shimekazari

正月に門戸に飾るもので、魔よけの意味があります。しめ縄は神を迎える清浄な場所を示すために張るものですが、そのしめ縄をもとに橙やシダ、伊勢エビなどの縁起物を付けて作った飾りがしめ飾りです。橙は子孫の繁栄を意味するなど、縁起物はそれぞれ意味を持っています。正月が終わると門松などと一緒に神社へ持って行き、焼いてもらいます。

Sacred straw festoon : *Shimekazari* decorates doors at **New Year** and serves as a charm against evil spirits. The **sacred Shinto rope** is hung to indicate a purified place for receiving divinities. The *shimekazari* is made by attaching **good luck charms** like bitter oranges, ferns and lobster to the **sacred Shinto rope**. The **good luck charms** each have significance, the bitter oranges, for example, indicating prosperity of one's descendants. When the **New Year** period ends, the **New Year's pine and bamboo decorations** and the other decorations are taken to **Shinto shrines** and burned.

【門松】 Kadomatsu／かどまつ

門松は、松の枝を組み合わせて作った飾りに竹や梅が添えられたもので、正月の間、家の門前に一対置きます。日本では松竹梅は縁起がよいとされており、特に松は古来、長寿を意味するものとして尊ばれてきました。本来、門松は年神を迎えるためのものでしたが、最近は正月飾りの1つと認識されることが多いようです。

New Year's pine and bamboo decorations : *Kadomatsu* are decorations made with assembled **pine** branches enhanced by stems of **bamboo** and sprays of **plum trees**. During the **New Year** period, a pair of them, one for each side, are placed in front of the house gate. In Japan **pine**, **bamboo**, **and plum trees** are taken as good luck, and **pine** in particular has been regarded as meaning longevity and valued since ancient times. Originally, *kadomatsu* were for receiving the **year god**, but in these days they are mostly considered just as another set of **New Year**'s decorations.

【初夢】 Hatsuyume はつゆめ

初夢とは、元旦の夜から２日の朝にかけて見る夢のことです。縁起のよい夢を見るとその年がよい年になるといわれ、「一富士、二鷹、三なすび」というように吉夢の順番があります。よい初夢が見られるようにと、**七福神**が金銀を積んだ宝船の絵を枕の下に敷いたり、悪い夢を食べてくれるようにと獏（夢を食べる動物）の絵を敷いたりする習慣もありましたが、今ではすたれたようです。

First dream of the New Year : *Hatsuyume* refers to the dream that occurs the night of New Year's Day to the morning of the 2nd. If it is an auspicious dream, it is said that that year will be a good one. Good dreams, counting from the top, are said to be "Mt. Fuji at the first, hawk at the second, eggplant at the third." To have a good *hatsuyume*, a picture in which the **Seven Gods of Luck** have piled gold and silver in a treasure ship is placed under the pillow, or a picture of a *baku*(an imaginary animal that eats dreams) is placed there to have bad dreams eaten, but these practices appears to have gone out of fashion.

【雑煮】 Zōni ぞうに

雑煮は、**餅**や野菜を入れた汁で、新年を祝うために**正月**には欠かせない料理の１つです。関東地方の雑煮は四角い**餅**を入れたすまし汁仕立て、関西地方の雑煮は丸い**餅**を入れた**味噌**仕立てというのが一般的ですが、味付けや中に入れる具は、その地方や家庭によって違います。ほかに魚や鶏肉を入れたり、地方の特産物を入れたりと、郷土色が色濃く出るのが雑煮の特徴です。

Soup with rice cakes and vegetables : *Zōni* is a soup with **rice cakes**(*mochi*) and vegetables, and is an essential dish for celebrating the **New Year**. In the Kantō area, *zōni* is generally prepared as a clear soup with square *mochi*, while in the Kansai it is made with **bean paste** and round *mochi*. But the seasoning and other ingredients are different according to each region and household. It is the special feature of *zōni* to bring out the richness of local color with additional ingredients, like fish, chicken or special regional items.

【鏡餅】 Kagami-mochi かがみもち

　鏡餅は、10〜20センチくらいの大小2つの平たくて丸い餅を、台の上に重ねたものです。**正月**には**床の間**に飾り、神仏に供えます。日本には、**正月**には**年神**という尊い神が家々を訪れるという古い信仰があり、その**年神**に鏡餅をお供えしてまつるというのがもともとの意味でした。しかし最近ではそのようなことを意識する人は少なく、鏡餅も**正月**飾りの1つになってしまっているようです。

Round mirror-shaped rice cakes : *Kagami-mochi* is a set of two round, flat rice cakes, one large, one small, about 10-20 cm in size stacked on a stand. At **New Year**, they are displayed in the **alcove** and offered to the Shinto and Buddhist deities. In Japan there is the old belief that at **New Year** the revered divinity known as the **year god**(*toshigami*) visits homes and the original significance of *kagami-mochi* was as worship offerings to the **year god**. Recently, however, few people are aware of such practices and *kagami-mochi* has become just another **New Year** decoration.

【鏡開き】 かがみびらき／Kagami-biraki

　鏡開きとは、**床の間**に飾っておいた**鏡餅**を1月11日に下ろして、食べる行事です。元来は20日に行われていましたが、1651年1月20日に徳川幕府三代将軍家光が亡くなったため、11日に改められたといわれています。11日にもなると、**鏡餅**は固くひび割れてきますが、**縁起物**なので刃物で「切る」ことを避け、手か槌でたたいて割ります。**餅**が割れて開くから鏡「開き」といわれるのです。

The opening of New Year's rice cakes : *Kagami-biraki* is an event that occurs when **round mirror-shaped rice cakes** (*kagami-mochi*), which have been on show in the **alcove**, are taken down on January 11 and eaten. Originally, this occurred on the 20th, but with the death of the third Shōgun, Iemitsu, in the Tokugawa shogunate, on January 20, 1651, it was changed to the 11th. By the 11th, *kagami-mochi* hardens and cracks, but, since it is a **good luck charm**,"cutting" it with a sharp edge is avoided and it is split open by hand or with a hammer. It is called *kagami-biraki*(literally, opening the mirror,) because the *mochi* is split opened.

【七草がゆ】
ななくさがゆ／Nanakusa-gayu

日本での米の調理法の1つに「かゆ」（米に水を多く入れて柔らかく煮る）があります。そして1月7日には、かゆにセリやナズナなどの「春の七草」を入れたかゆを食べるという習慣があります。この日にかゆを食べると、万病を遠ざけるといわれているからです。地方によっては、雑炊や雑煮にして食べたり、代わりに小豆を入れたかゆを作って食べたりするところもあります。

Seven-herb rice porridge : In Japan rice porridge(*kayu*) is one way to prepare **rice**(add lots of water to **rice** and boil until soft). And there is the custom that on January 7 *kayu* is eaten which has been enhanced by the **seven spring herbs**, such as Japanese parsley and shepherd's purse. Eating *kayu* on that day is said to ward off all kinds of diseases.

In some regions, seven spring herbs are served in **rice and vegetable porridge** or **soup with rice cakes and vegetables**, or they are substituted with red beans.

【成人の日】
せいじんのひ／Seijin-no-hi

1月15日は成人の日です。国民の祝日の1つで、1948年に制定されました。この日、全国の市町村では、20歳になった人たちを祝福して、成人式を催します。女性の多くは、華やかな振袖姿でこの式に臨みます。

日本では、20歳になると成人と認められます。20歳とは選挙権をはじめ、市民権を与えられる大切な節目なのです。飲酒や喫煙が許されるのも20歳からです。

Coming-of-Age Day : January 15 is *Seijin-no-hi*. It was established as a national holiday in 1948. On this day, those who have turned 20 are blessed and a coming-of-age ceremony is held. Most women attend this ceremony in a colorful, **long-sleeved kimono**.

In Japan, on turning 20, one is recognized as an adult. The age of 20 is an important juncture when one is granted full rights as a citizen, beginning with the right to vote. Drinking and smoking are also approved from this age.

【節分】
Setsubun
せつぶん

節分とは本来、「季節の分かれ目」を意味していましたが、現在では特に、**立春**の前日である２月３日ごろがこれに当たります。この日の夜、人々は炒った大豆を家の内外にまきながら、「**鬼**は外！　福は内！」と唱えます。その年の健康を祈るため、大豆を自分の年の数だけ食べるという習慣もあります。また、**寺**や**神社**でも大がかりな**豆まき**が実施されます。

The eve of the first day of spring : *Setsubun* actually signifies "the parting of the seasons;" especially nowadays it falls on about February 3, the day before the **first day of spring**. On the evening of this day, people yell, "Out with the **ogre**! In with the happiness!" while scattering parched soy beans inside and outside their homes. To pray for good health for that year, there is also the custom of eating only the number of soy beans as one's age. At **temples** and **shrines**, too, **bean scattering** is practiced on a grand scale.

【建国記念の日】
Kenkoku-kinen-no-hi
けんこくきねんのひ

２月11日は建国記念の日で、国民の祝日の１つです。「建国」といっても、アメリカの独立記念日のように歴史的な日ではありません。初代天皇である神武天皇が即位したのは２月11日だという神話に基づき、その日を日本が始まった日と定めたのです。第２次世界大戦後に歴史的根拠がないためにいったん中止されましたが、1967年に復活しました。

National Founding Day : February 11 is *Kenkoku-kinen-no-hi* and is a national holiday. Even though it is called "*kenkoku"(*National Founding), it is, unlike Independence Day of the United States, not a specific historical date. It is based on the myth that the first **Emperor** Jinmu ascended to the throne on February 11; and that day, it was decided, was the beginning of Japan. After the Second World War the observance was discontinued, because there was no historical basis for it, but in 1967 it was reinstated.

【針供養】

Harikuyō
はりくよう

供養とは**仏教**で、死者の霊に供え物をして冥福を祈ることですが、人間以外に対する**供養**も古くから行われています。例えば、かわいがっていた動物が死んだり、長い間使い続けてきた道具がその役目を終えたりしたときは、哀惜の情や感謝を込めて**供養**すべきだとする日本独自の考えから、それらのものへの**供養**も行われてきたのです。

今はややなじみが薄くなった感がありますが、2月8日または12月8日に行われる針供養は、その代表的なものです。1年間使ってきて折れたり曲がったりした針を**供養**するため、当日は裁縫を休んだり、折れた針を**豆腐**やこんにゃくに刺し、**神社**に納めたり土に埋めたりします。

Needle memorial services : In **Buddhist memorial services**, offerings are made for the spirits of the dead and prayers said for the repose of their souls, but since ancient times there also have been held **memorial services** for other than human beings. For example, when a beloved animal has died and the things used for a long time has been broken or has become useless, a **memorial services** for those things is held because of the peculiarly Japanese way of thinking that, filled with feelings of grief and thanks, one should do **memorial services**.

Nowadays, familiarity with this appears to have faded, but the *hari-kuyō* carried out on February 8 and December 8 are typical of the practice. To do **memorial services** for break or bent up needles that have been used for a year, the sewing stops on that day, **tofu** or a paste made from devil's-tongue are pierced with the bent needles, offered to a **Shinto shrine** and buried in the earth.

【春分の日】
しゅんぶんのひ／Shunbun-no-hi

春分の日は、３月21日ごろ、太陽が春分点に達する日で、昼と夜の長さが等しくなります。日本では自然をたたえ、生物をいつくしむ日として、国民の祝日にも制定されています。春分の日をはさんで前後３日ずつの７日間を「春の**彼岸**」といいます。**彼岸**とは**仏教**で「あの世、極楽」を指し、**仏教**信者でなくてもこの期間には**墓参り**をします。墓をきれいに掃除して花や線香などを供え、故人の霊を弔うのです。

Vernal Equinox Day : *Shunbun-no-hi* occurs on about March 21, the day when the sun reaches the vernal equinox, and the length of day and night is equal. In Japan, it is designated as a national holiday for venerating nature and cherishing all kinds of life. The seven-day period, including the three days immediately before and after *Shunbun-no-hi*, is called the spring **equinoctial week**(*higan*). In **Buddhism**, *higan* indicates "the next world" or "paradise", and during this time even those who are not **Buddhist** believers **visit graves**. They clean up the gravesites, offer flowers and incense, and mourn for the spirits of the dead.

【おはぎ】
Ohagi

おはぎは日本の伝統的な菓子です。もち米にうるち米を混ぜて炊き、軽くつぶして丸めたものに、あん、またはきなこやごまなどをまぶして作ります。年２回、春と秋の**彼岸**には欠かせない食べ物で、元来は先祖の霊にお供えするために家庭で作っていたものですが、今では一般的な**和菓子**の１つとなりました。

Rice dumpling covered with bean jam : *Ohagi* is a traditional Japanese pastry. It is made by mixing together and cooking glutinous and nonglutinous rice, lightly squashing and molding this into balls, which are covered with bean jam, orelse soybean flour or sesame seeds. This is an essential food twice a year, for the spring and autumn **equinoctial weeks**. Originally, it was made in the home to offer to the spirits of the ancestors, but now it is a typical **Japanese confectionery**.

【彼岸】Higan／ひがん

彼岸は年に2回あり、それぞれ**春分の日**と**秋分の日**を真ん中に挟んだ1週間をさします。彼岸とは**仏教**用語で「死者が渡る川の向こう側」を意味するもので、こちら側が生きた者の世界であるのに対し、向こう側は死者の世界というわけです。その向こう側にいる先祖の霊を慰めるため、彼岸には**墓参り**に行きます。なお、丁寧に「お」を付けて「お彼岸」と呼ぶのがふつうです。

Equinoctial weeks : *Higan* occurs twice a year and each lasts one week, with the **Vernal** and **Autumn Equinox Days** occurring in the middle of their respective weeks. In **Buddhist** terms, *higan* means "the other side of the river crossed by the dead," which means that, while this side is the world of the living, the other side is the world of the dead. In order to comfort the spirits of the ancestors on the other side, people **visit graves** during *higan*. By the way, it's generrly called "*ohigan*," with a preffix "*o*" to make it sound polite.

【ひな人形】ひなにんぎょう／Hina-ningyō

ひなとは女の子が遊ぶ小さな人形で、**平安時代**（794-1185）からありましたが、**江戸時代**（1603-1867）に現在の形になりました。赤いもうせんを敷いた5段か7段のひな段の最上段に**天皇・皇后**を模した一対の「**内裏びな**」が並び、以下「**右大臣・左大臣**」「**三人官女**」「**五人ばやし**」などが各段を飾ります。しかし最近では簡略化して**内裏びな**だけを飾る家も増えています。

Dolls for the Doll's Festival : *Hina* are small dolls for girls and have existed since the **Heian Period**(794-1185). They took their present form in the **Edo Period**(1603-1867). A "**doll Emperor and Empress in ancient costume**", patterned after the **Emperor** and **Empress**, are placed on the highest tier of a five- or seven-tiered stand covered with a red carpet, and under them come the "**Minister of the Right**, **Minister of the Left**", the "**three court ladies**", and the "**five court musicians**", among others. However, in recent times, more and more homes have simplified this by setting out only the **Emperor and Empress dolls**.

【ひな祭り】
Hinamatsuri
ひなまつり

ひな祭りは3月3日、女の子の成長や幸福を願う行事です。女の子のいる家庭の多くは**ひな人形**を飾り、桃の花や**ひなあられ**、**菱餅**、**白酒**などをひな人形に供えます。ひな祭りの起源は、身のけがれや災いを人形に移し、川に流して厄払いしたという古代中国の風習にあります。これが日本に伝わると女の子の人形遊びと結び付き、**江戸時代**（1603～1867）からはひな祭りとして行われるようになりました。

Doll's Festival : *Hinamatsuri* occurs on March 3 and is an occasion to pray for young girls' growth and happiness. Most homes with girls display **dolls for the Doll's Festival** and dedicate to them peach blossoms, **rice cake cubes**, **special colored and diamond-shaped rice cakes**, **white sake**, and other items. The origin of *hinamatsuri* is an ancient Chinese practice in which the sin of the body and misfortune are transferred to a doll and washed away by setting the doll in a river to drift away. When this practice spread to Japan, it was linked to girl's playing with dolls and, in the **Edo Period**(1603-1867), was developed into the *hinamatsuri*.

【花見】
Hanami
はなみ

　美しく咲いた**桜**を観賞し、遊び楽しむため公園などに出かけることを花見といいます。日本では３、４月に**桜**の花が満開になると、家族や職場の仲間、友人たちと一緒に花見に出かける習慣があるのです。**桜**の花の下にござなどを敷いて**酒**を飲んだり、歌を歌ったりして春の到来を楽しみます。都会では特に夜桜見物に人気があります。春の夜空には、満開の**桜**の美しさがよけいに強調されます。

Flower-viewing : *Hanami* is going out to places such as parks to enjoy leisurely while appreciating the beautifully bloomed **cherry blossoms**. The custom in Japan, in March and April when the **cherry blossoms** are in full bloom, is to do *hanami* with family, colleagues from work, or friends. People spread a mat under the **cherry blossoms**, drink **sake**, sing songs, and enjoy the coming of spring. In cities, viewing cherry trees in the evening is especially popular. Against the spring night sky, the beauty of the **cherry blossoms** in full bloom is abundantly emphasized.

【緑の日】 みどりの日／Midori-no-hi

4月29日は緑の日です。この日は亡くなられた昭和天皇の誕生日だったのですが、環境問題に関心の高かった天皇にちなみ、1989年から緑の日として新たに国民の祝日となりました。日本はこの日からゴールデンウィークに入ります。5月3日の**憲法記念日**、4日の国民の休日、5日の**子供の日**のほかに土・日曜日も入るため、**正月**休みと夏休み以外では、いちばん休日が多い週となるのです。

Greenery Day : April 29 is *Midori-no-hi*. This was the birthday of the Shōwa Emperor Hirohito who died in 1989 and, given his deep concern for the environment, the day has been renewed as a national holiday in the form of *Midori-no-hi*. This day ushers Japan into "Golden Week", a succession of holidays. May 3 is **Constitution Day**, the 4th is a National Holiday, the 5th is **Children's Day**, and, when Saturdays and Sundays are included, this week has more holidays than any other except for the **New Year** and summer vacations.

【憲法記念日】 けんぽうきねんび／Kenpō-kinenbi

1947年5月3日に現行の**日本国憲法**が施行されたことを記念して、国民の祝日として制定されました。**日本国憲法**は、第2次世界大戦の反省から第9条で戦争放棄を定め、軍隊を持たないことを規定しています。しかし自衛のための軍隊は許されるとする解釈もあり、現在自衛隊が存在する根拠となっています。平和主義のほか国民主権、基本的人権の尊重などが**日本国憲法**の基本精神です。

Constitution Day : This was established as a national holiday to commemorate the present **Constitution of Japan** that took effect on May 3, 1947. Taking the Second World War into consideration, the **Constitution of Japan** renounced war in Article Nine and made no provision for an army. But there was also an interpretation that an army for self-defense was permitted, and this became the basis for the existence of the present Self-Defense Force. In addition to pacifism, the fundamental spirit of the **Constitution of Japan** embraces sovereignty of the people and respect for fundamental human rights.

【田植え】 Taue たうえ

　田植えは、稲の苗を苗代から水田に植え替える作業で、5月から6月にかけて行われます。稲の種まきは、**立春**から数えて88日目に当たる**八十八夜**（5月2日ごろ）前後がピークとなり、**梅雨**に入ってから水田に移します。米は日本人の主食であるため、収穫の出来不出来は1年の生活を左右します。従って田植えは重要な行事であり、かつては村人の協同作業であり神事でもありました。

Rice planting : *Taue* is the activity occurring from May to June of transplanting rice seedlings from nursery to rice paddy. Planting rice seeds is at its peak before and after the **88th night**(around May 2) that corresponds to the 88th day counting from the **first day of spring**, and the transplanting to rice paddys follows the beginning of the **rainy season**. Because rice is the principal food of the Japanese, the success or failure of the harvest impacts life for a year. Accordingly, *taue* is an important event, which formerly was a cooperative activity and even a Shinto ritual for village people.

【茶摘み】 Chatsumi ちゃつみ

　緑茶は日本人の主要な飲み物です。この**茶**の木の若芽や葉を摘み取る茶摘みは、4月中旬から5月下旬の間に3週間くらいかけて行われ、特に**八十八夜**（5月2日ごろ）から2、3週間の間が最も盛りとなります。摘んだ葉は、蒸した後、その日の夜には揉みあげます。かつては赤いたすきがけに手拭いをかぶり、**茶摘歌**を歌いながら摘んでいたものですが、機械化が進むとともに昔の情緒も失われてきました。

Tea-picking : Green tea is the main drink of the Japanese people. Picking the young sprouts and leaves of the **tea** bush occurs over some three weeks from mid-April till the end of May, especially during the two to three weeks following the **88th night**(around May 2) when the tea-picking season is at its height. After the picked tea leaves are steamed, they are massaged the same evening. In the past, tea used to be picked with one's sleeves tucked up with a red sash and a rolled-up towel tied around one's head while singing a **tea-picking song**, but, along with the advance of mechanization, the artistic effect of old has been lost.

A doll for the Boy's Festival

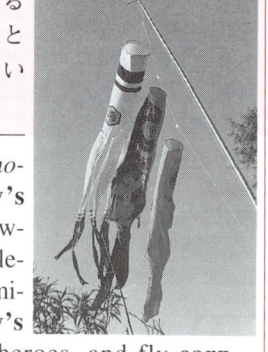

【子供の日】
Kodomo-no-hi
こどものひ

　５月５日は子供の日です。もともとは**端午の節句**といって、男の子の成長を祝う日でしたが、今は一般に子供のためのお祝いの日となっています。この日、男の子のいる家庭では武者や英雄を模した**五月人形**を飾ったり、空高く**こいのぼり**を立てたりします。**鯉**は滝でも泳いで登ってしまう力があり、昔から立身出世のシンボルとされてきたことによります。この日には薬効があるといわれる**菖蒲**を風呂に入れて入る習慣が昔からあり、**ちまきや柏餅**といった伝統的な**和菓子**も欠かせない供物となっています。

Children's Day : May 5 is *Kodomo-no-hi*. Originally it was called **Boy's Festival** and was for celebrating boys' growing up, but now it has become a day to celebrate children in general. On this day, families with boys set out **dolls for the Boy's Festival**, patterned after warriors and heroes, and fly **carp streamers**. **Carp** have the strength to even swim up waterfalls and have long been taken as symbols of success in life. The day also features the practice from long ago of taking a bath with **flag**, reputed to have medicinal effect, and it is also essential to make an offering of the traditional **Japanese confections** of **rice dumplings wrapped in bamboo leaves** and **rice cakes wrapped in oak leaves**.

【七夕】
たなばた
Tanabata

　七夕は７月７日に行われる星祭りです。天の川を挟んで両岸にさかれたアルタイ（牽牛星）とベガ（織女星）が年に１度この日の夜に出会う、という中国の伝説が日本の信仰と一緒になったもので、もとは朝廷の貴族の間で行われていた祭でしたが、**江戸時代**（1603〜1867）から一般庶民の間に定着しました。

　６日の夜には、色とりどりの短冊に願いごとを書いたり、歌を書いたりして**笹**につるし、７日の夜に庭先に出します。夏のクリスマス・ツリーといえるほど美しいものです。近年では、仙台や平塚などの市が大規模な飾りを商店街のアーケードに飾って観光客を集めています。

The Star Festival : *Tanabata* is the Weaver Star Festival, which occurs on July 7. The Chinese legend, which has it that Altair(the Cowherd Star) and Vega(the Weaver Star) were split apart by the two banks of the River of Heaven(the Milky Way) and come together once a year on this night, has aligned with Japanese belief. Originally a festival carried out among the Court nobility, it has since the **Edo Period**(1603-1867) become established among the people at large.

On the night of the 6th, people write their wishes or poems on strips of poety paper in various color. And hung them on leafy **bamboo**; then on the night of the 7th, they are put out in the garden. These are attractive enough to be called summer Christmas trees. In recent years, cities like Sendai and Hiratsuka attract sightseers by decorating their shopping street arcades with these *tanabata* decorations on a large-scale.

【花火大会】
はなびたいかい／Hanabi-taikai

花火大会は夏の代表的な風物です。**江戸時代**（1603〜1867）に江戸（現在の東京）の隅田川で、玉屋と鍵屋という花火メーカーが競って打ち上げた花火大会がその起源です。夏には各地で花火大会が行われます。日本の夏は暑く、湿気が多いので、眠れぬ夜の慰みにふさわしいにぎやかな催しです。夜空に美しく咲いてパッと消える様子は、**桜**と同様、潔さや**無常**の象徴にたとえられます。

Fireworks display : *Hanabi-taikai* constitute a typical summer scene. They originated in the **Edo Period**(1603-1867) with the exhibition of fireworks held competitively between Tamaya and Kagiya which were firework factories. In summer, fireworks displays occur throughout Japan. Because Japanese summers are hot and humid, these are appropriately lively gatherings for amusement on nights when one is unable to sleep. The spectacle of fireworks blooming beautifully, then disappearing with a pop can be taken as a symbol of graceful resignation or **transiency** like **cherry blossoms**.

【盆】
ぼん Bon

7月13日から15日、または8月に行われる**仏教**行事の1つで、先祖の霊を**供養**するものです。このときに霊が戻ってくるといわれているため、霊が道に迷わないよう家の門口で迎え火をたいたり、室内にちょうちんをともしたりするほか、**仏壇**をきれいにし、野菜や果物などの供物を飾ります。そして盆が終わると霊を送り返します。これを精霊送りといい、送り火を門口でたき、供物を川や海に流すのです。

Bon Festival : This is a **Buddhist** event occurring from the 13th to 16th of July or August to **hold a memorial service** to the spirits of ancestors. Because the spirits of the dead are said to return at this time, fires are lit at the entrances to homes so the spirits do not lose their way, and, in addition to lanterns being lit inside homes, the **Buddhist family alters** are tidied up and vegetables and fruit are set out as offerings. And when *bon* is over, the spirits are sent on their way. This is called the **escorting of the spirits** and fires to speed their seeing off are lit at entrances of homes and offerings are floated on rivers and the ocean.

【終戦記念日】しゅうせんきねんび／Shūsen-kinenbi

　第２次世界大戦は、連合国のポツダム宣言を日本が受諾し、無条件降伏をしたことによつて終了しました。1945年８月15日、**天皇**がラジオ放送で日本国中にそのことを伝えたのです。現在ではこの日を終戦記念日として、戦没者を慰霊する行事が各地で行われています。悲惨な戦争の記憶を後世に伝え、２度と戦争を繰り返してはならない、という決意を新たにする日でもあります。

The Day commemorating the end of the Second World War : The Second World War ended with Japan's unconditional surrender on accepting the Potsdam Declaration of the Allies. On August 15, 1945, the **Emperor** conveyed this with a nation-wide radio broadcast. This day is now *shūsen-kinenbi*, and observances are held in every area of the country to memorialize the war dead. It is a day to renew the determination to convey the memories of the wretched war to posterity and not to repeat a war again.

【月見】Tsukimi／つきみ

　東洋には月を鑑賞する習慣があり、日本でも旧暦８月15日の夜には**月見団子**やすすきの穂、季節の果物などを窓辺に飾つて月に供え、満月を鑑賞します。澄んだ秋空に浮かぶ満月は格別美しく見えるものですが、農耕民族である日本人の月見の原型は、月を神に見立て、これから実る稲の豊作を祈るための行事だつたとされています。それが現在でも月見として広く行われているのです。

Moon viewing : In the Orient there is a custom of appreciating the moon; in Japan, too, on the night of August 15 by the lunar calendar, **dumplings offered to the moon**, eulalia, seasonal fruits are set out by the window offered to the moon and the full moon is appreciated. The full moon floating in the clear autumn sky appear especially beautiful, but the prototype of *tsukimi* for the Japanese, who are a farming people, is to liken the moon to a divinity and to pay for abundant subsequent harvests of ripened rice. That is currently how *tsukimi* is generally observed.

【敬老の日】
けいろうのひ／Keirō-no-hi

　９月15日は敬老の日で、国民の祝日です。老人を敬い、長寿を祝うとともに、今後の健康を祈り、さらには老人福祉の問題に対する理解を深める日でもあります。

　この日には、地方自治体や**敬老会**などが演芸会をはじめさまざまな催しを開いたり、記念品を贈呈したりします。有志による老人ホームの慰問も行われます。世界一の長寿国として、これから重要な日になることでしょう。

Respect-for-the-Aged Day : September 15 is *Keirō-no-hi* and is a national holiday. It is a day to honor the aged, celebrate their long life, pray for their good health in the future, and, in addition, deepen understanding on the issues of welfare for senior citizens.

 On this day, regional governments and **respect-for-age associations** organize all kinds of events such as variety shows and they donate mementos. Volunteers make sympathy visits to old people's homes. Because this country has the world's longest life expectancy, this holiday will likely become increasingly important.

【秋分の日】
しゅうぶんのひ／Shūbun-no-hi

　秋分の日は９月23日ごろで、国民の祝日です。秋分の日を中日とする１週間は秋の**彼岸**といい、**寺**では法事が行われ、人々は**墓参り**をして先祖の霊を慰めます。

　この日はまた、**春分の日**と同様に、昼と夜の長さが等しくなる日でもあります。このころを境に夏の暑さも終わりを告げ、秋が深まってくるのです。

Autumn Equinox Day : *Shūbun-no-hi* occurs around September 23 and is a national holiday. The week in which *Shūbun-no-hi* is the middle day is called the autumn **equinoctial week**, during which memorial services take place at **temples** and people **visit graves** to comfort the spirits of their ancestors.

 On this day, like on the **Vernal Equinox Day**, the length of day and night is the same. This period is a boundary marking the end of the summer heat and the coming of fall.

【体育の日】 たいいくのひ／Taiiku-no-hi

10月10日は体育の日です。1964年10月10日に東京オリンピックが開催されたのを記念して、1966年から国民の祝日となりました。スポーツに親しみ、健康な心身を養うことを目的としています。秋は気候がいいため、スポーツも盛んになりますが、とりわけ体育の日には、学校や地域の運動会やスポーツ大会が数多く開催されます。

Health-Sports Day : October 10 is *Taiiku-no-hi*. It is to commemorate the opening of the Tokyo Olympics on October 10, 1964, and since 1966 it has been a national holiday. Its purpose is to familiarize with sports and nurture physical and mental health. Sports flourish in autumn because the weather is good, but, especially on *taiiku-no-hi*, numerous school and regional athletic meets and sports tourneys are held.

【文化の日】 ぶんかのひ／Bunka-no-hi

文化の日は11月3日です。もとは明治天皇の誕生日を祝うための日でしたが、現在では「自由と平和を愛し、文化をすすめる」ための国民の祝日となっています。この日には文化祭や芸術祭などが各学校や地域で開催されるとともに、日本文化に貢献した人たちには政府から文化功労賞が授与され、特に文化の発展に尽くしたとされる人には**皇居**で**文化勲章**が授与されます。

Culture Day : *Bunka-no-hi* is November 3. Originally, it was for observing the birthday of the Meiji Emperor, but now it is a national holiday dedicated to "the love of freedom and peace and the promotion of culture." On this day, along with cultural and art festivals held by each school and regional society, the government confers cultural service awards on individuals who have contributed to Japanese culture. In particular, the **Imperial Palace** confers **the Order of Cultural Merits** on people who have rendered special service for the development of Japanese culture.

7 years-old girl in her gala dress.

【七五三】
しちごさん
Shichi-go-san

　11月15日に子供の成長を祈って行う行事です。日本では奇数はめでたい数とされてきたため、子供の成長にとって大切な時期の奇数年、すなわち男の子は3歳と5歳、女の子は3歳と7歳に祝うのです。この日、子供たちは晴れ着を着て両親と**神社**に行き、**氏神**に参詣します。子供たちには**千歳飴**という、**鶴**や**亀**の描かれた袋に入った紅白の細長い飴が買い与えられます。「千歳」は千年を意味し、**鶴**も**亀**も日本では長寿の象徴です。また赤と白は日本人にとってめでたい色の組み合わせで、ここには子供の健康と成長への祈りが込められているのです。

A gala day for children of three, five and seven years of age : This is an event occurring on November 15, when prayers are offered for children's growth. Because odd numbers are auspicious in Japan, the odd numbered years of this important period of a child's growth–that is, the ages of three and five for boys, three and seven for girls–are celebrated. On this day, children dress up in their gala dresses and go with their parents to a **Shinto shrine** to pay a visit to the **tutelary deity**. Children are given **thousand-year candy**(*chitose-ame*), which is long, thin, red and white candy in bags with **crane** and **turtle** illustrations. *Chitose* means "one thousand years" and in Japan both the **crane** and the **turtle** are symbols of long life. Also, red and white are an auspicious color combination for the Japanese. All these indicate the wish for children's health and growth.

【勤労感謝の日】 きんろうかんしゃのひ / Kinrō-kansha-no-hi

11月23日は勤労感謝の日です。1948年に「勤労を尊び、生産を祝い、国民が互いに感謝しあう日」として国民の祝日となりました。この日には昔から、**新嘗祭**（にいなめ）と呼ばれる行事が宮中で執り行われてきました。これは、**天皇**がその年の新米を神に捧げ、初めて食するという行事で、その祭儀は現在も**皇室**で行われています。

Labor Thanksgiving Day : November 23rd is *kinrō-kansha-no-hi*. In 1948, it was designated a national holiday "for the people to honor labor, celebrate manufacturing and give thanks to one another." From ancient times, this day has been an observance known as the **Shinto Harvest Festival**, carried out at the imperial court. For this, the **Emperor** dedicates that year's new rice to the gods and tastes it for the first time. This observance is held still today in the **Imperial Household**.

【天皇誕生日】 てんのうたんじょうび / Tennō-tanjōbi

日本の象徴であり、日本国民統合の象徴である**天皇の**「誕生を祝う」日で、国民の祝日です。平成元年（1989年）からは今上天皇の誕生日である12月23日となりました。当日は**皇居**で各省大臣を招いての宴会や、各国大公使を招いての茶会が行われます。多くの国民が**皇居**を訪れ、**天皇**と皇族は、**皇居**のバルコニーに立ち、参賀者にあいさつをします。

Emperor's birthday : This is a national holiday to celebrate "the birth of the **Emperor**," who is a symbol of Japan and a symbol of the unity of the Japanese people. Since the first year of the **Heisei Period**(1989), it occurs on December 23rd, the current Emperor's birthday. The day is marked by banquets at the **Imperial Palace**, to which Cabinet ministers are invited, and tea ceremonies to which foreign ambassadors and officials are invited. Many people visit the **Imperial Palace**, and the **Emperor** and the Imperial family stand on the balcony of the **Imperial Palace** and greet those who come to offer congratulations.

【クリスマス】 Kurisumasu

日本ではクリスチャンに限らず多くの人がクリスマス・イブに家族や恋人にプレゼントを渡したり、一緒に食事をしたりして楽しみます。消費意欲を刺激するデパートや企業の戦略が、このようなクリスマス文化を作ったともいえます。11月後半になると繁華街には大きなツリーが飾られ、デパートや街の商店街などではクリスマス・セールの宣伝が行われるのです。

Christmas : Most people in Japan, not only Christians, enjoy Christmas Eve by exchanging presents with family and sweethearts and by eating together. The strategy of department stores and businesses, which is to stimulate consumer desire, has created this sort of Christmas culture. By the end of November, large trees decorate shopping districts and the advertising for Christmas sales in department stores and shopping street arcades is in full swing.

【年越しそば】 としこしそば／Toshikoshi-soba

大晦日に年越しそばを食べる習慣は**江戸時代**（1603〜1867）以降広まりました。この起源は**大晦日**の大掃除の際、金細工師が仕事場に飛び散った金粉を**そば**を練った団子で集め、それを**火鉢**で焼いて金粉を取ったことにあります。このため**そば**は金を集めるといわれ、**大晦日**に**そば**を食べる風習ができたようです。しかし今では、**そば**のように細く長くという長寿の願いを込めて食べます。

Year-crossing noodles : The custom of eating *toshikoshi soba* on **New Year's Eve** became widespread in the **Edo Period**(1603-1867). It started when a goldsmith, at the time of the general house-cleaning on **New Year's Eve**, gathered the gold dust that had scattered around in his workplace with kneaded *soba* dumplings, then burned these dumplings to ashes on a **brazier**(*hibachi*) and collected the gold dust left behind. Thus, it is said that *soba* collects money, and the practice came about of eating *soba* on **New Year's Eve**. Now however, because *soba* is fine and long, it is eaten with the wish for long life.

【大晦日】
Ōmisoka
おおみそか

　1年の最後の日、12月31日を大晦日といいます。新しい年を気持ちよく迎えるため、家中の大掃除、**畳**や**障子**の張り替えなどはこの日までに済ませておき、帰省してきた家族をも交え、一家だんらんのうちに**正月**を迎えます。

　夜の12時近くなると、全国の**寺**では**除夜の鐘**をつき始めます。**仏教**の教えによれば人間には108の煩悩があり、**除夜の鐘**を108回つくことによって、その煩悩を取り除くのです。そして人々は除夜の鐘の音を聞きながら、翌年の健康や長寿を願って**年越しそば**を食べます。

New Year's Eve : The last day of the year, December 31st, is called *ōmisoka*. To welcome the new year with good feelings, a general house-cleaning is completed, the **flooring rush mats**(*tatami*) are re-covered and the **sliding paper screens**(*shōji*) are repapered by this date; family reunions are held and the whole family brings in **New Year** with a sense of togetherness.

At about midnight, **bells speeding the old year** begin to be rung all at **temples** all around the country. According to **Buddhist** teaching, human beings have 108 worldly desires which are removed by striking the **bell speeding the old year** 108 times. While listening to the sound of the bells, people eat **year-crossing noodles**, wishing for health in the coming year and long life.

日本の祭り

　日本の祭りは大きく2つに区分されます。伝統的に行われている祭りは、**神道**の神と人間とが特定の日に儀式にのっとった交渉を行うことです。これはさまざまな民間信仰も交ざっているため形式はいろいろですが、**神社**があれば日本のどの地域でも必ず行われています。一方、伝統的な祭りが地域住民のすべてが参加して日常とは別の空間を現出することから、似たような形になる記念・祝賀のための集団的な行事も、あえて「祭り」というようになりました。さらに、一定の人数が集まってにぎやかな空間が作られれば「祭り」となり、また集団的な恍惚状態になるようなときには、これを「お祭り騒ぎ」というのです。

Festivals : Japanese festivals are roughly divided into two kinds. Traditionally-held festivals are that in which **Shinto** deities and the people communicate through certain rites on specific dates. Formalities vary, for these festivals are mixed with a diversity of folk beliefs, yet they are invariably held in any region in Japan where there is a **shrine**. Meanwhile, out of traditional festivals in which the regional people all participate to realize a separate space from daily life, mass events for commemoration and celebration, which resemble the form of the traditional festivals, have also become to be called "*matsuri*." And when a certain number of people gather and create a lively space, that too is called "*matsuri*", and the a collective state of excitement is called the "state of making a fete of it(*o-matsuri sawagi*)."

【雪祭】
Yukimatsuri
ゆきまつり

　北海道は、**日本列島**を構成する主要4島の中で最も北にある島です。その北海道の中心地・札幌は冬期五輪が開催された街でもありますが、冬は雪祭でも有名です。これは神をまつる伝統的な**祭り**とは違い、第2次大戦後に行われるようになった雪像の**祭り**です。毎年札幌の大通り公園で行われ、海外からの観光客も含めて数十万人の見物客が集まります。

　自衛隊を初めとする大きな組織から市民個人まで、多くの人が参加して雪像を作ります。城や怪獣など巨大な像は、市外から大量の雪を運んで何週間もかけて作られ、人々の人気を集めています。

Snow Festival : Hokkaidō is the farthest north of the four main islands that constitute the **Japan Islands**. As the center of Hokkaidō, Sapporo has been a host city of winter olympics, and is famous for its winter snow festival. Unlike traditional **festivals** that enshrine Shinto deities, it is a **festival** of snow sculptures that began after the Second World War. The festival is held in a park on the main avenue in Sapporo every year, attracting hundreds of thousands of spectators including tourists from overseas.

　Quite a few people participate in making snow images, varying from large organizations like the Self-Defense Forces to individual citizens. Gigantic images such as castles or monsters are constructed with a large amount of snow carried in from outside the city, taking several weeks, and they are very popular with people.

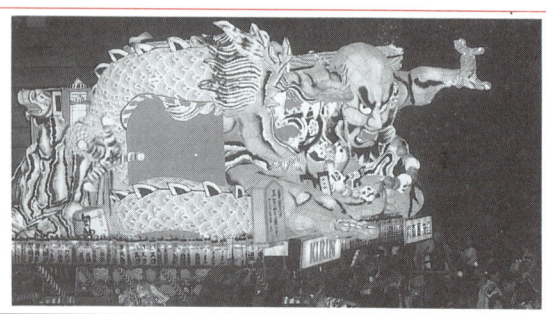

【ねぶた祭】
Nebutamatsuri.
ねぶたまつり

北国の夏は短い。その短い夏に激しい情熱を発散する祭りが、東北で行われるねぶた祭です。そもそもは七夕の行事として行われていたもので、極彩色の武者絵などを大きな灯篭に描いて街中を引き回しますが、その灯篭の周囲に、多い場合は数千人も集まって踊りながら一緒に街を回ります。このねぶたが多いときで60台が出ますから、その人出と熱気にはすさまじいものがあります。8月1日から7日にかけて東北地方の青森市、弘前市を中心に行われています。近年の観光客数は330万人が記録され、海外の祭りにも参加するので、日本を代表する祭りの1つといえるでしょう。(注：弘前市では「ねぷた」といいます)

Nebuta **Festival :** Summer is short in the northern provinces. The *Nebuta* Festival, held in the northeastern district of Japan, radiates strong passions during the short summer. Originally started as an event for the **Star Festival**, it is a parade around the city of *nebuta*, gigantic multi-colored floats with luminous paper effigies of warriors and at a maximum thousands of people gather around the *nebuta* and go through the town dancing. As many as sixty *nebuta* turn out, causing tremendous crowds and incredible heat. The festival takes place from the first to the seventh of August primarily in the cities of Aomori and Hirosaki in northeastern Japan. Since it has made a record of 3,300,000 tourists in recent years, and has participated in **festivals** abroad, it can be referred to as one of Japan's representative **festivals**.(Note: They call it "*neputa*" in Hirosaki City)

【竿灯祭】
Kantōmatsuri
かんとうまつり

　青森の**ねぶた祭**、仙台の**七夕**祭とともに東北三大祭りの１つで、８月４日から７日にかけて秋田市で行われます。「夏になると、暑さと激しい労働のために睡魔に襲われ、眠り病にかかる」と信じられていた時代に、その睡魔を追い払うために、灯篭付きの杉の木を門前に立てていたのが竿灯祭の起源です。現在では農作物の豊作を祈って、竿灯は稲穂を型どり、高さ10メートルの竹竿に９本の横棒を付け、それに多いもので46個のちょうちんを付けます。このような竿灯が180本も連なり、夜の街を埋めつくします。

Kantō **Festival :** It is one of the three major festivals of north-eastern Japan, together with the *Nebuta* **Festival** in Aomori and the **Star Festival** in Sendai, and is held on August 4-7 in Akita city. The *Kantō* Festival originated at a time when people believed that "during summer, you are overcome by sleepiness from heat and intense labor and catch a sleep disease"; so, to drive sleepiness away, people set up Japanese cedar trees with lanterns in front of their house gates. Today, those trees have been replaced by *kantō*; bamboo poles ten meters tall to each of which nine horizontal poles are attached to hang a maximum of forty-six lanterns. They were modeled after the ear of the rice plant, in the hope for a bountiful harvest of crops. As many as one hundred and eighty of these *kantō* stretch out in a row and fill the town at night.

【三社祭】 Sanjamatsuri. さんじゃまつり

東京の三大祭りの1つ。5月の半ばに浅草神社の祭礼として行われます。江戸（今の東京）の**祭り**はみこしを数十人でかついで街々を巡る渡御が主体です。この三社祭は、浅草という伝統的な町並みの中で、各**町内会**のみこしが数十基と大きなみこし3基が勇ましく練り歩くことで人気があり、毎年数十万人の見物人を集めています。**神社**の境内では古式の田楽が舞われ、3日間の期間中は**正月**の**初詣**期間とともにこの街が最もにぎやかなときです。

*S*anja **Festival :** One of the three major festivals of Tokyo. It is held as a ritual ceremony of the Asakusa Shrine in the middle of May. **Festivals** of Edo(present-day Tokyo) are mainly designed for scores of people to carry the portable shrine on their shoulders and parade around the area. This *Sanja* Festival is popular, with scores of the portable shrines from each **block association** and three big portable shrines energetically parading through the old traditional streets of Asakusa, and hundreds of thousands of spectators gather for it every year. Ancient ritual music and dancing is performed in the precincts of the **shrine**. The three days of this festival, together with the **first temple or shrine visit of the New Year** is the time when this town is most enlivened.

【神田祭】 Kandamatsuri. かんだまつり

　神田生まれは江戸っ子の代表といわれるほど、神田は江戸（今の東京）の繁華街の中心でした。神田祭は神田明神で5月に行われる祭礼です。他の東京の祭りと同様、みこしの渡御が主体です。江戸っ子は威勢がよくて喧嘩っ早いといわれますが、その中でも神田祭は威勢がよく、江戸の華ともいわれました。現在は昔ほどのにぎわいは見られませんが、東京の三大祭りの1つとなっています。

Kanda Festival : Kanda was so popular as a center of a commercial and residential district of Edo(present-day Tokyo), that those born in Kanda were said to be typical Edoites(*Edokko*). The Kanda Festival is a ritual ceremony that is held at the Kanda Shrine in May. Like other festivals in Tokyo, the procession of the portable shrines is the main event. Edoites are often described as high-spirited and combative, but even among them the Kanda Festival was high-spirited and was even called the essence of Edo. Today, it is not as bustling as it used to be, but it is still one of the three major festivals of Tokyo.

【秩父夜祭】 ちちぶよまつり／Chichibuyomatsuri.

　京都の**祇園祭**、飛騨高山の高山祭と並んで日本三大曳山祭として有名で、300年以上の歴史があります。12月2、3日に埼玉県秩父神社の祭礼として行われます。笠鉾2台と屋台4台が山間の寒い夜の街を巡ります。6台にはすべて無数のちょうちんやぼんぼりが灯され、にぎやかに花火が打ち上げられて冬の夜空を彩り、その美しさに数十万人の見物客は酔いしれるのです。

Chichibu Festival : It is famous as one of the three major giant-float festivals as well as the **Gion Festival** in Kyoto and the Takayama Festival in Hida of Gifu prefecture, and has a history of over three hundred years. It is held on the second and the third of December as a ritual ceremony of the Chichibu Shrine in Saitama Prefecture. Two elaborately ornamented floats and four other floats parade through the town among the mountains at cold night. All of the six floats are lighted up with countless paper lanterns, fireworks are cheerfully set off to color the winter night sky, and the beauty fascinate hundreds of thousands of spectators.

【祇園祭（会）】
Gionmatsuri きおんまつり

　京都の八坂神社の毎年7月17日〜24日まで行われる豪華絢爛な祭礼です。もとは**平安時代**（794〜1185）初期に疫病をなだめるためにまつられた**神社**で、初め疫病を退散させるために6メートル余りの鉾数十を立てて祭礼を行いました。この鉾がいろいろに飾り付けられ、江戸の**祭り**が勇壮なみこしが中心であるのに対し、こちらは豪華絢爛な鉾が有名です。この鉾は2階建てになっており、上では伝統的な伴奏楽器をつかったお囃子がにぎやかに演奏されます。7月になるとこのお囃子の稽古が街々で行われ、京都に夏が来ることを人々に印象付けるのです。

Gion Festival : This is a splendid Shinto festival held at Yasaka Shrine in Kyoto on July 17-24. The **shrine** was originally built to calm an epidemic which was sweeping the city at the beginning of the **Heian Period**(794-1185). The festival at first was in the form of a ceremony to stamp out the epidemic, featuring scores of standing halberds, each measuring over six meters tall. These halberds were replaced by giant festival floats with decorative halberds and became famous for their gorgeousness, in contrast to the bold and energetic procession of the portable shrines that are the focus of Edo(Tokyo) **festivals**. These festival floats are built in two stories, featuring on the second floor, festival music played in a lively way with traditional accompaniment instruments. When July comes, practice for this festival music is held in various towns, giving an impression for the people that summer is coming to Kyoto.

【どんたく】Dontaku

　5月3、4日に九州博多で行われる櫛田神社の祭礼です。「どんたく」とはオランダ語のZontagがなまったもので「日曜・休日」の意味です。神社から稚児が乗った曳台が出発し、馬に乗った恵比寿・大黒・福禄寿の3福人が続きます。多数の傘鉾や趣向を凝らしたさまざまな山車がこれに続き、街々を練り歩き、要所では稚児が舞を舞います。**三味線**や鼓などで松囃子がにぎやかに演奏されて**祭り**の雰囲気を盛り上げます。この松囃子は、800年前に、当時の領主、平重盛に感謝するために始められたといいます。

D*ontaku :** This is the festival of Kushida Shrine held in Hakata, Kyūshu on May 3-4. "*Dontaku*" is a corruption of the Dutch word Zondag, meaninig Sunday and holiday. *Chigo,* children disguized as heavenly beings for the festival, start from the shrine on a float, followed by the three deities of good fortune, Ebisu, Daikoku, and Fukurokuju, on horses. Numbers of *kasahoko,* elaborately ornamented floats, and *dashi*, decorated gigantic-wheel floats, proceed behind, and the whole parade marches through towns, with *chigo* performing dances at certain spots. **The festival** atmosphere is enlivened by cheerfully played music of ***shamisen and Japanese hand drums. This festival music is said to have started 800 years ago, in order to express gratitude to TAIRA no Shigemori, a feudal lord of the time.

3. 自然を通して見る日本

動物

【鯨】
Kujira
くじら

　日本の捕鯨には1,200年以上の歴史があります。昔は日本近海にも数多く、古代の原始的なモリ漁法でも十分採れたので、『**古事記**』という日本最古の神話集にも捕鯨の歌が収録されています。**江戸時代**（1603〜1867）には捕鯨の基地も数カ所あって、栄えました。

　第2次大戦後には、日本には大変な食糧難の時代があり、その際に鯨は重要な動物性たんぱく源として日本人を飢餓から救ったのです。また鯨は「捨てるところがない」といわれるほど利用価値が高く、例えば、油は工業用油や洗剤、化粧品の原料となり、歯や骨、ひげなどは工芸品に、筋はテニスラケットのガットにも使われました。

Whales : Whaling in Japan has a history for 1,200 years. Because in the past *kujira* were plentiful even in Japan's coastal waters and were sufficiently caught by an ancient and primitive harpoon method, whaling songs are recorded among Japan's oldest myths in "**Kojiki**"(the record of ancient matters). In the **Edo Period** (1603-1867), whaling thrived with a number of whaling bases.

After the Second World War when it was difficult to obtain food, *kujira*, as an important source of animal protein, rescued the Japanese people from hunger. In addition, the utility value of *kujira* is so high that it is said, "there is no part to be wasted ." For example, its oil becomes the raw material for industrial lubricants, cleansing agents and cosmetics; its teeth, bones and whale bone are used in objects of craftwork; and its sinews are used as the gut for stringing tennis rackets.

【鯛】 Tai たい

鯛は「めでたい」という言葉との語呂合わせから、**結婚式**などの祝いや**祭り**の席に出される、縁起のよい魚とされています。また、その姿と色の美しさから海の魚の王とも称されます。鯛をその形のまま食べると運に恵まれるともいわれ、料理して出すときは特に「尾頭付き」が好まれます。日本近海で採れるため漁法も発達し、**江戸時代**（1603〜1867）には生きたまま搬送する技術も考案されました。

Sea bream : Because the word *tai* rhymes with "*medetai*"[meaning "happy" or "auspicious"], the fish are served on the occasion of celebrations like **weddings** and **festivals**, and are regarded as good luck fish. In addition, from the beauty of their shape and color, they are termed the king of ocean fish. To eat *tai* in their natural shape is said to bless one with good fortune, so, when preparing them to serve, "the whole fish"(*okashira-tsuki*) is preferred. A method of catching the fish in Japan's coastal waters was developed, and in the **Edo Period**(1603-1867) a technique was devised to transport them while still alive.

【鯉】 Koi こい

鯉は、激流をさかのぼりあらゆる障害を克服できる魚と信じられており、大きな目的を成し遂げる強さと勇気、忍耐力を備え持つものとしての象徴とされています。

このことから、日本ではこの鯉にあやかって男の子が強く生きていけるようにと願い、5月5日の**子供の日**には、鯉の形をした「こいのぼり」を立てる習慣があります。

Carp : *Koi* are believed to be fish capable of climbing upstream against rapid currents and overcoming all manner of obstacles, hence they are taken as a symbol of the strength, courage and patience to accomplish major goals. From this comes the custom in Japan for boys to pray that they will take after *koi* and live their lives strongly and of hanging out **carp streamers**, shaped like *koi*, on May 5, **Children's Day**.

【金魚】 Kingyo きんぎょ

日本人が好む観賞魚で、たいていは金魚鉢というガラスの鉢の中で飼います。16世紀初頭に原種が中国から輸入され、**江戸時代**（1603〜1867）には種類も増えて、金魚を観賞用に飼うことが盛んとなりました。1960年代までは、東京でも金魚を入れた水桶を天秤棒でかついだ金魚売りが存在しました。夏祭りや**縁日**の露店では「金魚すくい」という遊びが行われ、今でも夏の風物詩となっています。

Goldfish : The Japanese enjoy these fish and usually keep them in a glass gold fish bowl. A pure breed was imported from China at the beginning of the 16th century, different kinds increased in the **Edo Period**(1603-1867), and keeping *kingyo* for enjoyment became widespread. Until the 1960s, *kingyo* sellers  flourished in Tokyo, carrying around *kingyo*-filled buckets suspended from a shoulder carrying pole. A game called "*Kingyo sukui*"(Dip up gold fishes) is played at street stalls at summer festivals and **fairs** and even today is a lyrical feature of summer.

【海老】 Ebi えび

腰が曲がり髭の長い海老は、その形が長生きした老人に似ているため、**鶴・亀**同様、長寿の象徴とされています。中世には「海の翁」などとも呼ばれていました。これを表す日本語の文字も「海の老人」という意味です。

特に伊勢海老は、その大きさ・姿・色の点で最も好まれ、**結婚式**などのお祝いの席によく出されます。ロブスターと似ていますが、大きなハサミはありません。

Shrimp, prawn, lobster : With their bent backs and long whiskers, *ebi* resemble long-lived old people and, like **cranes** and **turtles**, are considered symbols of long life. In the medieval times, they were called the "old men of the sea," and the Chinese characters for *ebi* also have the same meaning. Other characters in Japanese that express this mean "old people of the sea".

The size, shape and color of *ebi* from Ise are particularly well liked and are served on celebratory occasions such as **weddings**. They resemble lobsters but without the large claws.

【鶴】Tsuru つる

大型で頸と脚が長く、その美しさから日本古来の民話や絵画に多く登場しています。10月にシベリアや蒙古から日本に飛来し、翌年3月には帰って行く冬の渡り鳥です。日本では特に長寿を象徴する動物として尊ばれ、祝いごとの図案や装飾によく使われます。**折り紙**の**千羽鶴**は、病気の回復と長寿を祈って病人に贈られます。鶴の生息環境を保護する運動も盛んで、鶴は環境保護の象徴にもなっています。

Cranes : Many classical Japanese folktales and paintings have appeared, featuring the beauty of *tsuru* in their long necks and legs. They are winter migratory birds that fly to Japan in October from Siberia and Mongolia, returning the following year in March. In Japan they are valued especially as animals symbolizing long life and are often used for festive designs and decorations. **One Thousand Cranes** of **folded paper** are sent to the sick to pray for recovery from illness and for long life. The movement to protect the habitat of *tsuru* is active, and *tsuru* have become a symbol for environmental protection.

【亀】Kame かめ

日本には「鶴は千年、亀は万年」ということわざがあり、鶴とともに亀は長寿の動物としてめでたいものとされています。古代中国と朝鮮が鶴と亀を長寿と繁栄の象徴としたのが日本に伝わり、今では日本人の生活に深く根差したものとなっています。

琴や**能**などの日本の伝統芸能には、「鶴亀」という作品があり、これを祝辞の代わりに演じることもあります。

Turtles : In Japan there is the proverb, "**Cranes** live 1,000 years, turtles 10,000." Together with **cranes**, *kame* are thought to be animals symbolizing long life. In ancient China and Korea, **cranes** and *kame* were considered to be symbols of long life and prosperity, and that was conveyed to Japan; that belief has taken deep root in lives of the Japanese people.

In traditional Japanese performing arts like **Japanese harp** and **Noh**, there is a work called "*Tsurukame*" which has been performed to take the place of congratulatory messages.

【うぐいす】
Uguisu

独特の美しい鳴き声で春を告げる鳥として、古来より日本人に愛されてきた日本特有の小鳥です。ちょうど**梅**が咲くころ里に来て鳴き始めるので、**梅**とうぐいすの組み合わせは絵や詩歌の題材になります。**江戸時代**（1603〜1867）には飼っているうぐいすを鳴き競わせることも盛んに行われました。声の美しい、女性の電話オペレーターやアナウンサーなどを「うぐいす嬢」ともいいます。

Japanese bush warbler : These are small birds, peculiar to Japan, that have been beloved by the Japanese people since ancient times as birds that announce springtime with their uniquely beautiful cry. They come down to village and start to cry just about the time when **plum trees** bloom, so the combination of **plum trees** and Japanese bush warbler has become subject matter of paintings, poetry and songs. In the **Edo Period**(1603-1867), singing competitions for pet Japanese bush warbler were often held. And the term "Miss *Uguisu*" is applied to female telephone operators and announcers with beautiful voices.

【蛙】
Kaeru
かえる

蛙は古くから日本人に親しまれてきました。日本の農業は水稲が主であり、そのため水田にはさまざまな生き物がいました。蛙もその水田や池、川に多く住んでいます。『古今和歌集』（905年）にも「蛙の鳴き声を聞くと歌を詠みたくなる」と書かれているように、日本人は蛙の声にさえ季節を感じ、歌を詠みました。蛙の子であるおたまじゃくしは子供に人気があります。

Frogs have been closely associated with Japanese life for a long time. Agricultural products in Japan were mainly rice-paddy plants, and there were many creatures in paddy fields. Frogs inhabit the paddy fields, ponds, and rivers. As written in the "**Kokinwakashū**"(905 a.d.), "a frog's croaking inspire one to compose a poem," the Japanese people sensed the season even in a frog's croaking and composed poems. Tadpoles, baby frogs, are popular with children.

【犬】
いぬ Inu

　犬は、人間が野生動物の中から家畜として獲得した最初の動物です。従って、日本でも新石器時代から家畜としての犬がいました。しかし、農耕文化の日本では、ヨーロッパやユーラシアの牧畜民族と違い、猟犬よりも番犬としての役割の方が多かったようです。**江戸時代**（1603〜1867）には愛玩用としての犬も出てきました。日本を代表する犬には、秋田犬、土佐犬、柴犬などがいます。

Dogs : Among wild animals, dogs were the first that humans kept and domesticated. Thus, domesticated dogs have existed in Japan since the Neolithic era. However, in Japan with its farming culture, as distinct from the cattle-raising peoples of Europe and Eurasia, the role of house dog appears to have been that of watching dog rather than of hunting dog. In the **Edo Period**(1603-1867), dogs also emerged as pets. Typical Japanese dogs include Akita, Tosa and Shiba breeds.

【猫】
ねこ Neko

　日本の猫は、縁起のよい動物でもあり、恐ろしい動物でもあります。猫が顔をなでるしぐさは福を招いているようにも見え、その形が「招き猫」として縁起のよい置物になっています。一方、猫は化けて出ると考えられた時代もあり、日本の妖怪の中には「化け猫」がいます。ペットブームともいわれる現代は、世界中の猫が日本で飼われていますが、伝統的に優れた猫とされているのは三毛猫です。

Cats : In Japan, cats are regarded as both auspicious and fearful. The way cats wash their faces looks as if they are inviting good luck, so cats with in that gesture, are represented in an auspicious ornament as the "beckoning cat." On the other hand, there was a time when cats were thought to transform into monsters, among the many Japanese monsters is the "goblin cat." Today, with a pet boom under way, cats from all over the world are kept in Japan, but one that is traditionally valued is the tortoise-shell cat.

【狸】
Tanuki
たぬき

狸は東アジア（日本、朝鮮半島、中国）にのみ生息する穴熊に似た夜行性の動物です。非常に驚くと仮死状態となつて人を欺くため、「狸寝入り」といえば寝たふりをすることをいいます。日本の民話では、いろいろなものに化けて人をだますが失敗ばかりするユーモラスな動物として描かれています。また狸は腹で鼓を打つと信じられ、その様を歌つた『証誠寺の狸ばやし』は英語でも歌われました。

Raccoon dogs : Living only in East Asia(Japan, Korean Peninsula, and China), they are nocturnal animals resembling badgers. When they are very surprised they fall into a state of apparent death; from this deception comes the phrase "the raccoon dog's sleep," indicating a pretense of sleeping. In Japanese folktales, raccoon dogs are depicted as humorous animals, appearing in disguise and deceiving people, but always failing. Raccoon dogs are believed to beat a drum on their bellies, and the song that sings of this has even been sung in English.

【狐】
Kitsune
きつね

狐は日本人にとっても『イソップ童話』に出てくる狐と同様、人をだます悪賢い動物というイメージがあり、民話や伝説などでもしばしば悪役を演じています。また人間に憑（ひょう）いして狂わせる悪霊でもあります。

一方、稲荷神社の境内で見かける座った狐の石像は、神の使者としての狐を表しています。

Foxes : Just as with fox that appears in "Aesop's Fables," in Japan, too, the image of fox is one of cunning creatures who deceive people, and they often play the villain in folktales and legends. In addition, they are also evil spirits that possess human beings and make them go crazy.

On the other hand, the stone idol of a seated fox, which one can see in the precincts of the *Inari* Shrine, represents the fox as messenger of the gods.

【蝶】
Chō
ちょう

日本人にとって、蝶は美しい昆虫の代表の1つです。日本にいる蝶は約260種を数えますが、よく目にするのはもんしろちょうとあげはちょうです。また、国の蝶はおおむらさきといいます。

蝶は古くから**和歌**に詠まれ、歌に歌われてきました。特に菜の花に飛び交うもんしろちょうは、春を告げる光景として親しまれています。

Butterflies : The butterfly is a representative of beautiful insects. There are about 260 different kinds of butterflies counted in Japan. But common ones are Cabbage butterflies and swallowtails. The national butterfly of Japan is named the giant purple butterfly.

Butterflies have long been included in the **classical Japanese poems** and songs. In particular, the sight of cabbage butterflies flying around rape blossoms is beloved by the people as announcing the beginning of spring.

【蟬】
Semi
せみ

蝶や**とんぼ**などと並び、日本人に親しまれている昆虫で、夏になると山や里の木々で一斉に鳴き始めます。その数が多いとまるで鳴き声のシャワーのようになるため、これを「蟬時雨（せみしぐれ）」といいます。歌や**俳句**にも数多く詠まれており、俳聖・**芭蕉**の俳句には有名な蟬時雨を詠んだ句があります。蟬は生まれてわずか1週間ほどで死んでしまうため、かげろうなどとともに、人のはかない命にもたとえられます。

Cicadas : *Semi,* together with **butterflies** and **dragonflies**, are insects familiar to the Japanese people. When summer comes, they start to sing all together on trees in mountains and villages. When there are many cicadas, the dronings become like a shower, which is called "*semi-shigure*"(shower of cicadas). This word is often found in **poems in seventeen syllables**(*haiku*) and other poems; there is a famous *haiku* on *semi-shigure*, by the "greatest master" of *haiku*, **Bashō**. Since cicadas die only about a week after birth, they are compared, together with Mayflies, to transient life of man.

【とんぼ】 Tonbo

日本を昔は「あきつしま」といいましたが、「あきつ」とはとんぼのことです。初代天皇の神武（神話による）が蚊に刺されたとき、とんぼが飛んできてこの蚊を食べたので名付けられたという伝説があります。夏から秋にかけてさまざまな種類のとんぼを見ることができ、日本の代表的な昆虫といえるでしょう。特に子供たちに親しまれ、『赤とんぼ』という、秋の詩情を表した童謡の名曲もあります。

Dragonflies : Long ago Japan was called "*akitsu-shima*," "*akitsu*" meaning dragonflies(*tonbo*) [and "*shima*" meaning an island]. According to the legend, this name of Japan came from the time when Jinmu, the first Emperor(by myth), was bitten by a mosquito and a dragonfly flew in and ate it.

One can see various kinds of *tonbo* in summer and autumn; it is a common Japanese insect. Children especially like it, and there is even a well-known children's song called "Akatonbo"(red dragonflies) that expresses lyrical sentiments of autumn.

【蛍】 Hotaru ほたる

この昆虫は、清流の茂みなどに住み、初夏の5月ごろから7月中旬に姿を現わします。尾のあたりから青白い光を発するため、夏の夜などに虫籠に入れてその光を鑑賞することも盛んに行われていました。しかし近年清流が少なくなるとともに蛍もその数が減り、昔行われていた蛍狩りもできなくなりました。昔は、蛍の光は戦争で死んだ兵士の魂が姿を変えたものだと信じられていたこともありました。

Fireflies : This insect inhabits bushes by clear streams and appears from around May in early summer until the middle of July. Since they emit a pale glow from their backs, appreciating the glow through an insect cage filled with fireflies has been a popular activity during summer nights. However, with the decrease of clear streams in recent years, fireflies have also decreased in number, making it hard to hunt them as in the past. The glow of fireflies at one time was thought to be the altered form of the souls of soldiers who had died in war.

【天然記念物（動物）】

てんねんきねんぶつ／Tennen-kinenbutsu

　自然の中で貴重・希少なものを保護する目的で、日本では文化財保護法が制定されています。これを天然記念物といい、捕獲は禁止されています。対象となっている動物には、アマミノクロウサギ・トキ・アホウドリ・メグロ・オオサンショウウオなどの日本特産種がいます。また、特産ではありませんが分布が限られているものとしては、タンチョウなどがあげられます。そのほか、生物群集として鹿児島県の鶴とその渡来地、ゲンジボタルの発生地、千葉県の鯛生息地、カブトガニ繁殖地などがあります。

Natural monuments (animals) : A cultural properties protection law is in effect in Japan for the purpose of protecting what is valuable and rare in nature. It is called *tennen-kinenbutsu* and the law prohibits capturing of corresponding animals. The object animals are such as an Amami hare, Japanese crested ibis, short-tailed albatross, a bulbul, and a giant salamander, which are peculiar to Japan. There is, also on the list, the Japanese crane, which is not peculiar to Japan, but has a limited range of distribution. In addition, there are animal preserves, such as the stopping off point for **cranes** flying from overseas in Kagoshima Prefecture, a Genji-firefly habitat, a **sea bream** habitat in Chiba Prefecture, and a breeding ground for horseshoe crabs.

植物

【松竹梅】
Shōchikubai
しょうちくばい

　松、竹、梅という3種の木の名を1つの熟語にして、松竹梅といい、めでたいものの象徴的な表現となります。これらの植物は寒さに強いことから冬の間に珍重され、**正月**の**門松**や**結婚式**などの祝いごと、めでたいときの飾りとして使われます。**琴**や**長唄**などの曲の中にも歌詞としてよく使われ、やはり祝儀用とされています。

　松は、日本を代表する木で、**日本画**の背景にもよく描かれています。**竹**は、細工物や**笛**の材料として使われてきました。**梅**は、その花を観賞するだけでなく実を食品や薬品にし、古くから重要な保存食となっていました。

Pine, bamboo and plum trees : Putting these three names of the trees together makes the phrase *shōchikubai,* which is the symbolic expression of auspicious matters. These plants are highly valued in winter because they are strong against the cold, and they are used as felicitous decorations for celebratory, events, as with the **New Year's pine and bamboo decorations** or at **weddings**. They are also frequently found in the lyrics of melodies for **Japanese harp***(koto)* and **long epic songs***(nagauta)*, and there too they are for celebration.

　The **pine**, as the tree that stands for Japan, is often drawn in the background of **Japanese paintings**. The **bamboo** is used as raw material for handicrafts and **flutes**. The **plum tree** is not only enjoyed for its flowers, but its fruit is used for food, in medicine, and, since ancient times, as an important keepable food.

【紅葉】 Momiji, Kōyō もみじ・こうよう

　日本の多くの落葉樹は秋になると葉の色が紅や黄色に変わり、山々を美しい色で染めます。これを紅葉といって、日本人は春の**桜**と同じように美しい景色としてほめたたえ、古くから詩歌にその美しさを詠み込んでいます。秋になると人々は紅葉を見に山野へと繰り出します。**桜**を見るのを**花見**というように、山野に紅葉を見に行くことを「もみじ狩り」に行くともいいます。そうして赤や黄色の葉が散ってしまうと、**日本列島**は冬へと季節を変えるのです。日本の紅葉が美しいのには理由があります。晴れた良い天気が続くと葉の同化作用が盛んになり、炭水化物がたくさん蓄積され、紅葉のもととなる花青素が増えるからです。

Tinted autumnal leaves : In autumn, the leaves on most Japanese deciduous trees change color to reds and yellows and coat the mountains in beautiful colors. The Japanese people have admired this—they call it *momiji* or *kōyō*—as a beautiful scene in the same way as with springtime **cherry blossoms**, and they have expressed that beauty in poems and songs since long ago. In autumn, the people go out to hills and fields to see tinted autumnal leaves. Just as viewing **cherry blossoms** is called "**flower-viewing**," going to the hills and fields to see *momiji* is called "Momiji-hunting." And once all the red and yellow leaves have fallen, the **Japanese Islands** experience a change of season toward winter. There is a reason for the beauty of Japanese tinted autumnal leaves. It is because with continued clear, good weather, leaf metabolism speeds up, carbohydrates are stored, and anthocyan that is the cause of tinted leaves increases.

【キノコ】 Kinoko

キノコは森林の生植物で木やその根元に生えるものが多いことから、昔の日本人が「木の子」と名付けたのが由来です。古い言葉では「タケ」といい、そのためキノコの和名には「〜タケ」とつくものが多くあります。

食品としてのキノコは独特の風味によって大変親しまれています。日常の食卓にのぼる主なものには、シイタケ・エノキダケ・シメジ・ナメコ・マイタケなどがあり、焼いたり、汁の身にしたり、油炒めや茶碗蒸しにしたりします。「香りマツタケ、味シメジ」といわれ、マツタケは芳香のため非常に珍重されていますが、高価で一般の家庭の食卓にはあまりのぼりません。

Mushrooms : *Kinoko* reproduce in forests, mostly growing on or beneath trees, thus the Japanese long ago named them *"kinoko"*(children of trees). An old word for mushroom is *take*, and this is often added to the Japanese mushroom name as "name + *take*."

Mushrooms are enjoyed very much for their unique flavor as food. Among the main items for daily dining are mushrooms (*shiitake*), winter mushrooms(*enokidake*), champignons(*shimeji*), Japanese endemic mushrooms(*nameko*) and *maitake*, which are grilled, put in soup, fried in oil or put in a steamed custard of vegetables, eggs and meat. As in the saying, "pine mushrooms for aroma, champignons for flavor," the *"pine mushroom"* are very highly valued for their fragrance; but they do not often appear on the dining tables of ordinary families, because they are so expensive.

【果物】
Kudamono
くだもの

日本は四季がはっきりしているのでそれぞれの季節に果物がとれます。中でも秋は果物の季節といっていいでしょう。「桃栗3年、柿8年」という言い方があり、桃や栗は種をまいてから3年で実がなり、柿は8年かかる、という意味です。これらの果物は古くから日本人に親しまれて民話にもよく登場します。桃は「桃太郎」、栗や柿は「猿蟹合戦」などです。そのほかの秋の果物はナシ、リンゴ、ぶどう、秋から冬にかけてはみかん、夏には梅、びわなどが収穫されます。梅からは梅干しを作りますが、これは昔から優れた保存食として親しまれています。

Fruit : Since in Japan there are clear distinctions among the four seasons, there is fruit for each season. Among these seasons, particularly autumn can be said to be the season for fruit. There is an expression, "three years for peaches and **chestnuts**, eight years for Japanese persimmons," meaning that it takes three years for peaches and **chestnuts** and eight years for Japanese persimmons to bear fruit after sowing the seeds. These fruits have been popular among the Japanese people since a long time ago, and have often appeared in folktales; for example, peaches appear in "Momotarō" and **chestnuts** and Japanese persimmons appear in "Saru-Kani Gassen." Other autumn fruits are pears, apples, and grapes. From autumn to winter, mandarin oranges, and in summer, **plums** and loquats are harvested. **Pickled plums** are made of the **plums**, and they have been favored as excellent preserved foods since long ago.

【朝顔】
Asagao
あさがお

　アジア原産の一年草のツル草で、朝顔は盛夏のころから初秋にかけて咲きます。日本には西暦900年代に遣唐使によって薬用として持ち込まれ、栽培されるようになりました。「朝の顔」という日本語名の意味通りで、朝咲き、すぐに花を閉じてしまいます。**江戸時代**（1603〜1867）に栽培が盛んになり、多くの品種ができました。湿気が多く暑い日本の夏には、朝の涼しい空気の中に咲く朝顔が人々の心をなごませるのです。こんな有名な**俳句**もあります。

　朝顔に　つるべとられて　もらい水　（千代女）

　東京の下谷では毎年7月6日から8日まで、鉢植えの朝顔を売る朝顔市が開かれます。

Morning glory : An annual climbing plant originally produced in Asia, *asagao* blooms from midsummer to early fall. It was brought to Japan for medical purposes by an envoy to China sometime in the 900s and began to be cultivated. In keeping with the meaning of its name in Japanese, "morning face," it blooms in the morning and the blossoms close up immediately. Cultivation flourished in the **Edo Period**(1603-1867) and many varieties were developed. In the hot, humid Japanese summer, *asagao* blooming in the cool morning air soften people's hearts. There is even a famous *haiku*(a **poem in seventeen-syllables**):

　For morning glories taking up a well bucket,
　I get water from next-door. (by Chiyojo)

 In the Shitaya district in Tokyo every year from July 6-8, an *asagao* market opens for selling potted *asagao*.

【ほおずき】 Hōzuki

ナス科の多年生植物で、夏にはオレンジ色をした風船のような袋の中に、丸いさくらんぼのような実が熟します。日本の女の子たちは、その実をよくもみ、小さく開けた穴から柔らかくした果肉を出し、舌と歯に当てて笛にして、よく遊んだものです。

毎年7月には、東京の浅草でほおずき市が開かれ、多くの人々が集まります。

Ground cherries : A perennial plant of the eggplant family, its fruit ripens in summer like a round cherry inside a balloon-like, orange-colored pouch. Japanese girls frequently used to play by rubbing the fruit, taking out its softened flesh from a small hole, and inserting it between tongue and teeth as a whistle.

Many people gather every year in July for a *hōzuki* market in the Asakusa district in Tokyo.

【藤】 Fuji ふじ

藤は、発音すると**富士**と同じですが、晩春に咲く薄紫色の蔓性の美しい花です。山野に自生していますが、観賞用としては棚を作りその上に蔦をはわせ、花はその棚から垂れ下がるようにします。この花の房は数十センチから1メートル数十センチになり、風が吹くと波のように揺れるのが藤波といって美しいのです。薄紫色は一般に藤色といわれます。

Japanese wistaria : *Fuji*, pronounced the same way as **Mt. Fuji**, are beautiful pale purple flowers with vines that bloom in late spring. They grow wild in fields and mountains, but, to appreciate their beauty, the vines are trained over a trellis and the flowers are drooped down from it. Each bunch of *fuji* measures

from scores of centimeters to one meter and scores of centimeters in length, and beauty is found in the bunches swaying(like waves) in the wind, which are referred to as fuji waves. A pale purple color is generally called fuji color.

【菖蒲】
Shōbu
しょうぶ

根や茎は水の中に横たわり、長い葉を持ち、初夏に花を咲かせます。葉には芳香があり、邪気を払うとされ、5月5日の**端午の節句（子供の日）**には、その葉や根を湯の中に入れて風呂に入ります。これを「菖蒲湯」といい、古くからの習慣で**銭湯**でも行われています。菖蒲や、似た形のアヤメは姿が美しく、大きく繊細な花弁が開く様は、美しい女性を形容する比喩にも使われます。

Sweet flag : Its roots and stems lay sideways in water, its leaves are long and it blooms in early summer. Its leaves are fragrant and it is believed to get rid of evil; for **Boy's Festival**, also known as **Children's Day**, on May 5, baths are taken with *shōbu* leaves and roots added to the hot water. This is called "*shōbuyu*"(sweet-flag baths) and is a custom of long standing that can be enjoyed even at **public baths**. The manner in which the beautifully-shaped *shōbu* and *ayame*, an iris which is similar to *shōbu* in shape, open their large, delicate flower petals also has been used as a metaphor to describe beautiful women.

【柳】
Yanagi
やなぎ

春を告げる緑の中でも、柳は真っ先に芽を吹き、新しい季節の到来を告げるので、昔から日本人に親しまれ、歌にも多く詠まれています。日本中どこにでも植えられて日常親しまれているためか、柳を用いた諺も数多くあります。種類も多く90種以上を数えますが、しだれ柳がその代表です。中でも東京の銀座の柳の街路樹は、古い流行歌にも歌われて有名です。

Willows : Because *yanagi*, even in the midst of the greenery announcing springtime, send forth their sprouts before all others and announce the coming of a new season, they have been enjoyed by the Japanese people since ancient times and are often included in poems. Perhaps because they have been so enjoyed and have been planted everywhere throughout Japan, there are many proverbs using *yanagi*. One can count more than 90 different kinds, with the weeping willow most typical. The streetside *yanagi* in Tokyo's Ginza district are so famous that they are even sung about in an old popular song.

【栗】 Kuri. くり

　秋の味覚の中では、栗は最も親しまれているものの1つです。そして柿とともに秋を象徴する果物でもあります。実を覆ういちばん外側の皮は針ネズミのように針がたくさん生えています。この実はゆでてそのまま食べるか、ご飯に炊き込んで栗ごはんにします。また、ようかんや饅頭など、日本の菓子類にもよく使われます。栗の濃い茶色は栗色ともいわれます。

Chestnuts are one of the most common and beloved tastes of autumn, and together with persimmons they symbolize autumn. The outermost shell covering the fruit of the nut is covered with prickles, like a hedgehog. These nuts can be eaten simply boiled or cooked with rice to make chestnut rice. They are also used as ingredients in Japanese confectionery such as sweet bean jelly(*yōkan*) and buns with a bean-jam filling(*manjū*). In Japan, dark brown color is called chestnut color.

【竹・笹】 Take,Sasa たけ・ささ

　竹は古くから日本全土に分布し、建築材や細工ものによく使われてきました。また、筍は食用として古くから日本の料理によく使われています。

　小さな竹のことを笹といいます。竹も笹も観賞用として植えられます。日本最古の物語『**竹取物語**』は竹の中からかぐや姫が拾われ、最後は月へ帰っていくという美しい内容で、日本人に最も親しまれている物語の1つです。

Bamboo, bamboo grass : Since long ago, *take* is found all over the land of Japan and is frequently used for construction material and in craftsmanship. Moreover, bamboo sprouts have long been used as edible material in Japanese cuisine.

　Small *take* is called *sasa*. Both *take* and *sasa* are planted in gardens for visual appreciation. The Japan's oldest story, the "Taketori monogatari"(**Tale of Bamboo Cutter**), is about the Princess of the Moon found inside a bamboo stalk and in the end returns to the moon, and it is one of the most beloved stories in Japan.

【稲】 Ine
いね

　稲を脱穀して精米すると米になります。この稲はもともと熱帯産で、インドや東南アジアが原産地とされています。2,000年以上前に温帯の日本に渡り、気候に適応するようにさまざまな改良が加えられて高い生産性を示すようになりました。稲を育てるには多くの水が必要ですが、その点夏は高温多湿で、冬を除けば雨量も多い日本は水稲に適していました。山岳地帯が国土の61％を占める日本で稲を育てるには、村が共同で治山治水作業や農作業をすることが必要でした。集団で物事を決めて遂行していく日本人の習慣の原点がここにあります。現在ではさらに改良が加えられ、新種のおいしい米が競って作られています。

Rice plants go through a process of threshing and polishing to become **rice**. This plant originally came from tropical regions, and is native to India and Southeast Asia. It was brought to Japan, which is in the temperate zone 2,000 years ago and, with adjustments to fit the climate, it yielded high productivity. Rice cultivation requires much water, and, in this regard, Japan with its high heat and humidity and large amount of rainfall except in winter was suited to paddies. To grow rice in a country like Japan where the mountainous regions occupy 61% of the land, it was necessary for the whole villagers to cooperate in flood control and agricultural endeavers. This is the source of the Japanese tendency to decide and carry things out in groups. Today, new species of **rice** are being made competitively with even more improvements.

地理・気候・風土

【面積と人口（都道府県別）】Menseki to jinkō めんせきとじんこう

◎都道府県別面積と人口（1991年10月1日現在）
Area and Population by Prefectures(as of October 1st, 1991)

○面積／Area（km²）
●人口（千人）Population(unit：1,000 persons)

	○	●		○	●
北海道／Hokkaidō[1]	78,415 (83,411)	5,649	香川／Kagawa	1,875	1,023
青森／Aomori[2]	9,606	1,477	愛媛／Ehime	5,674	1,513
岩手／Iwate	15,275	1,415	高知／Kōchi	7,104	821
宮城／Miyagi	7,284	2,264	福岡／Fukuoka	4,966	4,831
秋田／Akita[2]	11,613	1,223	佐賀／Saga	2,439	877
山形／Yamagata	9,323	1,257	長崎／Nagasaki	4,089	1,557
福島／Fukushima	13,782	2,108	熊本／Kumamoto	7,402	1,843
茨城／Ibaraki	6,093	2,870	大分／Ōita	6,336	1,235
栃木／Tochigi	6,408	1,947	宮城／Miyagi	7,733	1,167
群馬／Gunma	6,363	1,974	鹿児島／Kagoshima	9,185	1,792
埼玉／Saitama	3,797	6,483	沖縄／Okinawa	2,265	1,229
千葉／Chiba	5,156	5,614	全国／Total	372,754 (377,750)	124,043
東京／Tōkyō	2,183	11,887			
神奈川／Kanagawa	2,413	8,044			
新潟／Niigata	12,582	2,474			
富山／Toyama	4,246	1,121			
石川／Ishikawa	4,185	1,166			
福井／Fukui	4,188	824			
山梨／Yamanashi	4,465	858			
長野／Nagano	13,585	2,160			
岐阜／Gifu	10,598	2,072			
静岡／Shizuoka	7,779	3,686			
愛知／Aichi[3]	5,147	6,724			
三重／Mie[3]	5,775	1,802			
滋賀／Shiga	4,017	1,234			
京都／Kyōto	4,612	2,604			
大阪／Ōsaka	1,886	8,737			
兵庫／Hyōgo	8,383	5,437			
奈良／Nara	3,690	1,389			
和歌山／Wakayama	4,722	1,076			
鳥取／Tottori[3]	3,498	616			
島根／Shimane[4]	6,626	778			
岡山／Okayama	7,111	1,929			
広島／Hiroshima	8,473	2,858			
山口／Yamaguchi	6,109	1,569			
徳島／Tokushima	4,143	830			

建設省国土地理院「1991年全国都道府県市区町村別面積調査」
Ministry of Construction, Geographical Survey Institute "National Survey of Land Areas by administrative divisions of all Japan 1991"
総務庁統計局「1991年10月1日現在推計人口」
Management and Coordination Agency, Statistics Bureau "Estimated Population as of October 1st, 1991"
1)北方領土を含む。2)十和田湖（61km²）は水面境界不明のため両県の面積に含まず。3)境界未定地域（5km²）を含ます。4)中海（87km²）と境水道（2km²）は水面境界不明のため両県の面積に含まず。ただし全国計には2)、3)、4)を含む。
1)Includes Northern Territories.
2)Does not include Towada Lake in neither areas of the two prefectures for an unidentified border on the water surface.
3)Does not include districts with an unidentified border(5km²).
4)Does not include inland seas(87km²) and channels(2km²) in neither areas of the two prefectures for an identified border on the water surface. Note: all 2), 3), 4) are included in the national total.

【日本列島（都道府県）】

Nihon-rettō
にほんれっとう

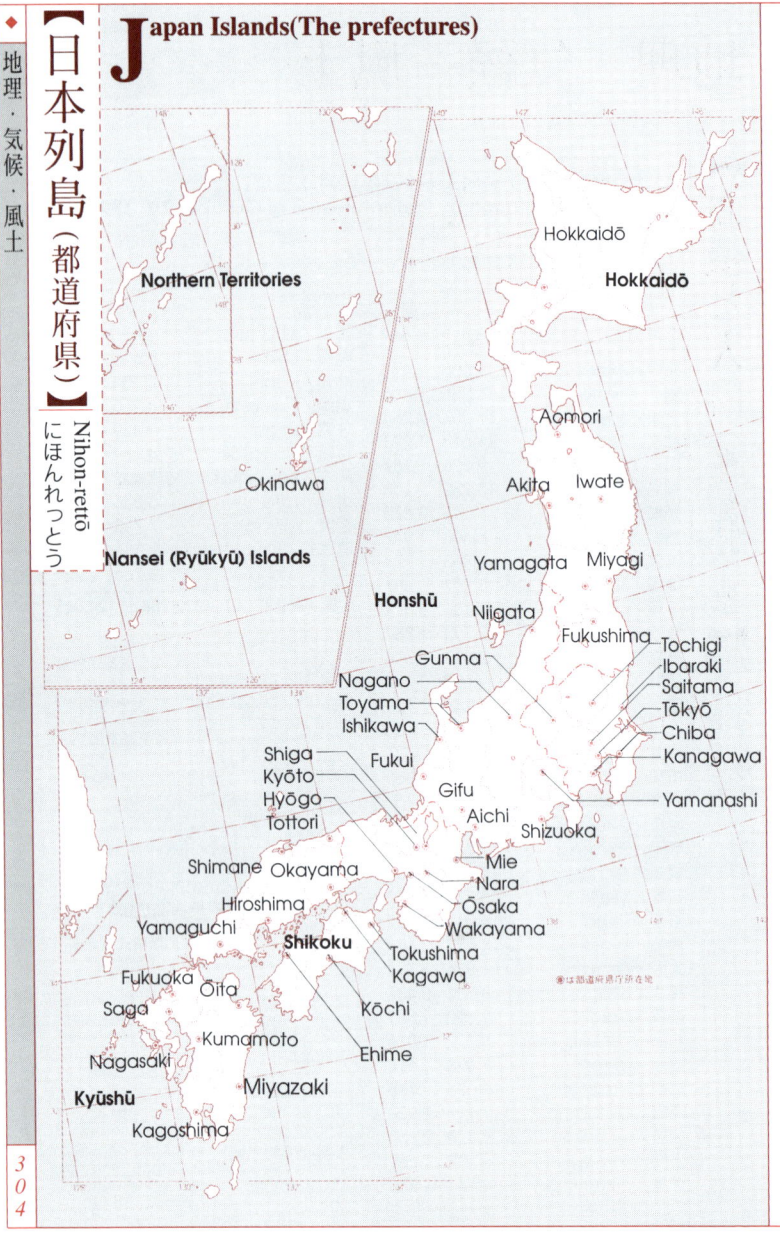

Northern Territories

Hokkaidō

Hokkaidō

Okinawa

Aomori

Akita   Iwate

Nansei (Ryūkyū) Islands

Yamagata   Miyagi

Honshū

Niigata

Fukushima   Tochigi

Gunma   Ibaraki
Saitama
Nagano   Tōkyō
Toyama   Chiba
Ishikawa   Kanagawa

Shiga   Fukui
Kyōto   Yamanashi
Hyōgo   Gifu
Tottori   Aichi
Shizuoka

Shimane   Okayama   Mie
Nara
Hiroshima   Ōsaka
Yamaguchi   Wakayama
Shikoku
Tokushima
Fukuoka   Ōita   Kagawa
Saga   Kōchi
Kumamoto
Nagasaki   Ehime
Kyūshū   Miyazaki
Kagoshima

◉は都道府県庁所在地

【日本列島（地勢）】

Nihon-rettō

にほんれっとう

Japan Islands(Natural features)

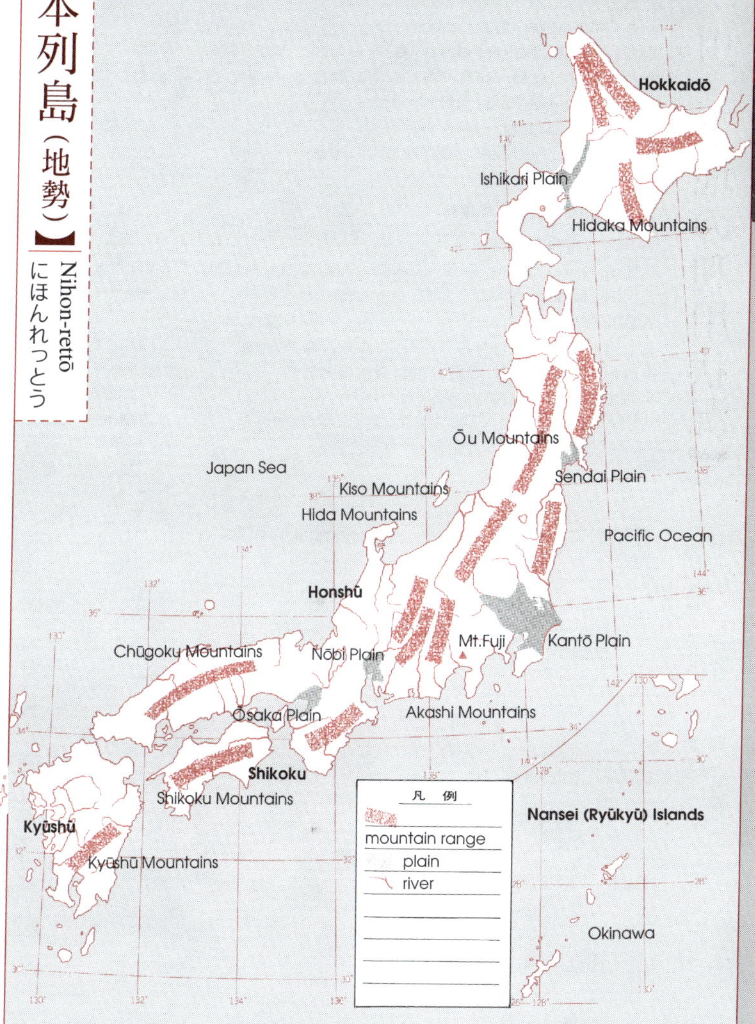

Hokkaidō
Ishikari Plain
Hidaka Mountains
Ōu Mountains
Japan Sea
Sendai Plain
Kiso Mountains
Hida Mountains
Pacific Ocean
Honshū
Chūgoku Mountains
Nōbi Plain
Mt.Fuji
Kantō Plain
Ōsaka Plain
Akashi Mountains
Shikoku
Shikoku Mountains
Kyūshū
Kyūshū Mountains
Nansei (Ryūkyū) Islands
Okinawa
凡　例
mountain range
plain
river

【山・川・土地の利用状況】

やま・かわ・とちのりようじょうきょう

Yama, kawa, tochi no riyōjōkyō

◎主な山／Major mountains

Name （所在／Location）	高さ／Height
富士山／Fuji-san （山梨／Yamanashi、静岡／Shizuoka）	3,776m
北岳／Kita-dake （山梨／Yamanashi）	3,192m
奥穂高岳／Okuhotaka-dake （長野／Nagano、岐阜／Gifu）	3,190m
間ノ岳／Aino-take （山梨／Yamanashi、静岡／Shizuoka）	3,189m
槍ケ岳／Yari-ga-take （長野／Nagano）	3,180m
東岳／Azuma-dake （静岡／Shizuoka）	3,141m
赤石岳／Akaishi-dake （長野／Nagano、静岡／Shizuoka）	3,120m

◎主な川／Major rivers

Name （流域／Course）	流域面積／River basin area	長さ／Length
利根川／Tone-gawa （群馬／Gunma、千葉／Chiba,etc.）	16,84k㎡	322km
石狩川／Ishikari-gawa （北海道／Hokkaido）	14,330k㎡	268km
信濃川／Shinano-gawa （長野／Nagano、新潟／Niigata,etc.）	11,900k㎡	367km
北上川／Kitakami-gawa （岩手／Iwate、宮城／Miyagi）	10,15,k㎡	249km
木曾川／Kiso-gawa （岐阜／Gifu、愛知／Aichi,etc.）	9,100k㎡	277km
十勝川／Tokachi-gawa （北海道／Hokkaido）	9,010k㎡	156km
淀川／Yodo-gawa （京都／Kyoto、大阪／Osaka,etc.）	8,240k㎡	75km

◎地形による国土の区分／Classification of land

低地／Lowland 13%
山地／Mountainous area 53%
台地／Plateau 12%
山麓／Piedmont 4%
丘陵／Hill 11%
火山地／Volcanic zone 7%

Mountains, rivers, current land use

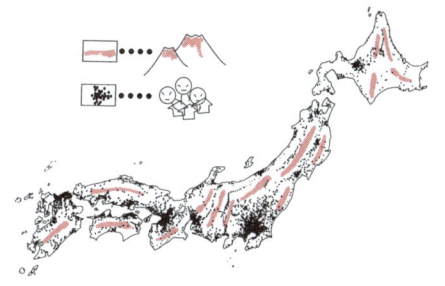

【地形】
Chikei
ちけい

　日本は東北から南西に長く伸びた弧状の列島で形成されています。列島を構成する主な島は北海道、本州、四国、九州の4島で、さらに沖縄を主体とする南西諸島を加えれば、その長さは3,500キロになります。地形の特色から本州のほぼ中央を境にして東北弧と南西弧とが合体して**日本列島**が形成されたと考えられています。国土面積の61%は急峻な山岳地帯であり、森林に覆われています。一方、人が住める平野や山間の盆地を合わせた平地の面積は24%にしか過ぎません。ここに人口の65%が集中しています。そのため美しい山々と豊かな緑に恵まれている反面、居住可能面積当たりの人口密度は世界有数となっています。

Geographical features : Japan is an arc-shaped archipelago that stretches a long way from northeast to southwest. The four islands Hokkaidō, Honshū, Shikoku and Kyūsyū are the main islands making up the archipelago, and, if the southwestern islands centered around Okinawa are included, the length of the archipelago comes to 3,500 km. Based on its *chikei*, the **Japan Islands** are thought to have been formed by the merging of the northeast arc and the southwest arc, taking the approximate middle of Honshū as the boundary between the two. Sixty-one percent of the land is precipitous mountains covered with forests. Meanwhile, the flat areas, including the open country and mountain valleys where people can live, amount to only 24 percent. Sixty-five percent of the population is centered there. They are therefore blessed by beautiful mountains and lush greenery, but, on the other hand, the population density on the land that is habitable is among the highest in the world.

	東京/Tokyo 35°41′	ロサンゼルス Los Angeles 34°03′
最寒月の平均気温 the average temperature of the coldest month	4.1℃	13.2℃
最暖月の平均気温 the average temperature of the warmest month	26.7	22.8
年格差 the range in a year	22.6	9.6

【気候】
Kikō
きこう

　日本列島は、南西諸島が亜熱帯気候に属すほかはほぼ温帯地帯に属しますが、アジア大陸の東端、太平洋の西端に位置しているため、夏は太平洋の高気圧から吹き込む南東の季節風を受けて高温多湿、冬はシベリア高気圧の影響で北西の季節風が吹き込んで寒くなります。この寒暖の温度差を東京と同緯度のロサンゼルスと比較すると、上の表のようになります。この寒暖の差に現われているように、日本の気候の特色は季節がはっきりしていることと、温帯の中でも最も降雨量の多いことです。農耕民族である日本人はこの季節の特色の下、農事と結びついた季節感が鋭く、それが美意識に反映して日本人の感性を形成してきました。

The climate : Except their the southwestern islands belonging to the subtropical zone, the **Japan Islands** belong to the temperate zone. They are located on the eastern edge of the Asian Continent and the western edge of the Pacific, so their summers, with seasonal southeast winds that blow in from the high pressure of the Pacific Ocean, have high temperature and humidity; and its winters, with the seasonal northwest winds blowing under the influence of Siberian high pressure, are cold. The above graph shows the difference in temperature between this heat and cold compared with Los Angels, which is at the same latitude as Tokyo. As it is indicated by this great changes of temperature, the special characteristics of *kikō* in Japan are clearly distinguished seasons and having the highest precipitation rate even among the other temperate zone countries. With these characteristics of the seasons, the Japanese, who are an agricultural people, have developed a keen sense of the seasons in relation to agriculture; that has influenced their aesthetic senses and has shaped their sensibility.

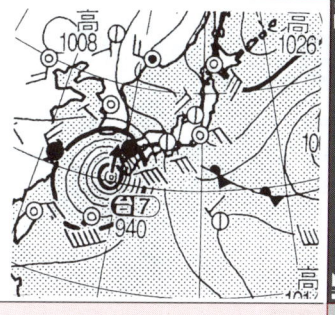

【台風】
Taifū
たいふう

　南太平洋の熱帯性低気圧が発達して大きな勢力を持ち、日本を襲うようになると、それは台風と呼ばれます。台風は夏から秋にかけて毎年多くの風水害を**日本列島**にもたらします。日本の風水害の80％は台風によるものです。風による被害としては建造物破壊、作物減収、塩風による送電線の故障などがあり、豪雨による被害は建造物の浸水・流失、地滑り、山崩れ、土石流などがあります。アメリカのハリケーンなどと比較して日本の台風被害の特色を挙げれば、急峻な山岳地帯のために起きる地滑り・山崩れなどが多いということでしょう。毎年このために何人もの死者が出たり、家屋が破壊され交通が遮断されたりします。

Typhoons : When a subtropical low pressure zone in the South Pacific develops, and start to hit Japan, it is called *taifū*. Every year from summer into autumn, *taifū* cause the **Japan Islands** great storm and flood damage. 80% of storm and flood damage in Japan is caused by *taifū*. There are destruction of buildings and reduction of crops from storm damage and breakdown of power lines from the salt winds, and there is damage from torrential rain such as floods, things being swept away, mudslides, landslides, and rock slides. Compared to hurricanes in America, the main characteristic of *taifū* damage in Japan is probably that there are mud and landslides that occur because of its geography featuring the precipitous mountains. Due to *taifū*, every year a number of people die, houses are destroyed, and traffic cur off.

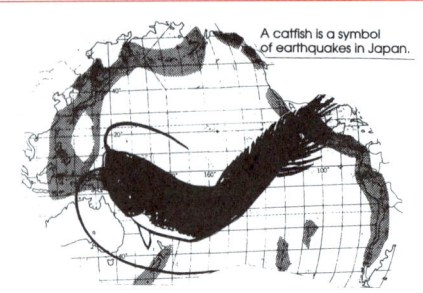

A catfish is a symbol of earthquakes in Japan.

【地震】
Jishin
じしん

　世の中の恐ろしいものの順位を、日本人はユーモアを交えて「地震、雷、火事、おやじ」と表現します。地震は恐ろしいものの第一に挙げられるほど被害が大きく、また日本列島各地で頻繁に発生します。地球規模でこの地震の発生地帯を見ると、日本列島は環太平洋地震帯に区分されます。1923年の関東大震災では、家屋倒壊と火災により約9万人が死に、最近では北海道南西沖地震により一夜にして奥尻島がほぼ全滅してしまいました。このように頻発する地震の被害を最小限に食い止めるために、日本では地震予知の研究が進み、また建造物にも世界最高水準の安全基準が設けられています。

Earthquakes : The Japanese humorously express the ranking of things to be feared in this world as: "earthquakes, thunder, fires, fathers." *Jishin* produce so much damage and occur so frequently in every region of the **Japan Islands** that they are ranked as the number one phenomenon to be feared. When one looks at *jishin* on a global scale, the **Japan Islands** are part of the circum-Pacific *jishin* belt. In the catastrophe of the Great Kantō Earthquake of 1923, about 90,000 people died from houses collapsing and from fires, and recently Okushiri Island was almost completely destroyed overnight by a *jishin* off the southwest coast of Hokkaidō. In order to minimize the damage of such frequently occurring *Jishin*, research in *jishin* forecasting is advancing in Japan and the world's highest safety standards are established for buildings.

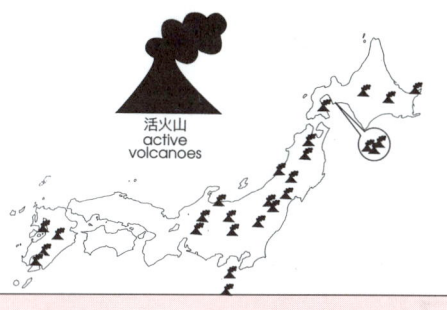

活火山
active
volcanoes

【火山】
Kazan
かざん

地震地帯にほぼ重なるようにして火山地帯が**日本列島**を走り、世界でも最も**地震**・火山活動が活発な地域を形成しています。各地の火山はときどき大噴火をして山麓に被害をもたらします。1991年から続く長崎県の雲仙普賢岳の噴火はふもとの町を火砕流と土石流で襲い、全滅の危機に陥れています。**富士山**も歴史的に何度も大爆発を起こしていますが、やがてまた爆発するだろうといわれています。

この火山は**日本列島**に被害をもたらすだけでなく、各地に**温泉**を湧出せしめて、人々の健康に寄与しています。**温泉**は古くからさまざまな病気に効くことが知られ、各地に湯治場が形成されています。

Volcanoes : *Kazan* regions run along the **Japan Islands**, almost overlaying the **earthquake** belts, and together they form the world's most active **earthquake** and *kazan* region. *Kazan* in some regions occasionally have major eruptions causing damage at the foot of the mountains. The eruptions of Mt. Unzen fugen in Nagasaki Prefecture that have continued since 1991 have assaulted the surrounding villages with lava and earth and rock flows and the villages have fallen into a crisis of total destruction. **Mt. Fuji** too has had large eruptions a number of times in the past, and it is believed to erupt again.

These *kazan* not only cause damage to the **Japan Islands**, they also cause **hot springs** to gush out in various parts of the country and so are conducive to the good health of the people. Known for a long time to be effective against various illnesses, there are **hot springs** all over Japan.

【森林】
しんりん | *Shinrin*

　日本の国土の67％は森林です。森林がこのように多い理由には、まず降水量が多く、どこでも森林が生育する条件が整っていることがあげられます。東京の1日当たり平均降水量は11ミリ、**雪国**の新潟で8ミリですが、他の温帯に属する諸国はその2分の1程度にしかすぎません。さらに、山岳地帯が国土の61％を占めているのも森林地帯が多い理由です。また氷河期に**日本列島**が氷河に覆われなかったため、ヨーロッパやアメリカ大陸の温帯地域に比べて植物の種類も豊富です。また植林を初めとする森林の管理も進んでいます。このような条件の下で日本は木の文化を育んできました。奈良の**法隆寺**は世界最古の木造建築物です。

Forests : Sixty-seven percent of the land in Japan is *shinrin*. The reason why there are so many *shinrin* is, first of all, that there is a lot of precipitation that prepares the conditions for nurturing *shinrin*. The average precipitation per day in Tokyo is 11 mm and in Niigata in the **snow country** it is 8 mm, but it is no more than half in the other temperate zone countries. The fact that mountainous regions comprise 61% of the land is a further reason why *shinrin* areas are plentiful. Besides, in the ice age the **Japan Islands** were not covered with glaciers, so it is rich in varieties of plants by comparison with the temperate zones of the European and American Continents. In addition, the management of *shinrin*, such as reforestation, is in progress. Under these kinds of conditions, Japan has nurtured its culture of wood. The **Hōryūji**, a temple in Nara, is the world's oldest wooden structure.

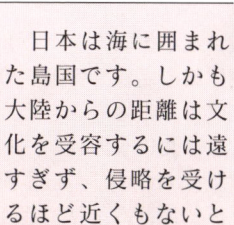

暖流
warm current

寒流
cold current

リマン海流
Liman Current

対馬海流
Tsushima Current

親潮
Oyashio
(Kuril Current)

黒潮(日本海流)
Kuroshio (Japan Current)

【海】
Umi.
うみ

　日本は海に囲まれた島国です。しかも大陸からの距離は文化を受容するには遠すぎず、侵略を受けるほど近くもないという、独自の文化圏を作るに極めて適した位置にあります。太平洋側は南から暖流の黒潮が流れて、北からは親潮が下って列島のほぼ中央でぶつかり、そこに世界の3大漁場の1つが形成されています。日本海側にはそれらの支流が流れ込んでいます。北海道の北東部は、春になるとオホーツク海から流氷が大量に流れてきます。南の沖縄の海には世界有数の珊瑚礁があり、美しい海として世界的に有名です。

Oceans : Japan is an island nation surrounded by *umi*. And it is at such a location, where the distance from the Asian Continent was neither too far to accept the culture from it nor too close to be invaded, that it was suitable for Japan to create peculiar cultural realm. On the Pacific side, the warm Black Current flows from the south and the Kurile Current comes down from the north, meeting almost at the center of the archipelago, forming one of the world's three "big catch" fishing spots. In the spring, ice floes in large quantities drift from the Sea of Okhotsk to the northeast coast of Hokkaidō. The sea of Okinawa, on the south of Japan, is famous worldwide for the clear water and one of the world's most noted coral reefs.

【雪国】
Yuki-guni
ゆきぐに

「国境の長いトンネルを抜けると雪国であった」……これは、ノーベル賞作家・**川端康成**の名作『雪国』の冒頭部の有名な1節です。この表現は日本の地形をもよく表しています。冬はシベリアから吹く冷たい季節風が、本州中央部を北東から南東へ連なる山脈にぶつかり、日本海側に大雪を降らせます。山脈の太平洋側にはあまり雪は降りません。そのため太平洋側から日本海側へトンネルを抜けるといきなり深い雪の積もった雪国が劇的に出現するのです。このように雪国とは本州の日本海側一帯と東北地方及び北海道全域を指します。

Snow country : "The train came out of the long tunnel of a border area into the snow country." That is the famous opening of Nobel Prize-winning novelist KAWABATA Yasunari's masterpiece "Snow Country". This phrase accurately indicates a geographical feature of Japan. In winter, a chilly seasonal wind blows from Siberia, striking the mountain range that runs through the central part of Honshū from the northeast to the southwest and causing heavy snowfall on the Japan Sea side. There is not much snowfall on the Pacific Ocean side of the mountain range. Thus, when one comes out of the tunnel from the Pacific side to the Japan Sea side, the *yuki-guni* with snow piling high dramatically appears. The term *yuki-guni* therefore indicates the regions on the Japan Sea side of Honshū, the Tōhoku area and all of Hokkaidō.

【川・湖】

かわ・みずうみ / Kawa, Mizuumi

　急峻な山岳地帯が61％もあり、降水量が多い**日本列島**には当然ながら川も湖も多くあります。川は地形を反映して急流が多く水量も豊富です。また、山岳地帯の森林がよく水を保持しながら地下水となって流れているため湧水も多く、きれいな水が湖や川に流れ込んでいます。北海道の摩周湖は、かつて世界で最も透明度の高い湖でした。

　しかし、全国の川では大規模なダム建設や堤防工事が治山治水のために行われてきたため、自然が破壊されてきたり、工場排水で汚染されたりしてきました。今、日本人は美しい自然が人々の安全とどうすれば両立できるか、再び考え始めています。

Rivers, Lakes : Because the **Japan Islands** are 61% composed of steep mountainous regions and have a lot of rainfall, naturally there are many of both *kawa* and *mizuumi*. Reflecting those geographical features, *kawa* have rapid currents and abundant amounts of water. In addition, forests in the mountainous regions preserve water well : because this turns into underground water, there is a lot of spring water and clean water flows into *kawa* and *mizuumi*. Mashū Lake, a lake in Hokkaidō, was formerly the world's clearest *mizuumi*.

　However, with large scale dam and levee constructions being undertaken on rivers throughout the country for flood control, nature has been destructed and polluted by construction drainage water. Currently, the Japanese people have begun to reconsider the beauty of nature and whether it can coexist with the security of the people.

歴史年表

8000B.C.–300B.C. JŌMON PERIOD	
300B.C.–3C YAYOI PERIOD	
	Introduction of rice cultivation.
A.D.57	Dispatch of Japanese mission to China.
3C–710 YAMATO PERIOD	
552(or 538)	Official introduction of Buddhism from Korea.
596-622	Prince Shōtoku was appointed regent.
607	Construction of the Buddhist temple, Hōryūji.
630	Start of the Japanese envoys to China.
645	Taika Reformation and the collapse of the SOGA family; institution of the use of era names.
710– 784 NARA PERIOD	
710	Establishment of Heijō capital (Nara).
712	Compilation of "Kojiki."
720	Compilation of "Nihon shoki."
752	Construction of Great Buddha (Daibutsu) in Nara.
c.760	Compilation of "Man'yōshū."
794–1185 HEIAN PERIOD	
794	Establishment of Heian capital (Kyoto).
801	Subjugation of the people in northern Japan.
805	Saichō(Dengyō Daishi) introduced the Tendai Buddhism.
806	Kūkai(Kōbō Daishi) introduced the Shingon Buddhism.
858	FUJIWARA no Yoshifusa became the first non-imperial regent.
894	Abolition of Japanese envoys to China.
905	Compilation of the "Kokinwakashū."
939 - 940	Rebellion of TAIRA no Masakado in the Kantō district.
995 -1027	FUJIWARA no Michinaga seized the sovereign power.
c.1002	"Makura no sōshi"(Pillow Book) was written by Sei-Shōnagon.
c.1008-1020	"Genji Monogatari"(Tale of Genji) was written by Murasaki-Shikibu.
1051 -1062	Earlier Nine Years' War : MINAMOTO no Yoriyoshi destroyed the ABE family of northen Honshū.
1053	Construction of the Buddhist temple, Byōdōin.
1083 -1087	Later Three Years' War : MINAMOTO no Yoshiie destroyed the KIYOWARA family of northern Honshū.
1156	Hōgen War : Leading members of the MINAMOTO family were sent exile.
1159 -1160	Heiji War : TAIRA no Kiyomori destroyed MINAMOTO no Yoshitomo.
1175	Genkū (Hōnen Shōnin) founded the Jōdo(Pure Land) sect of Buddhism.

1180-1185	源平合戦
1185	壇の浦の戦いで平家滅亡
1185-1333	**鎌倉時代**
1185	源頼朝、鎌倉に幕府を開く
1191	栄西、中国から禅宗の一派・臨済宗を紹介
1192	頼朝、将軍の肩書を受ける（征夷大将軍となる）
1221	承久の乱
1224	親鸞、真宗（浄土真宗）を興す
1227	道元、中国から禅宗の一派・曹洞宗を紹介
1232	貞永式目（鎌倉法典）が制定される
1253	日蓮、日蓮宗を興す
1274	初の蒙古襲来〈文永の役〉
1281	２度目の蒙古襲来〈弘安の役〉
1333	鎌倉幕府滅ぶ
1336-1392	**南北朝時代**
1334	建武の中興
1338	足利尊氏、征夷大将軍となる
1392	南北朝の統一
1392-1573	**室町時代**
1397	足利義満、金閣寺を建立
1404	明と勘合貿易開始（～1547）
1467-1477	応仁の乱
1543	種子島にポルトガル人が上陸、鉄砲を伝える
1549	フランシスコ・ザビエル九州を訪れ、キリスト教の布教を開始する
1573	室町幕府滅ぶ
1573-1603	**安土桃山時代**
1576	織田信長、安土城に入城
1582	信長暗殺される〈本能寺の変〉；天正少年使節渡欧（～90）
1585	羽柴秀吉、関白となる
1586	秀吉、太政大臣となり、豊臣姓を授かる
1587	バテレン（キリスト教宣教師）追放令を公布する
1592	朝鮮を侵略〈文禄の役〉；スペイン・フランシスコ会、布教活動を開始
1597	朝鮮出兵再開〈慶長の役〉；ヨーロッパ人伝道者と日本人改宗者を死刑に処す〈26聖人の大殉教〉
1598	秀吉没、朝鮮から撤退
1600	家康、関ヶ原の戦いで勝利

1180-1185	War between the MINAMOTO and TAIRA family(Gempei wars).
1185	Annihilation of the TAIRA at naval battle of Dannoura.

1185–1333 KAMAKURA PERIOD

1185	MINAMOTO no Yoritomo established the Kamakura government.
1191	Eisai introduced the Rinzai Buddhism (a branch of Zen Buddhism) from China.
1192	Yoritomo is granted the title of shōgun(the commander-in-chief).
1221	Jōkyū Disturbance.
1224	Shinran founded Shinshū (the True Pure Land) sect.
1227	Dōgen introduced the teachings of the Sōtō sect of Zen Buddhism from China.
1232	Enactment of the Jōei Shikimoku (Kamakura law code).
1253	Nichiren founded the Nichiren sect of Buddhism.
1274	First Mongol invasion of Japan.
1281	Second Mongol invasion of Japan.
1333	Overthrow of the Kamakura government.

1336–1392 PERIOD OF THE NORTHERN AND SOUTHERN COURTS

1334	The Kenmu Restoration.
1338	Appointment of ASHIKAGA Takauji to the Shogun, the commander-in-chief.
1392	Unification of the northern and southern courts.

1392–1573 MUROMACHI PERIOD

1397	Construction of the Kinkakuji by ASHIKAGA Yoshimitsu.
1404	Tally trade is initiated with China (continued until 1547)
1467-1477	Ōnin wars.
1543	Portuguese arrived at Tanegashima and introduced firearms.
1549	St.Francis Xavier arrived in Kyūshū and began the Christian propagation.
1573	Overthrow of the Muromachi government.

1573–1603 AZUCHI–MOMOYAMA PERIOD

1576	ODA Nobunaga entered the Azuchi castle on Lake Biwa.
1582	Assassination of Nobunaga in the Honnōji Incident; the mission of four Christian Japanese boys to Europe in Tenshō Era (until 1590).
1585	HASHIBA Hideyoshi was appointed the chancellor.
1586	Hideyoshi was appointed the Minister-President and was granted the surname TOYOTOMI.
1587	Issuance of an anti-christian edict to expel Christian missionaries.
1592	First invasion of Korea; Spanish Franciscans began Christian propagation.
1597	Second invasion of the Korea; European missionaries and Japanese converts were executed in Twenty-six martyrs.
1598	Death of Hideyoshi and withdrawal from Korea.
1600	TOKUGAWA Ieyasu won victory at the battle of Sekigahara.

1603-1867	江戸時代
1603	家康、征夷大将軍となり、江戸幕府を開く
1609	平戸にオランダ商館開設
1612	キリスト教信者の迫害が再開される
1613	平戸にイギリス商館開設
1633	奉書船以外の海外渡航を禁じ、海外渡航者の帰国を制限
1635	外様大名に参勤交代を制度化
1636	すべての日本船の海外渡航を禁ずる
1637-1638	島原の乱
1639	ポルトガル商船を追放
1641	オランダ商船を平戸から長崎港の出島に移す
1657	江戸の大火〈明暦の大火〉
1758	竹内式部、京都の廷臣に尊王論を説き、罰せられる〈宝暦事件〉
1772	田沼意次、老中となる
1792	ロシア人・ラックスマン北海道に来航
1801	間宮林蔵、サハリンを探検
1804	ロシア人使節・レザノフ、長崎に来航
1808	イギリス船・フェートン号、長崎に来航〈フェートン号事件〉
1823-1830	シーボルト滞日
1825	異国船打払令
1837	大坂で儒教学者・大塩平八郎率いる百姓一揆が起こる〈大塩平八郎の乱〉；アメリカ船・モリソン号、浦賀に来航
1846	アメリカ海軍提督・ビッドル、浦賀に来航
1853	マシュー・C・ペリー提督、浦賀に到着
1854	神奈川条約〈日米和親条約〉締結、鎖国の終焉
1856	総領事・タウンゼント・ハリス、下田に到着
1858-1860	井伊直弼、最高権力者〈大老〉となる
1858	日米修好通商条約締結
1860	井伊直弼、水戸浪士により暗殺〈桜田門外の変〉
1864	英・仏・蘭・米の連合艦隊が下関を砲撃〈四国艦隊下関砲撃事件〉
1867	王政復古の大号令、大政奉還
1868-1912	明治時代
1868	明治維新
1869	諸藩の大名が領地を返還する〈版籍奉還〉；封建的に割拠された領地を整理し、府や県を置く〈廃藩置県〉
1872	東京・横浜間に鉄道開通
1873	徴兵令公布；地租改正条例公布
1875	サハリンを千島列島と交換する協定〈樺太・千島交換条約〉をロシアと結ぶ

1603–1867	EDO PERIOD
1603	Ieyasu was granted the title of shogun and opened the Edo government.
1609	The Dutch factory was established at Hirado.
1612	Resumption of Christian's persecution.
1613	The English factory was established at Hirado.
1633	Prohibition of Japanese travel abroad except for ships with an official permission; restriction on return of Japanese travellers abroad.
1635	Institution of the mandatory "alternate-year attendance to Edo" (sankin-kotai) for "outer" (tozama) daimyo.
1636	Prohibition of any Japanese travel abroad.
1637 -1638	Uprise of Shimabara.
1639	Portuguese trading vessels were expelled from Japan.
1641	The Dutch factory was transferred from Hirado to Dejima in Nagasaki harbor.
1657	Great Fire of Edo.
1758	TAKENOUCHI Shikibu was punished for teaching loyalist doctrines to the Kyoto courties.
1772	Appointment of TANUMA Okitsugu to a member of the Shōgun's Council of State
1792	Visit of the Russian Laxman to Hokkaido.
1801	Exploration of Sakhalin by Mamiya Rinzō.
1804	Visit of the Russian envoy Rezanov to Nagasaki.
1808	Visit to Nagasaki of the British ship Phaeton.
1823 -1830	Siebold in Japan.
1825	Enactment of the Foreign Ships Repelling Order.
1837	A Confucian scholar ŌSHIO Heihachirō led a peasants' uprising in Osaka; visit of the American ship Morrison to Edo Bay and Nagasaki.
1846	Visit of American Commodore Biddle to Uraga.
1853	Commodore Matthew C. Perry arrived at Uraga.
1854	Peace Treaty between U.S. and Japan; the end of Japan's Isolation Policy.
1856	Arrival of Consul General Townsend Harris at Shimoda.
1858-1860	II Naosuke held the sovereign power as Chief Minister of the Shōgun.
1858	Commercial treaty with the U.S.
1860	Assassination of Ii Naosuke by Mito samurai.
.1864	Bombardment of Shimonoseki forts by British, French, Dutch, and American ships.
1867	Return of power to the Emperor.
1868–1912	MEIJI PERIOD
1868	Establishment of Tokyo (Edo) as the new capital.
1869	Return of their domains by the daimyo appointment of the daimyo; as governors of their former fiefs.
1872	Opening of the railway between Tokyo and Yokohama.
1873	Inauguration of universal military service; adoption of the new land tax system.
1875	Agreement with Russia over the exchange of Sakhalin for the Kuril Islands.

1889		大日本帝国憲法公布
1890		教育勅語発布
1894		清国との宣戦布告〈日清戦争〉
1895		下関条約〈日清戦争講和条約〉により日清戦争終結；ロシア、フランス、ドイツによる三国干渉の結果、遼東半島を清に返還
1897		金本位制確立
1900		義和団の変に日本軍参加
1902		日英同盟締結
1904		日露戦争始まる
1905		ポーツマス条約〈日露講和条約〉により、日露戦争終結
1910		韓国併合；朝鮮総督府を設置
1912		明治天皇崩御
1912-1926		**大正時代**
1914		ドイツに宣戦布告、第1次世界大戦参戦
1915		対華21か条要求提出
1923		関東大震災
1925		普通選挙法成立
1926		大正天皇崩御
1926-1989		**昭和時代**
1927		金融恐慌
1930		ロンドン海軍軍縮条約締結
1931		満州事変
1932	5.15	犬養毅暗殺（5.15事件）
1933		国際連盟脱退
1936	2.26	暗殺および暗殺未遂のクーデター（2.26事件）
1937		日中戦争開始
1939		モンゴルのノモンハンでロシア人と衝突〈ノモンハン事件〉
1940		ドイツ、イタリアと3国軍事同盟調印〈日独伊3国軍事同盟〉
1941		日本軍、真珠湾を攻撃、太平洋戦争開始
1942		ミッドウェー海戦
1945		東京に大焼夷弾投下〈東京大空襲〉；ポツダム宣言〈日本に降伏勧告〉；広島と長崎に原子爆弾投下；8.14ポツダム宣言受諾；8.15終戦
1946		天皇、自らの神性を否定〈人間宣言〉
1947	5.3	日本国憲法施行
1951		サンフランシスコで、48カ国との平和条約調印、および米国との安全保障条約〈サンフランシスコ平和条約・日米安全保障条約〉調印
1952		日米行政協定調印；講和条約発効
1954		第5福竜丸、ビキニ島で水爆に被災；自衛隊発足

1889	Promulgation of the Constitution of the Empire of Japan.
1890	Imperial Rescript on Education.
1894	Declaration of war on China (Sino-Japanese War).
1895	Treaty of Shimonoseki concluding the Sino-Japanese War; return of the Liaotung Peninsula after the intervention of Russia, France, and Germany.
1897	Adoption of the gold standard.
1900	Participation by Japanese forces in the capture of Taku, Tientsun, and Peking during the Boxer Uprising in China.
1902	Signing of the Anglo-Japanese Alliance.
1904	Outbreak of Russo-Japanese War.
1905	Conclusion of the Russo-Japanese War through the Treaty of Portsmouth.
1910	Annexation of Korea; creation of the goverment-general of Korea.
1912	Death of Meiji emperor.

1912–1926 TAISHO PERIOD

1914	Japanese declaration of war on Germany; entry into World War. .
1915	Presentation of the Twenty-one Demands on China.
1923	Great Kantō earthquake.
1925	Adoption of universal manhood suffrage.
1926	Death of Taisho emperor.

1926–1989 SHOWA PERIOD

1927	Bank crisis.
1930	Signing of the London Naval Treaty.
1931	The Manchurian Incident.
1932	May 15, assassination of INUKAI (5-15 Incident).
1933	Withdrawal from the League of Nations.
1936	Februaly 26, assassinations and attempted coup d'etat (2-26 Incident).
1937	Outbreak of war with China.
1939	Fighting with the Russians at Nomonhan in Mongolia.
1940	Tripartite Alliance with Germany and Italy.
1941	Attack on Pearl Harbor and outbreak of the Pacific War.
1942	Battle of Midway.
1945	Great firebomb raids on Tokyo; <advice for Japan to surreder> by the Potsdam Proclamation; atomic bombings of Hiroshima and Nagasaki; August 14, acceptance of terms of the Potsdam Proclamation; August 15, the end of the war.
1946	Emperor's denial of his own divinity.
1947	May 3, New constitution goes into effect.
1951	Signing of the peace treaty with 48 nations and the security treaty with the U.S. at San Francisco.
1952	Signing of an administrative agreement on terms for the U.S. bases in Japan; peace treaty goes into effect.
1954	No.5 Fukuryū-maru involved in Bikini nuclear fallout; Self-Defense Agency is established.

1955	広島で第1回原水爆禁止世界大会開催；日本、GATT〈関税と貿易に関する一般協定〉に加盟；ソ連と正常国交の共同声明〈日ソ共同声明〉；12.12日本、国際連合加盟
1959	皇太子、民間出身の女性と結婚
1960	米国との相互安全保障および協力条約〈日米新安保条約〉に調印；条約締結に反対する大規模なデモが起きる
1964	日本、OECD〈経済協力開発機構〉に加盟；東京オリンピック開催
1968	小笠原諸島返還
1970	日本万国博覧会開催（大阪）
1972	冬季オリンピック開催（札幌）；沖縄返還；日中国交正常化〈日中友好平和条約〉
1973	石油危機起こる
1976	ロッキード事件；成田空港（新東京国際空港）開く
1979	第5回先進国首脳会議、東京で開催〈東京サミット〉
1989	昭和天皇崩御
1989–	**平成時代**
1990	バブル経済の崩壊
1991	湾岸戦争で他国籍軍を支援
1992	東京佐川急便事件；国連平和維持活動（PKO）法案成立
1993	自民党38年ぶりに政権を失い、連合政権誕生

1955	The First World Conference against Atomic and Hydrogen Bombs was held in Hiroshima; Japan joins GATT(General Agreement on Tariffs and Trade); the <Japan-Soviet joint statement >, declaring the normalization of Japan-Soviet relations; Japan joins the United Nations.
1959	The crown prince marries a commoner.
1960	Signing of the Treaty of Mutual Security and Cooperation with the United States; giant antitreaty demonstration.
1964	Japan admitted into the OECD (Organization for Economic Cooperation and Development); Tokyo Olympic Games.
1968	Agreement for the return of the Bonin Islands (retuned June 26).
1970	Opening of the Expo'70 in Osaka.
1972	Opening of the Winter Olympic Games at Sapporo; Okinawa was returned to Japan; the normalization of Japan-China relations <the Japan-China Treaty of Peace and Friendship>.
1973	Impact on Japan of the shock of the Arab oil crisis.
1976	Lockheed scandal ; opening of the Narita Airport (New Tokyo International Airport).
1979	Fifth summit meeting of the seven major industrial democracies held in Tokyo.
1989	Death of Showa emperor.
1989–	HEISEI PERIOD
1990	The collapse of Bubble Economy.
1991	Financial support to the multinational forces in the Gulf War.
1992	Tokyo Sagawa scandal; the PKO Bill passes the Diet.
1993	The LDP is out of power for the first time in 38 years; the birth of a coalition government.

索引

*項目見出しとなっている語およびそのページは、太字で示してあります。

●著者紹介

◎**杉浦洋一**（すぎうら　よういち）

明治大学政経学部卒業。月刊誌『翻訳の世界』編集長（バベルプレス）、『月刊日本語』（アルク）編集長を歴任。ニューヨーク駐在体験などを踏まえて異文化接触や日本の国際化をテーマに執筆・編集活動中。㈱イーストウェスト代表。
主著：ワードスター・クイックマニュアル（宝島社）
　　　英語で自己紹介（ナツメ社）

◎**ジョン・K・ギレスピー**（John K. Gillespie）

アメリカのヒューストン・バプティスト大学を卒業。インディアナ大学で比較文学博士号取得。ドイツ、フランス、日本の各地で日本と西洋の演劇の相互影響を研究。ジャパン・ソサエティー（ニューヨーク）で、Performing Arts Director。現在クラーク・コンサルティング・グループ、ニューヨーク支局長。
主著：*Alternative Japanese Drama*: University of Hawaii Press

●本文デザイン・図版作成
三浦廷子

●執筆協力
大橋牧子
折笠秀樹
長橋俊恵
西山理恵子
真鍋美佳子

日本文化を英語で紹介する事典

著　者	杉浦洋一、ジョン・K・ギレスピー
	© Yoichi Sugiura, John K. Gillespie 1993
発行者	田村正隆
発行所	**株式会社ナツメ社**
	東京都千代田区神田神保町1-52 加州ビル2 F　（〒101）
	電話　03(3291)1257　（代表）
	振替口座　東京3-58661
制　作	**ナツメ出版企画株式会社**
	東京都千代田区神田神保町1-52 加州ビル3 F　（〒101）
	電話　03(3295)3921　（代表）
印　刷	**ラン印刷社**

ISBN4-8163-1566-7　　　　　　　　　　Printed in Japan
〈定価はカバーに表示してあります〉

*

① Mr + Mrs Inoue (Keiko)
   555-51 Ayamei Keminami
   7-Chome Nara-shi Nara
   631   Japan   (oitto eat
   (06) 416-0530   School)

Nara - Ikuko Yonemoto
         5-6-16 Jinnan Ikaruga-cho
         Ikoma-gun Nara
         Japan 636-01
         0145-74-3145

② * Mr + Mrs Yasuo Masaka (Son in Law) New Baby March
      2006-1 Uchimiyachou
      Matsuyama Japan
      (0 899) 79-0333 file photo
      (Laundry Mat)   slippers
                      handkvefs.
                      post cards

   * Pastor Ikuo Nishida   Church service
     Japan Gospel Mission   Cable car
     21-1 Nishi-Ishii   pot luck meal
     Matsuyama Ehime   card gift
     790 Japan
     Phone: 0899-57-6651

③   Hiroshima — Fried Keiko
   * Cindy Kumamoto
     T 731-51
     6-1 Minega 1 Chome
     Saeki-Ka Hiroshima-shi
     Japan 731-51
     Phone: 0829-24-7550